BUILD
YOUR OWN
TENNIS COURT

CHARLES D. NEAL

BUILD YOUR OWN TENNIS COURT

Constructing, Subcontracting, Equipping & Maintaining Indoor & Outdoor Courts

CHILTON BOOK COMPANY

Radnor, Pennsylvania

Published in Radnor, Pennsylvania, by Chilton Book Company
and simultaneously in Don Mills, Ontario, Canada,
by Thomas Nelson & Sons, Ltd.

Designed by Anne Churchman

Manufactured in the United States of America

Library of Congress Cataloging in Publication Data
Neal, Charles D
    Build your own tennis court.

    Includes index.
    1. Tennis courts—Design and construction.
2. Tennis courts—Maintenance and repair.
I. Title.

GV1002.N42   624   76-51303
ISBN 0-8019-6573-X

1 2 3 4 5 6 7 8 9 0   6 5 4 3 2 1 0 9 8 7

Contents

Preface

This book contains detailed discussions and step-by-step instructions for every tennis buff—from beginner to professional—who is interested in building his own tennis court, doing his own maintenance, and purchasing his own equipment.

Whether you're a novice do-it-yourselfer or an old pro, you'll find this book packed with comprehensive information on everything required to build your own tennis court, including proper use of a transit and rod and chain saw, and how to install a fence. This information is like having money in the bank: long after your tennis court has been built, this book should be a source of valuable reference when trees require felling, yard fences are in the making, and patios and other concrete slabs are scheduled for building. For example, the techniques required to build a tennis court fence are very similar to those required to build any kind of chain-link fence.

In addition to providing a detailed approach to the whole problem of building tennis courts, I have tried to do two additional things in this book.

First, I want to explode the myth that you can't build a tennis court unless you're a tennis court contractor. You'll find clear, step-by-step guidance for building several different types of tennis courts, such as fast-dry, clay, grit, grass and concrete surfaces. A bonus is the platform tennis court presented in Chapter 7. Any person who can saw a board square, drive a nail, drill a hole, and use a paintbrush can build them.

Second, I want to emphasize self-evaluation as an important process for any do-it-yourselfer, including myself. I urge you to carefully read those parts of the book pertaining to a specific project—clearing the land, building the base and fence, selecting the surface, doing the maintenance, or whatever. Then decide which operations and how much of the projects are for you to do. It's surprising how many people discover four fingers and a thumb on each hand when they actually start building something.

There's another point I'd like to make regarding self-evaluation. Recognize natural barriers as well as strong and weak points where they exist. For instance, when large equipment is required, farm out the job to the pros. Don't try haphazard substitutions, for you'll not be happy with the results. Building an asphalt surface is a case in point: acceptable results call for the use of large equipment run by trained operators. But I'd be remiss if I didn't point out that you can do many other important jobs yourself prior to and following the building of the surface. You'll find these jobs carefully illustrated and explained as you read.

The sources of supply listing in the Appendix provides addresses of suppliers mentioned in the text as well as names and addresses of other suppliers of materials and equipment used to build, equip, and maintain tennis courts, including equipment used in playing tennis.

Because limited space prevented the inclusion of all suppliers of quality equipment and materials, random sampling was used in the preparation of the guide. I offer my humble apologies to those manufacturers and companies omitted.

Although lists of required materials are given, only a few cost estimates are included. Since prices of materials vary from time to time and location to location, you will want up-to-date estimates. Request suppliers in your area to submit bids from the list of materials you have selected.

Since construction techniques and quality vary and the availability of many materials fluctuates, I recommend that the purchaser follow the manufacturer's instructions carefully whenever directions accompany merchandise. Most manufacturers will honor their warranties only if the products are assembled and used as recommended. Although I mention certain manufacturers and products by their trade names, neither I nor the publisher necessarily imply any endorsements or make any guarantee of satisfaction. Here I suggest both warranty and end use be understood by the purchaser and the supplier at the time of actual purchase.

In some places I have changed names and places to protect the guilty and the innocent. Any similarity between these people and people living or dead is purely coincidental.

I hope this book will help the reader to build a tennis court that will give him, his family, and his friends many happy hours of enjoyment and relaxation.

Acknowledgments

I wish to pay special tribute to the following people for the many practical construction ideas found in this book: William Bost, Robert Bundy, H. C. Caldwell, David Cox, Joe Ebeling, Dan Fraioli, Robert Lee, Harold Little, Dave Pullman, and N. R. Seaman.

I am deeply indebted to the numerous tennis court contractors and their workmen who, without charge, gladly gave of their time and shared their ideas and knowledge with me to provide helpful construction techniques, including trade secrets that were gleaned from many years of doing successful construction work.

It is a genuine pleasure to mention my deep appreciation to Benton M. Arnovitz, for his encouragement and guidance. His suggestions and timely information on the latest developments in tennis court construction did much to make this book compact and comprehensive.

1

Preliminary Considerations

INTRODUCTION

A quiet revolution has been going on in sports during the past few years. Its goal—to bring tennis from obscurity to its rightful place in the world of sports—is well underway. New courts are being constructed to the tune of 8,000 a year to help meet the needs of the ever-increasing number of tennis players, which has soared from an estimated 5 million in 1960 to well over 40 million today. No question about it, we're now in the midst of a big tennis boom. And the end is nowhere in sight.

Only a few years ago, men and women played tennis on occasional weekends or when there wasn't anything else exciting to do. Children played tennis when their teachers literally forced them onto the courts as part of an organized physical education program.

Now folks who, until recently, scarcely knew the difference between a snowshoe and a tennis racket religiously take lessons so they can play the game intelligently. Parents urge their children to learn the game because "you can play it for the rest of your lives, and it's good for you."

What are the results of this sudden interest in tennis? For one thing, there is a shortage of public courts. For another thing, tennis clubs charge from $8 to $20 an hour, and usually there is a long waiting list at most courts. For still another thing, dedicated tennis players who would otherwise spend a lot to play on private courts are building their own. It seems as if every time you turn around these days someone is building a tennis court in his backyard.

As a point of interest, $10,000 is about the minimum cost of a respectable outdoor court if you turn the complete job over to a contractor. If you do it yourself and carefully shop around for materials, you can cut this cost considerably below half. If you do part of the work yourself and turn some of the work over to professionals, you can still save a big chunk of money from the total contractor's bid.

The foremost question in the mind of the average person inspired to construct something is, "Can I do it?" Having built many projects myself and having been often faced with this question, I was prompted to find some answers. So, for the past several years, I carried on a casual investigation. The results are interesting. In short, here is what I discovered: Most people turn out much better work than they anticipated when the project first got underway. It seems that people are not all thumbs, as some folks would have us believe. Since the beginning of man, hands have become increasingly useful tools for producing more and more surprising and satisfactory results.

It would be grossly misleading to say that no one who tries his hand at building something ever makes a mistake. To never make a mistake means to never try. All of us, I think, can take a lesson from the building trades people. When most of them make mistakes, they profit from them by not making the same errors twice. Sometimes they observe what went wrong and correct it. Sometimes they seek help from a fellow workman. At other times they study articles and books on the subject much as you are doing

1

now. All of us, no matter how little or how much we have built, can follow their examples as we travel along the road leading to success. I know of no better principle to recommend to you than the tried and proven philosophical statement, ''We learn by doing.''

If you still doubt your ability to do it yourself, think of a tennis court as a series of small separate segments. Take one small step at a time until you complete a single segment. For example, once the court is laid out, preparation and application of the surface will follow as naturally as day follows night. The step-by-step operations for these segments are discussed in Chapters 4 and 5, but I do want to make the point here that each step is part of a progression from beginning to end, in no sense of the word complicated.

Once the court is laid out and surfaced, remaining segments are obvious. Generally, they include installation of optional items, such as lighting, fencing, wind screens, and various pieces of equipment.

Nowhere in the construction program will you become involved in anything but the simplest kind of carpentry work and labor, calling for nothing more than a strong back and simple arithmetic calculations.

If you still wonder whether you should do it yourself, permit me to make this suggestion: Don't hesitate, for there is no better time to start than now. Even if you have only limited experience with tools, you can build many tennis courts like a pro. What you need to know is detailed in the appropriate chapter.

PHYSICAL SPECIFICATIONS

Space

Although a doubles lawn tennis court is 36 x 78 feet, tournament play requires an area of 60 x 120 feet—roughly one-sixth of an acre. However, where space is limited, many people shave the out-of-bounds space by a few feet, keeping the playing area of 36 x 78. This, of course, is never shrunk! So it is not uncommon to find private courts as small as 54 x 110 feet. Also, reducing the area recommended for tournament play can be a blessing in disguise. With less area to surface, coupled with a reduction in linear feet of fence, you save a small sum of money.

Site

If you have a choice of location, select one that doesn't lie lower than the adjoining ground. Otherwise, special provisions for drainage will add to your cost. Avoid, if possible, moving objects such as people or automobiles behind the ends of outdoor courts. If these cannot be avoided, install wind curtains, for they provide a desirable background as well as slowing wind speeds.

If possible, lay out your outdoor court with the long axis in the north–south direction so none of the players in action ever look directly into the sun.

Tall junipers or spruce-type evergreens near an outdoor court may serve as a windbreak in addition to providing a desirable background, provided they are so located as not to cast shadows on the playing area. Deciduous trees also form a pleasant background; however, in addition to the possibility of casting shadows on the court, falling leaves and protruding branches can interfere with play. In addition, roots may cause physical damage to the surface of the court.

Finally, avoid building an outdoor court where tall buildings are already located on either the west or east side of the proposed location: Distracting shadows can play havoc with the best of players, leaving only a few hours during the day of ideal playing conditions.

Platform Tennis

What if you don't have one-sixth of an acre? Should you give up in despair? Not at all. How about a space one-fourth the size of a lawn tennis court? If you have this much space, you're in business. This is all the area required for building a platform tennis court. Because, in part, of its smaller space requirements, even if it is on the side of a hill, it is a made-to-order game for tightly packed suburbs. The playing surface is 30 x 60 feet, and people are finding the game challenging and easy to learn. Because the court is made of either wood, aluminum, or built on a slab, the minimum price tag still comes to $10,000 if a contractor does the job. By doing part or all of the work yourself, you cut the cost to half or even less. For complete details on building a platform tennis court yourself, see Chapter 7.

LEGAL REQUIREMENTS

Zoning Regulations

Zoning regulations are the legal rules by which an entire community or section of it is governed and the nature of its growth controlled. Basically, restrictions on types of structures in specified locations are intended to be a genuine protection. Therefore, theoretically, all of them should be designed to protect property owners. Nevertheless, control in the hands of governmental amateurs can result in zoning *against* instead of zoning *for*. One of the first orders of planning is to be certain that a tennis court is permitted on your property. Once this is determined, find out all the ramifications. For example, most likely you'll find there is a statement giving the minimum number of feet tennis court boundary lines must be set inside property lines.

Deed Restrictions

In the legal profession, deed restrictions are known as deed covenants. These are formal agreements of legal validity, and they are further regulations to investigate before building your tennis court. They are intended to perpetuate the wishes of a previous owner. Generally, such an owner puts his demands in all forthcoming deeds when he subdivides property. The requirements of zoning ordinances and building codes can be mere child's play compared to rigid and complex deed covenants. On the other hand, a shady developer may find that many of his lots are not selling. He removes the deed covenants from all future deeds, allowing the purchasers complete freedom to build anything. By the time those purchasers having deed covenants bring suit against the developer, they find his land corporation dissolved, which means they have no one to sue. One final comment: Deed covenants cannot be superseded by zoning regulations or building codes.

Local Building Codes

The intent of building codes is to protect the public interest and safety. Codes are not intended to restrict or prevent the use of tried and proven materials and techniques. However, many conventional building codes have not been updated. Consequently, they are based on old products. For the past several years, many new products have been eliminated from construction, not because they conflict with public interest and safety but because no one has taken the time to include them in an updated building code. A case in point is air structures, or "bubble buildings," some of which are designed to house indoor tennis courts. There are many reputable firms today which manufacture safe and aesthetic air structures approved by responsible architects and engineers (*see* Sources of Supply). Yet such structures are not permitted in some communities because of outdated building codes.

Many rural areas and small towns do not have building codes; those that do may not have salaried building inspectors, and frequently codes are old-fashioned or out of date. Usually, such communities depend upon the services of volunteers and they are compensated with a percentage of the building permit fees. In such places, as long as the fee is paid, any kind of construction is permitted. If your community has a building code, check for two basic requirements: a performance code and a specification code.

A *performance code* defines a specified performance criteria, regardless of the materials used. Generally, it allows design choice and freedom in using regulation building materials.

A *specification code* generally defines the kinds of materials to use. One criticism of such a code is that it can be made-to-order for unscrupulous building suppliers and contractors.

Building Permits

If you are in doubt about building permit requirements before you can legally construct a tennis court, check with the city hall in your community. The fact that you live outside an unincorporated town or city may, in itself, not exempt you from the requirements. One town I know of requires building permits 1½ miles from existing corporate limits as well as within the city limits.

Sometimes securing a building permit may seem quite involved, but often this is necessary to protect the best interests of a growing city. For example, if I build a tennis court in Carbondale, Illinois, I must abide by the following procedure.

Building Permit Application

The building permit application, secured from the Planning Division in City Hall, calls for applicant's name and address, legal description of the property, type of construction, plot plan showing size of lot and location of structure(s), a set of drawings of proposed structure(s), and cost of construction.

Note: It is also a good idea to check with the city and county health departments to find out if a health permit is required before building a tennis court.

Application for Zoning Certificate

Following completion of the building permit application, it is taken to the Code Enforcement Department. Application is made for a zoning certificate, requiring the name and address of the land owner, property location, and legal description of the property.

Following approval by authorities in the Planning Division, a building permit and zoning certificate are issued. This may seem like unnecessary red tape, but it really isn't. Once the tennis court is approved for building within a specified zone, I will have little concern about lawsuits from city officials or disgruntled neighbors trying to stop the project.

REAL ESTATE VALUES

Effect on Property Tax

How much a tennis court will increase your property tax is a difficult question to answer specifically. Since a tennis court is legally considered a capital investment, it stands to reason that some increase in property tax is a certainty. Much depends upon the type of property assessments made in your community. Some tax assessors place a low valuation on home "extras," such as tennis courts, swimming pools, storm cellars, carports. Other tax assessors place as high a valuation on them as the law permits. Your best bet is to call on your own tax assessor and find out how much extra valuation he will place on your property for the kind of tennis court you have in mind. Then you can multiply the valuation by the tax multiplier times the tax rate to find out exactly in dollars and cents what extra property tax you can expect to pay. The answer should tell you whether or not this is a fair price to pay for your own pleasure.

Resale Value

When the Browns sold their home in St. Louis, they congratulated themselves on their good fortune.

After more than six months, they'd found a buyer who didn't quibble at $52,000—a not-too-modest sum in St. Louis for a used five-room ranch house with tennis court.

"Because John was transferred to Chicago," recalls Mrs. Brown, "we'd have settled for a much smaller figure."

The Browns' sale is a good example of a tennis court increasing home value. Is this true in all cases? It would be misleading to give a definite "yes" answer. My findings show two answers to the question. Some real estate experts claim that a tennis court boosts the value of home and property by as much as 200 percent. Equally reputable real estate agents are more cautious. They point out that when home swimming pools were in their heyday, they paid for themselves in added real estate value. Now some swimming pools are being filled to make room for tennis courts. Furthermore, they claim, "This is some evidence to show that swimming pools no longer add too much to home valuation." Therefore, they predict the same thing could happen to tennis courts if the boom should collapse.

All is not gloom. Even the most pessimistic realtor agrees that you can expect to recover a large percentage of your expense in higher resale value. Since these predictions are based on contractor prices, this is really good news for the do-it-yourselfer. Even if he hires professionals to do some of the work, he can gamble almost with certainty that a tennis court will add much, in terms of his investment, to the resale value of his home.

What it all boils down to is this: People value their own pleasure as priceless. They buy boats, vacation homes, expensive sports cars, go on trips to faraway continents. In light of this, a capital investment made in a tennis court is not really an extravagance.

2

Estimating Costs

IF YOU DO IT ALL YOURSELF

The pioneers were the first American do-it-yourselfers. Out of necessity, they made practically everything they needed. They had no other choice: They either did it or they did without. Passing years brought about change. Americans, as well as other peoples of the world, became more interdependent and less independent, so fewer and fewer people made what they wanted. Now with a deluge of higher and higher material and labor costs, people are again trying to make some of the things they want. Not only has making things become a prestige symbol, but people are discovering that if the pioneers could do it, so can they. Manufacturers and writers are recognizing the rebirth. Their brochures, magazine articles, and books are evidence enough to prove the point. They show how to do everything from soling shoes to building geodesic domes. And the materials are especially suited to the do-it-yourselfer.

Reviewing the Project

The more you consider building a tennis court, the sooner you are confronted with the question: Can I construct a tennis court myself? If you are experienced at do-it-yourself projects, you know you can, so skip to the next topic. If the question bothers you, begin to relieve your mind by carefully reading the step-by-step procedures presented later in this book. The first time

through, the different procedures may seem odd. Repeated reading gradually brings the whole project into sharper and sharper focus. Once you actually get underway, the information on each step makes more sense when combined with the section that you are actually building. What to do if you come to a dead end? Give up in despair? Not at all. You'll find your building supplier a great comfort. Generally, there is at least one person working for a supplier who knows material and equipment and how to install or build it. I have actually seen experienced building trades people take off from the job to seek information on a tough construction problem. Also, manufacturers are pleased to answer installation questions about their products if you will but write or telephone them.

Planning the Details

The way to determine exactly what you can do and what you want someone else to do is to carefully plan. First of all, decide on the type of surface you prefer. Will the location require filling, excavating, or a concrete base supported by pillars if you must build on a hillside? Do you want lights? How about a fence? If so, do you want it only along the ends of the court or do you want it all the way around? Is yours to be an outdoor or indoor court? Complete the list, including equipment than can be built on the job. Next decide what you want to build and what you want to farm out to professionals. For example, no one

5

in his right mind is going to do an excavation job with a shovel that requires big power equipment, so hire out this job if you have to do it.

Reaping the Benefits

Most of us gain a great deal of satisfaction from building a project ourselves, but satisfaction is not the only reason. By nature, man likes to save money, and building your own tennis court saves a tidy sum.

You can save up to 60 percent of the total construction cost, more if you're willing to scrounge around for bargains. During off-seasons, some material suppliers run sales or, for a cash payment, will reduce the price on certain items. Another advantage in building your own tennis court is that you get the kind of construction you want. For instance, a friend of mine paid for a 4-inch base course of crushed stone and a 2-inch asphalt binder leveling course. Sometime later, one of the laborers told him, "If you drilled a test hole anywhere in the court, you'd more than likely find only 3 inches of crushed stone and 1¾ inches of asphalt binder leveling course."

The moral is this: Even if you hire out part of the construction, be on the job or have someone else there to be sure you get what you pay for, especially on segments that later will be hidden from view. Also, as you progress from grading to applying the finish coat, you not only can make necessary changes and additions but you can make them with the least amount of additional cost. Nothing is more of a drain on your pocketbook, if the work is being done by professionals, than to request a radical change in part of the completed tennis court. On the other hand, a desire to change is natural. No matter how carefully you plan, you'll see opportunities for improvements as the project progresses. In any event, the more effort you spend in careful planning, the fewer the changes and additions during construction.

IF YOU EMPLOY PROFESSIONAL HELP

Finding a Reliable Contractor

If you decide to hire a contractor or subcontractor, how do you find a reliable one? Here are six ways to find out.

1. Ask the U.S. Tennis Court and Track Builders Association, 1201 Waukegan Road, Glenview, Ill. 60075, for their free Membership Directory. In it you will find a number of member contractors located throughout the country, some of which may be located right in your area.

2. Consult friends or other people in your community who may have had tennis courts built.

3. Contact owners of racquet clubs.

4. If you are still in doubt, select tennis court contractors from the Yellow Pages.

5. Check with your Better Business Bureau or Chamber of Commerce.

6. Sometimes banks will release credit ratings, a worthwhile indication of business stability.

Once you're ready to put the job out for bids, have each contractor or subcontractor you've selected prepare an estimate from your job outline. Once you've decided, but before signing on the dotted line, secure references, including other owners of tennis courts for whom he has worked. Then check each reference carefully. Consider as worthless letters of recommendation in the hands of the contractors themselves. Almost anyone can obtain a stock recommendation, especially if favors are exchanged for it. Also, check on the contractor's insurance to determine if his policy protects you or other people from injuries, as well as his own workmen if they are hurt on the job.

Here are some additional suggestions: If you hire professionals for building all the tennis court or subcontract only parts of it that you don't want to do yourself, take a lesson from the pros themselves.

Early one fall, a contractor friend of mine said, "I'm leaving in the morning for a month's vacation."

"I didn't know your subcontracts were taken care of for next year's construction," I replied.

"They're not," he said, "I wait till the subcontractors are hungry before accepting bids."

He explained that the time to let contracts was during off-seasons. During January and February he found that subcontractors' bids are made on a narrow margin of profit. As the building season approaches, bids become higher and higher, increasing as much as 50 percent.

Of course, my friend didn't mean the subcontractors were literally hungry! During off-seasons, contractors have few if any contracts for the future, so they are more likely to bid on a smaller profit because they realize it is likely that many bids are being made on the job at hand. Also, this is the time of year to get the better contractors to do the work for you. By the time the construction season rolls around, they'll be snowed under.

When the subcontracts are let and the building begins, it is much to your advantage to spend some time on the job. If your free time is limited, it may be necessary to have a friend or to hire someone to supervise the job in your absence. At any rate, try to be around during the day, even if it is only for a few minutes at a time. This can be time well spent in giving instructions and answering questions. This is not to imply that you will try to tell an experienced craftsman how to do his job. Rather, it means making a decision whenever there is a choice and answering questions that are sure to come up from time to time.

If you cannot visit the job during working hours, try to leave a telephone number where you can be reached. If you are hiring craftsmen by the hour, it is essential that you or someone of your choice be on the job. With the hourly wage what it is, you cannot afford to have them sit around hour after hour waiting for someone to show up to make a decision. Then, too, if you're there, you know you will get what you pay for—no skimping on materials that are covered over later.

IF YOU FORM A PARTNERSHIP

There are two kinds of partnership plans to consider before making a final cost estimate. If they are carefully organized, both can save you money. If either one is carelessly organized, you're headed for trouble and can expect nothing but headaches for your efforts. One is the work partnership, while the second is the ownership partnership.

Work Partnership

Under the *work partnership* plan, two or more do-it-yourselfers trade work to build each one a project. Experienced craftsmen do this all the time. If, for instance, an electrician wants to build a garage, he finds out about other tradesmen who plan to build a house or a cabin in the woods. The end result is that the partners agree to exchange an equal number of hours. Not only is each project swiftly completed, but while construction is taking place there are fewer errors made, for where one workman doesn't understand a particular job, another does. In addition, as long as no one receives money for services, a partnership building program like this generally has the blessing of the local building trade unions.

Generally, work partnerships are organized wholly on trust. The number of partners is usually fewer than five and all are close friends. In such cases, there's no real need to organize a legal partnership involving the services of an attorney. However, certain agreements should be put in writing. The specifics are at the discretion of the partners; as a starter, here are a few points to consider.

1. *Exactly* what is it each partner wants to build and when does he want to begin?
2. On what days of the week can each partner work and for how long each day?
3. What if one or more partners must drop out of the program? Is a monetary compensation earned? Generally, some small compensation is agreed upon, something like $1 an hour or a small gift to be decided upon by the remaining members. Usually, the small payment or gift cost is borne by the partner(s) for whom the work was done.

Ownership Partnership

The *ownership partnership*, sometimes known as a co-op, is by far the more complicated of the two types. In addition to the involvement of time, capital investment is shared by all; the number of partners for all practical purposes, can range from two to twenty.

Partnership tennis courts can cause the same problems as co-op apartment buildings, boats, summer homes, hunting lodges: arguments and/or fights, usually winding up in the courtroom. But jointly owned tennis courts are in existence, and problems can be kept to a minimum if the partnerships are well organized.

Let's suppose you plan to head up a partnership. Without question, you and your fellow tennis players want to form the partnership because of a desire to share costs and have a place to play. So don't begin by running head-on into trouble. Problems can develop, and when they do they'll not fade away by themselves. Suppose there are only ten partners. Not much of a problem, you think, but consider their wives, husbands, friends, and relatives. With little control, the number ten could be blown all out of proportion, creating untold problems.

Unlike the work partnership, you cannot afford to draw up a simple agreement. A legally binding document is a priority; you and your partners should put the engagement of an attorney as your first item of business. When he is selected, all of you must do your homework. Here are twelve questions to answer before meeting with him. You may come up with more.

1. What name do you want? Almost any name is acceptable. It may be a fictitious or trade name, but be sure it isn't similar to one already in existence. If you infringe on a copyrighted name, all of you can wind up in a lawsuit. If a trade name is decided upon, your attorney will recommend registering it with the proper government bureau, depending on the laws of your state.

2. What are the capital assets of the partnership, and how shall they be contributed?

3. If you rent the court(s) for profit, how shall the profits be divided and the losses borne?

4. If you want partners to have a drawing account, what are the provisions? Usually, this is not a problem with tennis court partnerships unless a number of courts are to be constructed.

5. What kind of accounting books shall be kept, and who keeps them? Most likely your attorney will recommend a time for balancing the books as well as having them available for inspection by the partners.

6. What bank shall be the depository?

7. What system shall be adopted for borrowing money or the endorsement of notes?

8. What procedure shall be used by members to retire from the partnership?

9. What provision shall be made if a partner wishes to sell all or part of his shares?

10. Upon the death or total incapacity of any partner, what is to happen to his shares? Do they go to his estate or to the remaining partners?

11. What kind of playing schedule shall be adopted, including prime time? Are guests of partners permitted to play? If so, under what conditions?

12. How shall this agreement terminate? Such things as cessation of partnership business, bankruptcy, receivership, and dissolution of the partnership should be thoroughly discussed with your attorney before he prepares the final partnership agreement.

When the attorney hears your proposal specifying exactly how you plan to carry on the tennis court co-op, he may recommend a corporation rather than a partnership. If he does, was your homework in vain? No, for answers to the previous questions will help him to either recommend a partnership or a corporation. He will point out advantages and disadvantages of both. But you and your partners must weigh the evidence and make the final decision as to which type of business will serve best.

ADDITIONAL COST FACTORS

Time to Build

I pointed out previously how to save money by letting contracts during building off-seasons. Now you can save even more money by not waiting until the last minute to begin construction. It takes from three to six weeks of full-time work, depending upon type of court, to do the job. Allow much more time than this if you expect to do it yourself on a part-time basis.

When you do the job yourself or have some outside help, the important thing is not to become discouraged if you fall behind schedule. We can all learn a lesson from contractors. Their discouragements ended long ago. With unforeseen circumstances, such as strikes, shortage of materials, inclement weather, they take jobs in stride, for their business soon teaches them that unpleasant surprises are part of the building game. Not so with the average novice. Soon he thinks he's only marking time, but most likely he's making more progress than he realizes. Of course, a certain amount of lost motion can always be expected, but surprisingly, keeping faith in oneself and working little by little finds the job soon completed. And you'll save money by pushing ahead, with less outside help to employ.

You can also save money by planning your part-time work schedule so as not to get caught in a bind, forcing the aid of unnecessary outside help to finish on time. For example, if you are building an indoor court where cold weather is a certainty, do the ground clearing, the grading, and put the court under roof before winter rolls around. Then you can work under roof when you have time to spare. Also, if you need additional help, there should be no problem, since most workmen prefer working indoors to working in blustery cold weather.

If you're building an outdoor court, do the preparation work as described above. Generally, weather conditions are such between fall and spring in many parts of the country, that you can do concrete work, such as surfacing, setting posts and filling their holes, and building fence curbing.

Take advantage of off-season building to purchase materials and equipment. Since it takes months to get delivery on some items, you'll have these on hand when you're ready to work. Also, you'll have more time to shop around for better prices on materials and supplies. If storage is a problem, use 4 mil polyethylene, secured from any lumberyard, as a covering. Used bricks and building blocks, used lumber, and tree limbs clean of branches are satisfactory materials for holding the polyethylene in place.

Tool Rental

"I saved $52," says a tennis court builder of Palo Alto, California. "I saved $78," says another court builder of Jackson, Mississippi.

A Detroit, Michigan, do-it-yourselfer "saved more than $350 in interest alone." A recently built private tennis court co-op in the midwest cut corners by more than $500.

Hundreds of people from coast to coast are paying less to build tennis courts by renting tools and leasing buildings to house the finished courts.

It is unnecessary and unwise to purchase all the tools required to build a tennis court. You should base the kinds of self-owned tools on their future use, not just their use to build the court. For instance, you wouldn't think of buying a bulldozer to use only once to do the grading. Reason would call for renting the dozer along with its operator. On the other hand, basic carpentry and concrete-working tools are well worth buying, because they have untold uses around the home long after the tennis court is finished.

Is it practical to purchase a lot of cheap tools, or is it better to divide your budget among quality tools? The answer to this is to propose another question: Would a surgeon perform an operation with a kitchen knife just because it is cheaper than a scalpel? Just as the surgeon demands quality tools in the operating room, you need the best tools on the market to do quality construction work.

How about borrowing tools? If I've learned anything at all about do-it-yourself construction work, I've learned this: If you value your friends, don't borrow their tools, for it is a sure-fire method of breaking up friendships. There is one exception: If you are a party to a building partnership, each workman can take advantage of the other's hand tools. Power tools are an entirely different ball game. Here the borrowing practice is acceptable if the owner, and *only* the owner, operates them. Maintenance and occasional repairs are accepted expectations with power tool usage. However, when operated by unskilled workmen, they tend to require frequent maintenance and break down more often.

Renting both hand and power tools has become big business during the past quarter of a century. Service agencies are now established all over the country, with California leading the field. Whether it is a carpenter's hammer or a chain saw, a tool rental agency usually has it, as well as myriad other tools. For tools used only a few times during a lifetime, the rental charge is extremely reasonable. Charges for similar tools vary slightly from agency to agency. However, the daily rental fee for long-lasting tools runs approximately 3 percent of retail price. For instance, a construction-type wheelbarrow at one agency rents for $1.50 per day, cheaper per day over longer periods of time. This same wheelbarrow sells for $41 at a lumberyard. This same agency rents a $225 chain saw for 8 percent of its retail value, or $18 per day or $10 for a half day. Another point to remember about rental tools is this: Generally, tool rental agencies buy nothing short of heavy-duty tools. To purchase anything less is impractical, considering the hard use they get from the most unskilled workmen to highly experienced craftsmen.

Leasing a Building

More and more park districts, private tennis clubs, and co-op court owners building indoor courts are leasing buildings rather than providing all the capital outlay at the outset of construction. There's a lot of sense to this line of reasoning. Taxes, club dues, and court rentals, as well as salaries, simply don't materialize at one time. Since income to pay the bill is spread over several years and the life expectancy of a building is over a period of several years, it makes good sense, in many cases, to lease rather than to purchase outright. One such structure company which leases or sells outright is the Seaman Building Systems (see Ch. 12 and Sources of Supply). Their Portomod structure is *not* air supported. Rather, it is a rigid steel frame with a fabric membrane, representing a new dimension—an entirely new concept in portable structures. Portomod is available on a most attractive lease contract basis; or it can be purchased directly. There is a structure designed for almost every requirement—single, double, or triple courts. Added attractions of the lease are the renewal and purchase options. Under the lease renewal option, at the end of each selected base period of three, four, or five years, the customer has the option of renewing the lease in minimums of one-year periods at 20 percent of the original yearly lease cost. Under the purchase option, at any point after the basic lease term or renewal term, the customer may purchase the Portomod based upon a qualified appraisal of the structure's true value at the time.

INSURANCE

Perhaps you think your tennis court is the most private place in the neighborhood, but it's really made to order for the professional accident faker helped along by a shady lawyer. And they're both ready to take you through the legal mill, whether you're prepared for it or not.

Most attorneys follow the letter of the law and will not touch an illegal case with a 10-foot pole, but not so with some. Last year more than 100 lawyers were disbarred in the U.S. alone. To make the situation even worse, for every shady lawyer, there're hundreds of characters just waiting to bring accident suits against law-abiding citizens, particularly if they don't carry liability insurance.

Suppose someone has an accident on your ground during construction or later gets hurt while playing tennis on your court without per-

mission. In either case you could be liable for a huge accident claim. Most likely, your retaliation would amount to no more than having the party arrested for trespassing. So before you complete cost estimates, be sure to have your insurance agent check your present home policy to find out whether or not it covers accidents on the court during the period of construction as well as thereafter.

If you are not protected against outsiders who might have accidents on your court, a homeowner's insurance policy could be your best answer. (If you live in Hawaii, Alaska, Oregon, or Mississippi, your insurance agent might recommend a Comprehensive Dwelling policy.) Any reliable agent will explain the policy best suited to your needs.

If you are borrowing money, your lending agent may require title insurance before granting the loan. Such insurance provides protection against such matters as disagreements over property lines and flaws that might appear in the property title. If you are building without financial aid, check with your attorney as to whether it is advisable to buy title insurance. He will give a definite answer once he examines the abstract and title of your parcel of ground.

FUTURE MAINTENANCE COSTS

In matters of future tennis court costs, everyone from grandmother to a seatmate on a jet plane is quick with well-meant advice.

Occasionally, it's sound. But unfortunately, the advice is often misleading, based on hearsay or misconceptions instead of facts.

There is no tennis court absolutely maintenance free, but some need less attention than others. For instance, clay requires constant watering, rolling, weeding, and TLC (tender loving care). To do it yourself requires much backbreaking labor. If you hire a gardener, you'll pay plenty. In addition, resurfacing is needed about every three years, and it will set you back approximately a couple of thousand dollars if you hire it done. Grass can cost more.

Synthetic courts last from five to ten years before requiring resurfacing. Figured on present-day costs, resurfacing runs anywhere from $2,000 to $6,000, depending on type. Replacing the nets should amount to anywhere from $25 to $50 a year, depending upon quality. An occasional repainting of the lines is a negligible cost, but it does have to be done.

If your court is lighted, bulbs or tubes need replacing occasionally, with price depending upon system of lighting.

Snow removal is not expensive if you do it yourself. Hiring it done is another matter. If you plan to install a heating system to remove it, find out now what it costs to operate. You may change your mind.

A chain-link fence should require no maintenance during the first twenty years.

Future costs of an indoor court are figured about the same way as home maintenance.

There is a close relationship between future costs and construction costs. Generally, the cheaper the original installation per square foot, the more the future maintenance costs.

So far I've presented a few general figures on construction and future costs. If you want a more specific estimate, I suggest you browse through the book. Jot down your first, second, and third choices, where practical, of the whole ball of wax, i.e., clearing of ground if required, grading, drainage, type of surface, fence, and other equipment. Then get estimates on those materials you plan to install yourself as well as obtain estimates on the jobs you plan to farm out. The results should help in keeping present and future costs within your set budget.

FINANCIAL RESOURCES

Paying the Bill

So you've looked through the book and found the kind of court and equipment you want but don't have enough money to pay the bill. Don't give up.

First, common practice permits payment in three installments as construction progresses. Second, more and more lending agencies are granting home improvement loans for tennis court construction. The fact that you are going to do most of the labor yourself means less money to borrow, which makes the loan easier to obtain.

If you don't have all the cash, seek the help of a reputable lending agency. It could be a savings and loan association, bank, mortgage loan company, building and loan association, or a private lender of impeccable reputation. Beware of the sharpie who promises quick loans with low interest rates along with almost unlimited time to repay the loan. If in doubt, contact your Better Business Bureau, your Chamber of Commerce, or your attorney.

Reputable lending agencies or individuals always operate within the letter of the law. They agree to supply a given amount of money to complete your court; you sign a note whereby you promise to pay the borrowed amount back in specific installments spaced over a given period of time, with interest set within the state legal limit. A collateral is required to assure payment of the loan. Your life-insurance policy might be enough collateral to cover a small loan. If the sum you wish to borrow is large, other collateral, like your home, might be required.

Under businesslike conditions it is sometimes advisable to borrow from a friend, relative, or a trustworthy individual in the community. But if you do, take nothing for granted. Have all terms, including amount of loan, amount of interest and principal required per month, or other period of payment, clearly in writing. Then before you sign your name, have your attorney approve the document. If you can possibly arrange it, have all document signing done in the presence of your attorney.

Financing Public Tennis Facilities

Revenue bonds and federal assistance matching funds from the Bureau of Outdoor Recreation (BOR) are two major sources used to finance indoor and outdoor public tennis facilities. There is also a new booklet available from the U.S. Tennis Association, prepared by its Education and Research committee, with guidelines for obtaining funds. Donations, grants, local tax funds, lease-back arrangements, and the generosity of a philanthropist are some minor sources.

Revenue bonds are issued by a government agency. These are not approved as general obligation bonds because the facilities do not benefit the average taxpayer. Selling of the bonds provides the money to construct the facility, while the revenue realized from the facility operations are obligated to retire the bonds over a prescribed number of years. If you are interested in this kind of financing, be sure the agreement calls for court fees as the primary source of repayment. Since revenue is required for maintenance, other facilities, such as concession stands, should be a part of the planning and construction stages.

If your city, school district, county, or recreation district is interested in securing grants for fund assistance, grant application for proposed tennis facilities should be made to the official liaison officer of the state. Generally, the grant applications are for fifty-fifty matching funds. Secure complete information from the Regional Director in one of the following cities:

NORTHEAST REGION

District of Columbia, Maine, New Hampshire, Vermont, Massachusetts, Rhode Island, Connecticut, New York, Pennsylvania, West Virginia, Maryland, New Jersey, Delaware

Federal Building
1421 Cherry Street
Philadelphia, PA 19102

SOUTHEAST REGION

Tennessee, Arkansas, Virginia, North Carolina, South Carolina, Georgia, Alabama, Mississippi, Louisiana, Florida, Puerto Rico, Virgin Islands

810 New Walton Building
Atlanta, GA 30303

PACIFIC SOUTHWEST REGION

Arizona, California, Nevada, Utah, Hawaii, American Samoa, Guam

450 Golden Gate Avenue
Box 36062
San Francisco, CA 94102

LAKE CENTRAL REGION

Ohio, Minnesota, Wisconsin, Iowa, Illinois, Michigan, Missouri, Kentucky, Indiana

3853 Research Park Drive
Ann Arbor, MI 48104

PACIFIC NORTHWEST REGION

Oregon, Washington, Montana, Idaho, Alaska

1000 Second Avenue
Seattle, WA 98104

MID-CONTINENT REGION

Texas, North Dakota, South Dakota, Wyoming, Nebraska, Colorado, Kansas, New Mexico, Oklahoma

Building 41
Denver Federal Center
Denver, CO 80225

If your proposal is accepted, it must meet the requirements of the BOR and state recreation plan and guidelines.

Caution: If you want the least amount of friction, secure the assistance of an expert in proposal writing. It is now a highly specialized field. Because of the widespread acceptance of government grants during recent years, there are probably several people in your community who have written a number of government proposals. To find the experts, check with your public school superintendent, county superintendent of schools, and heads of city, township, and county government agencies.

3

Selecting the Surface

"I don't mind the trouble involved in selecting a surface for my tennis court," a friend of mine moaned recently, "but you have to be a combination chemist and engineer to do it right."

He had a point. It's true that he talked to every court owner and builder from far and near, but he didn't have an organized list of points to talk about. So he reaped claims, counterclaims, confusion, and contradiction.

A number of backyard court owners select synthetic all-weather cushioned surfaces that require little maintenance other than removing leaves, and snow if they live in a cold region. But even if you follow in their footsteps and are dead set on having a synthetic surface, what kind will you choose? It seems as if most chemical companies, to say nothing of a few contractors, have plunged into the manufacture of synthetic court surfaces. And each one lays claim to manufacturing a material essential to quality surface texture, ball bounce, resiliency, and minimum player fatigue. In the mad rush to get into the act, some have made the grade; others have discontinued their lines or gone out of business.

Selecting a tennis court surface is an important decision, and should not be made haphazardly. It should be a choice made after considering a variety of factors, such as single or multipurpose use, protection, climatic conditions, amount of money allocated for construction, upkeep and maintenance costs, players' preference, and reputation of the contractor if you hire it done. Examine each one carefully, weigh the evidence, then make the decision.

SINGLE OR MULTIPURPOSE AREA

One important factor in the selection of a surface is whether you want a single or multipurpose playing area. A dyed-in-the-wool tennis player knows exactly what he wants. To talk to him about a multipurpose playing area borders on the sacrilege. He wants a tennis court and a tennis court only. Not so with others, especially those who want a backyard area to bring their families closer together. Here, providing there is room and budget enough, they want a multipurpose area.

Use the dimensioned sketches in Figures 6-1 through 6-5 to assist in reaching a decision on the area of surface required for your choice of activities. If you're multipurpose minded, plan the area for playing either tennis, volleyball, or basketball at one given time. Even if you have the money and space to build the courts close to each other, stray basketballs or volleyballs bouncing all over the tennis court during play doesn't do anything to win friends and influence people.

PROTECTED OR UNPROTECTED COURT

Another important factor deals with the amount of protection afforded against damage during and after construction. Surfaces such as grass, clay, cushioned, and fast-drying should be built only where persons wearing smooth-soled tennis shoes are permitted.

13

One advantage of encompassing the court with a high fence is to provide protection by locking the gate during nonplaying time. Having the court located in the same yard as the house is no insurance against vandalism and well-meaning children wanting to have some fun.

In some cases, protection is provided through supervision by professional tennis players or other responsible people in tennis clubs, country clubs, schools, and parks. Generally, supervision for backyard tennis courts is spotty at best. Where such courts lack protection, there's usually an unnecessarily high maintenance and upkeep cost. Children and adults wearing street shoes, bicycle riders, and roller skaters can do a good deal of damage in a matter of minutes.

If protection is questionable, consider the advantages of a noncushioned type of surface. Such courts as concrete, hot plant-mix asphalt, or job-mixed asphaltic composition are stronger and can withstand normal abuse without damage. Also, outside courts so constructed extend the playing season.

Climatic Conditions

Still another factor to consider when choosing a surface is climate. If you live in an area experiencing either extreme cold or extreme heat, you may be in trouble if you use an unsuitable material. Softening of some surfaces, surface cracking, heat radiation, and glare are some of the problems possible with extreme heat. Surface cracking and upheaval may damage certain surfaces where there is extreme cold and frost action.

SURFACE CHARACTERISTICS

Knowing what to look for before making selection of a tennis court surface is the best way to get satisfaction as well as the most for your money.

Consider each of the following points before making your decision.

What is your cash outlay? If you plan long-term payments, are you sure payments can be made when needed?

Is the court planned for recreational or professional use?

Are you planning to use the court for single purpose or multipurpose games? Some surfaces are not practical for multipurpose use.

What are the players' choices? If you're new to the game, learn from talking with other tennis players in your locality.

What is the construction cost and how much of it can you do? Bargain prices here are the most costly in the long run.

What are the maintenance costs and how much will be required? While you're investigating this point, find out how much of the maintenance you can do yourself.

How long before resurfacing is required? A surface lasting less than three years is a poor investment.

What are the resurfacing costs? A resurfacing job lasting approximately three years should cost in the neighborhood of 33⅓ percent of one requiring resurfacing about every ten years.

Be sure softness of surface is desirable for the players' comfort.

A surface on which players can slide relatively easily or not slide at all reduces possibility of injury.

Do you want a fast or slow surface? Generally, a fast surface applies to a smooth court, such as concrete, while a slow surface applies to a rough court, such as fast-dry or clay.

To what degree is the ball bounce uniform? A moderately hard-hit ball on a fast court is inclined to have a long skid and low bounce. A ball with spin is not diverted much. On the other hand, a moderately hard-hit ball on a slow court is inclined not to skid much, while it's possible for a ball with spin to be diverted.

If an outdoor court, what is the effect of color on glare and heat absorption? Here the answer is best found by examining nearby court surfaces and talking to their owners.

If an outdoor court, what is the drying time following a rain? Sometimes a slow-drying court, especially a porous one, is the result of inadequate drainage system installation during time of construction.

How does the surface hold its color and what is its effect on ball discoloration? Here again, visit and talk with owners of surfaces you are evaluating. This often provides an insight into what to expect from your court.

What are the effects of abrasive surfaces on falling players, as well as on shoes, balls, and rackets? Players falling or sliding on a highly abrasive surface can cause severe skin infection, to say nothing about shortening the lives of shoes, balls, and rackets.

Some materials used for lines have an adverse effect on ball bounce, cause players to trip, and require frequent maintenance.

If an indoor court, some porous courts cause special problems in meeting moisture requirements.

What, if any, are your climatic conditions? For instance, an outdoor tennis court built in a climate similar to the one found in Minneapolis may not have the freeze and thaw problems found in a climate like the one in Champaign, Illinois. In the first case, there's usually one big freeze that lasts throughout the winter. In the second case, there are periodic freezes and thaws, making it possible for serious damage due to punishment caused by frequent upheaval and settling.

If you farm out surface construction, determine the contractor's experience, qualifications, and dependencies. Check with tennis court owners who employed him to build their courts. If possible, find out if he pays his bills promptly. Sometimes a contractor operating with little experience and a shoestring budget has a way of going broke. Then if the court doesn't hold up, he is nowhere to be found. And if you can find him, there's not much point in going to court. After all, what is your gain from obtaining a judgment against a person with all liabilities and no assets?

Does the contractor carry insurance covering liabilities and surface damage, including vandalism, until his services are terminated?

Will the contractor be available when the court requires service? Of course, all contractors may retire, dissolve their businesses, or go broke, but a nearby contractor with an A-1 rating by his customers is more likely to be around when service is required.

Examine Chapter 5. Here you will find the degree of such items as glare, ball spin, ball skid, ball bounce, and other factors as they relate to the different court surfaces.

3-1. Last but not least, play on as many different kinds of courts as possible. This gives you the opportunity to discover many characteristics that meet your personal fancy, one of which is ball bounce. Professional tennis players know that when a tennis ball strikes an object, such as a court surface, part of the ball is flattened. Because the rubber in it is elastic, the ball springs

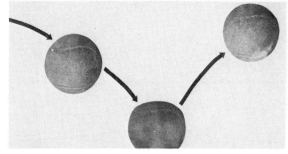

3-1

back to its original shape. Ball bounce is caused by the rubber returning to its original shape.

Bounce is also assisted by the air confined inside the ball. When the ball strikes an object, the air is compressed. This causes an increase in air pressure. As the air expands, the ball is forced outward until it regains its original shape.

As ball bounce varies among different type surfaces, so do several other playing conditions. After you know what to look for in selecting a surface, make an analysis of the players' requirements, or for a private court, your own requirements. Only then begin building the court.

PLATFORM COURTS

If a traditional tennis court is not for you, why not build a platform tennis court? This exciting paddle and ball game follows the basic rules of tennis with only a few variations.

Platform tennis has tremendous appeal. Once tennis players are exposed to it, they are attracted by the excitement and fast pace of the game. In the past few years the game has shown a growth of 25 percent every year, and its popularity is reflected by the American Platform Tennis Association, which now has over 250 clubs and sponsors annual televised tournaments.

Since the size of the court is 31 x 61 feet, generally built on a platform supported by pillars, it can be constructed on sites unthinkable for traditional tennis courts. Rooftops, marshy ground, hillsides, and backyards, all without extensive site work, are made to order for platform courts. And the beauty of building on reasonably level terrain is that any of the traditional tennis court surfaces can be substituted for the platform, as explained in Chapter 7.

4

Constructing the Court Foundation

Before actual on-site work begins, be certain you have planned well and thoroughly, making preliminary decisions that will help carry the project through to completion. Determine the type of surface you want, reviewing considerations in Chapter 3 and the information on specific surfaces in Chapter 5. From this point on, you'll carry out only those preparatory operations which apply to the particular surface you'll be installing.

Select a location, avoiding low, marshy ground, then ascertain where you want to locate the long axis of the court. If your site is well away from moving vehicles and tall buildings, fulfills code requirements or other restrictions (*see* Ch. 1), and you've obtained your building permit, you are ready to begin.

DETERMINING AXIS POSITION

Although directional layout of indoor tennis courts is left to the discretion of the builder, not so with outdoor courts. Here one should govern the most desirable court angle by site characteristics, specific weather, season or seasons of heaviest play, and latitude.

Because the sun helps dry the courts following a rain or watering the surfaces, it's a welcome sight to the players. But there's no need to penalize some of them for the service by having the sun shine in their eyes. As a preventive measure, courts should be laid out in a general north–south direction. Making the layout now

can save time and money when you clear the site, do the grading, build the base, and apply the surface.

True north, or the earth's geographic north, is used to determine the north–south axis, rather than the earth's magnetic north pole. Examine a globe or map of the world. The point where all north–south (longitudinal) lines meet at the top of the world is the true north or geographic pole. Do not use a compass to locate "north," for it points toward the magnetic north pole. In fact, the magnetic north pole lies at a distance of 1,000 miles from the geographic north pole. Also, it does not lie on the surface, but is located approximately 70 miles beneath the earth's surface. For example, in the District of Columbia, a compass needle points about 7° west of true north, while in San Diego, a compass needle points about 15° east of true north.

If you live in the northern United States, full-time outdoor play is approximately limited to the last days of March through the first days of November. Here the court axis of north–south seems to be the most desirable.

4-1. If you build a court in the southern United States below 42° north latitude, play is generally on a year-round basis. So plan the court location 20° to 22° west of true or geographic north, as shown. With this location, neither winter nor summer play will cause a hardship on right-handed players on the north court by having them look almost directly into the sun. This is especially true during the winter months.

16

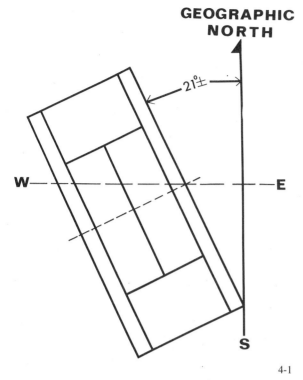

GEOGRAPHIC NORTH

21°±

W —— E

S

4-1

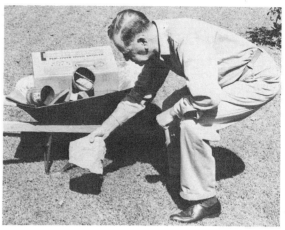

4-2

CLEARING THE SITE

The first order of business is clearing the site. Even if you're going to hire pros to do most of the actual construction, you can save a small bundle of cash by doing some of the preliminary work, such as removing rocks, clearing debris, felling trees and trimming limbs, and grubbing sprouts if they're in the way.

Removing Rocks and Debris

If you are not familiar with the subsoil in your area, you can readily find out about it by making test borings. In most cases, making several holes 3 or 4 feet deep with a posthole digger reveals enough of the subsoil to let you know whether or not it is suitable to support a tennis court.

Next begin clearing the site by removing rocks, bricks, and other objectionable items, both on the surface and to a depth of 12 inches, if they are within the boundaries of the grading area.

4-2. The picture shows a good example of a rock that is ideal to help make a beautiful rock garden in a part of the yard removed from the

court. Disposing of surplus debris, such as rocks, bricks, and broken pieces of concrete, may not present the problem you at first think. Covered with 18 inches of dirt, they provide ideal fill material for low places in your yard. On the other hand, if they're no use to you, try giving them away by placing an ad over a radio station "trading post" program, as well as post notices in public places such as laundromats and grocery stores that provide such services to individuals not in competition with local businesses. You may be surprised to discover how easy it can be to get free help in disposing of them.

If large boulders are present, about the only quick way to remove them is by blasting, certainly a must for the pros if this is your problem.

Felling Trees and Grubbing Sprouts

"Woodman, spare that tree" is as important today, and perhaps more so, than it was when the familiar old saw was first uttered by a thoughtful lover of nature. In fact, trees are loved more today than anytime in history—except by eager beavers removing leaves and twigs from the court or waiting for the sun and wind to dry a tree-shaded one. This is to say nothing of leaves and twigs which, if left over a period of time, will also discolor and deteriorate a hard-surface court, resulting in a premature resurfacing job. So regardless of how some people might feel about felling trees, you will be the one to pass final judgment on whether certain trees are transplanted, stand, or fall.

4-3

4-3.   Tag trees you plan to transplant with visible white bands, such as strips of white rags.

Chain Saws

I've witnessed people felling trees with every kind of hand-operated saw from a bucksaw to a crosscut timber saw, but they were doing the job the hard way. Nothing is more practical to fell trees and trim limbs than a chain saw. If you're renting or buying one, look into the merits of both the electric and gasoline-powered ones before making a selection.

I own an electric chain saw sold by Sears, Roebuck and Company. What I like best about an electric saw is its relatively quiet operation. It's so quiet it can be used indoors if required. I use a #12-gauge trailing cord 200 feet long, and this doesn't bother me as much as I expected, even when working from a ladder or up in a tree. My Sears saw features a self-sharpener, which only takes a few seconds to do a pro job. Every fifth sharpening it's a good idea to touch up each cutter with a 5mm round hand file. Also, the chain is self-oiling, and the built-in clutch prevents motor stalling and chain movement when the motor starts and stops. The saw has a double-insulated motor housing, so I feel perfectly safe from electric shock.

A gasoline motor-operated saw is extremely noisy, and sometimes there is a problem of the small-diameter gasoline line stopping up with small particles of dirt. Even so, this is the only saw to use if you do any camping or use it where electricity is lacking. You could use an electric saw in conjunction with a portable 120-volt alternating current generator, but such an arrangement would be both cumbersome and expensive. Gasoline motor-operated saws can be purchased with an automatic chain-oiling device, chain self-sharpener, and built-in clutch, as described above for the electrically operated saw.

Anyone can be careless and have an accident while using a power chain saw. On the other hand, it is almost impossible to have an accident if you will study the following tips provided for your safety. Most are directed to the operator of either a gasoline or electrically powered saw; a few tips are of special interest only to one as the other.

1. Do not allow children to operate saw, nor allow adults to operate it without full knowledge of these safety tips and instructions on felling and trimming trees.

2. Always keep adults, children, and pets at a safe distance when saw is in operation.

3. Be sure to keep your hands, any other part of your body, and clothing away from the moving chain.

4. Do not wear baggy clothes, and keep your shirttails tucked in at all times. Wear safety glasses, heavy shoes, and heavy gloves. If you're felling large trees, or any size trees with broken or dead limbs, wear a protective helmet such as a hard hat.

5. Work slowly! Many accidents happen when operators hurry.

6. Provide a good footing by clearing away all brush and debris entirely around the tree.

7. Provide an escape path, and be certain it is free of tools and other obstructions.

8. Carry saw with the engine or motor off and the bar to the rear.

9. With your footing secure and weight evenly distributed on both feet, grip both handles firmly when operating saw.

10. Don't refuel a gasoline-powered saw in the cutting area.

11. Don't start a gasoline-powered saw in the fueling area.

12. Don't smoke when refueling a gasoline-powered saw.

13. Keep cord on electrically powered saw clear of chain at all times.

14. Don't guess. Know exactly how your chain saw operates by becoming familiar with all the different sections of the manual before attempting to operate the saw. Know all the controls, and keep the chain sharp and oiled at all times.

15. Help keep saw in good working condition by keeping all nuts, bolts, and screws tight.

16. Never cut with chain-lubricating system out of order, and use only the type of oil recommended in the manual.

17. When cutting a log into desired lengths (bucking), always take an uphill position.

18. Stop saw and inspect for damage if chain strikes a foreign object. Be sure to repair any damage before operating saw.

19. Always stand to the side of saw when cutting. Never stand directly behind saw, in case the chain catches in a cut and kicks backward.

20. Watch for broken or loose limbs (widow makers) when felling a tree or trimming its branches.

21. Before felling a tree, practice making cuts on small, fallen logs as described later.

22. Don't cut when there's a hard wind.

23. Never work under lean of tree.

24. When trimming or pruning (removing unwanted limbs from a standing tree), fasten saw to a rope so you can pull it up into the tree. Keep the rope tied to the saw while cutting. Also, tie the remaining end of the rope to the tree or a tree limb so saw cannot strike a limb or the ground if it should fall. Be sure you are secured to the tree; use a safety belt or rope around the tree trunk so you can use both hands on the saw. Start saw only after assuming correct cutting position.

25. If you use felling wedges, be sure they're not made of metal. Use only those made of plastic or wood so as not to damage the chain should they meet.

26. If you use an ax, be sure it is kept sharp. You should use the head of a single-bitted ax or sledge to set the wedges. Be sure to keep ax head or sledge free of burrs.

Soundness and Height of Tree

Before deciding to fell a tree, see if it is sound enough and not too tall to tackle yourself. Sometimes a sound-looking tree is deceiving and has more rot at the core than will provide enough

togetherness to control it during the fall. Generally, such a tree's bark pulls away easily, exposing punky wood underneath. If the tree is very rotten on the inside, bits of bark and rotten core are generally found on the ground at its base.

Warning: Such a tree can be dangerous to both property and life while cutting! If you're inexperienced in felling trees, don't try it alone. Better hire a professional for this one and profit by observing his technique.

If you decide the tree is for you to cut, determine its height before felling it. If the tree is squeezed close to obstacles, such as power or telephone lines, buildings, or other trees, do not guess at its height. You can determine the exact height with a clinometer, priced between $13 and $16, or you can rent one from a tool rental store.

Direction of Fall

Natural fall is determined by inclination of tree from the perpendicular or plumb; also, by excessive weight of limbs on one side. Tree limbs growing close to other trees are usually smaller than the ones growing on the open side.

Caution: Never fell trees when wind is strong, as it affects direction of fall and could be dangerous.

Never leave lean of tree to chance. Know for certain by plumbing it from four different places, 90 degrees apart. If you don't have a plumb bob, tie a piece of cord to a heavy bolt as a substitute.

After determining direction of fall, you may want to support yourself on a strong ladder and use a chain saw to remove low-hanging limbs to improve weight distribution. Use a pruning saw to remove thin branches.

Note: When using a chain saw, always cut with spike bar of saw firmly against wood, also being sure chain is well oiled.

I don't recommend getting up into a tree with a chain saw unless you are a pro, but if you must, be sure to reread point "24" under tips for safe operation of chain saws in the preceding section.

Felling

4-4. If lean of tree is excessive from desired lay, leave the job to a professional. Assuming your tree is to drop in the direction of its natural inclination, slightly away from it, or is practically vertical, proceed to cut it. First clear an escape

4-4

path. Be prepared, when the tree begins to fall, to never run directly behind it as it might split vertically from the stump, throwing the back of the tree out toward you. Rather, be prepared to run away at a 45°-angle behind the line of fall. The pair of arrows at upper right indicate direction of lay (fall).

Begin sawing by making the undercut in two steps, called facing the tree. Using a chain saw, make horizontal *kerf cut 1* about one-fourth of the tree's diameter, on the side and at a right angle to the direction you want it to lay. Now angle *cut 2* into it about one-fifth the diameter of tree above cut 1, meeting the back edge of cut 1, squarely forming a notch. With resulting wedge removed, examine the cut. If it isn't clear, square it up with a chain saw or an ax.

Caution: This is an extremely important step, particularly in larger trees where a poor preparation can cause the hinge to break badly or too soon, thereby adversely affecting fall of tree.

Next make *cut 3* from the back side, 2 or 3 inches higher and parallel to bottom of notch. Saw an inch or two from the notch to form *hinge 4*. (The purpose of the hinge is to provide the tree with something to pull against while it is falling.) Once cut 3 is deep enough to allow you to start a wedge, do so. This is a safeguard against the tree pinching the saw. Also, alternating between saw-

ing backcut 3 and driving the wedge with a sledge gradually forces tree forward toward direction of lay. Never cut closer than 2 inches to the notch. If tree doesn't start to fall by this time, help it along by driving wedge or wedges deeper into the cut, always keeping a keen ear peeled for the cracking of wood, made just prior to the fall. Immediately, as tree starts to fall, pull out saw, stop the engine or motor and leave saw on the ground while you take off on your escape path.

Warning: During the tree-cutting operation, be sure people and animals are at a safe distance. Even the best woodsmen sometimes cut trees that don't fall according to plan.

Bucking

Bucking is a woodsman's term used to describe cutting a log into shorter lengths. The rule of thumb is not to saw until you know how the log is supported. Knowing this, you can have the cut opening away from your saw, rather than pinching it, as the final cut is made. Also, when sawing, avoid cutting into the earth. Doing so is a sure way of dulling the chain. The following three examples show how bucking is done.

4-5.   Trim limbs from a fallen tree by working from the base toward the top. Always cut limbs off the opposite side from where you are standing. To prevent limbs from binding saw, begin by cutting limbs (supported by branches) about halfway through from top side as shown. Then complete cut from bottom.

4-6.   If log is supported on one end, start cut from underneath side as shown and cut about

4-5

4-6

4-7

Note: Don't carry chain saw while climbing a ladder or tree. It's much safer to lift it with a rope.

4-8. Start *cut 1* from underside approximately 6 inches from trunk, sawing about one-third through its thickness. Then make *cut 2* approximately 3 inches farther out on the limb, sawing until it falls. Now make *cut 3* one-third through its thickness and as close to trunk as possible without damaging its bark. Complete *cut 4* from above limb and as close to trunk as possible to meet undercut 3. Be sure chain clears bark on trunk.

Note: Never leave limb stubs on trunk, for they will sooner or later decay and, quite frequently, do damage to the trunk.

When pruning job is completed, apply two coats of pruning and tree wound dressing to the pruned areas on the trunk. You can obtain it from most hardware stores and nursery supply houses. Two applications protect three wounds from insect damage by certain insect borers.

Removing Stumps

"With a few sticks of dynamite, a nitroglycerin cap, and three feet of fuse, I can blow that stump so it will lie just above the ground for easy removal," said Bert, my long-time friend and former neighbor. He blew the stump alright, but

one-third of the way through log. (Continued cutting would cause saw to pinch.) Then complete by cutting from top side to meet first cut.

4-7. If log is supported on both ends, start cut from top side and continue to cut about one-third of the way through log. Then saw from bottom side to meet first cut.

Pruning

Pruning is a term used by woodsmen and nurserymen for cutting unwanted limbs from standing trees.

If a limb is cut in only one operation, its weight can cause it to break prematurely, thereby tearing the bark of the trunk as the limb tumbles to the ground. Here's the correct way to do the job.

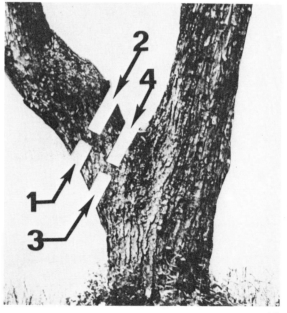

4-8

not "just above the ground." With the *boom* of the explosion, I was reminded of a missile heading for outer space. Its course was in an arc, roughly 60 feet high and 40 feet down range, where it landed right side up on Bert's pickup truck. Fortunately, there were no people or animals within the immediate area. Since he was not a licensed demolition expert, his insurance did not cover the damages.

Warning: No matter how much knowledge anyone claims to have about the properties of explosives, never allow anyone but a demolition expert to use dynamite in any form or any other highly explosive materials on your construction site.

There are chemicals, available from garden supply houses, to help deteriorate a stump. They are poured into predrilled holes made in the top of the stump. This method is not only time consuming, but eventually you'll need fill dirt to fill in the hole left by the stump. Since the chemicals are toxic, wear rubber gloves if you decide to use them. This method of disposal is out of the question with stumps located in the future playing area, although treatment also aids in combustion if you decide to use kerosine to "burn it out." *Never use gasoline* for burning stumps. The risk of danger is much too great. If kerosine is used, be sure it is poured on a flaming fire. Pouring kerosine on a smoldering fire will generate gas, causing a dangerous explosion.

The best way to remove stumps is to let the operator of heavy equipment do it. He will hook a heavy log chain around the stump, pulling it out of the ground quicker than a dentist can pull a tooth.

Grubbing Sprouts

You can use a shovel to dig the ground and an ax to cut the roots of sprouts, but it is faster to use a special tool called a grubbing hoe if you have many sprouts to remove. Most tool rental stores charge only a small fee for the use of one.

To prevent voids forming later from decaying roots in the subsoil, cut out the sprouts and their root systems to a minimum depth of 12 inches. Then treat the soil with a sterilant (carried by most hardware stores) that will effectively inhibit future growth of flora.

If your site requires excavating, there is no point in your taking time to grub out the sprouts. They will be removed with the soil at that time by the excavator.

GRADING AND EXCAVATION

Regardless of the kind of tennis court you decide upon, its serviceability will depend largely upon proper preparation for the base: establishing grade lines, excavation, fill material, and base. The weight of the court structure itself must be ultimately carried by earth through all kinds of weather conditions. A sound understructure, which provides an even base for the court proper to rest upon, will do much to prevent uneven settlement resulting in cracks and additional maintenance costs.

With site cleared of trees and growth including root systems, the next job is to excavate and/or fill. You may be one of the lucky ones with a level site, thin layer of topsoil to remove, and a small amount of fill soil to be delivered. In such a case, most likely you'll want to do all the work yourself, using a long-handled shovel and a wheelbarrow.

4-9.   On the other hand, you may be one of the court builders not so lucky. If so, arrange to contract with an excavation subcontractor who uses either a bulldozer or shovel dozer (sometimes referred to as a front-end loader) to excavate the dirt. If your site has rocky ledges, you'll need an operator using a back hoe, clamshell, or regular power shovel.

Excavation charges vary with type of equipment used, amount of time required to move machinery to and from the job, and amount of work required. Start by discussing the nature of your site with two or more excavation subcontractors. They will want to know about type of soil: amount of rock, if any; slope of the land; amount of soil to dispose of; amount of fill dirt to deliver, if required; and whether you or they are responsible for establishing the grade lines. You'll learn

4-9

which one has the type of equipment best suited for the job. Equipment is one thing to discuss, but so is price. Some subcontractors rent their equipment with an operator by the day. When this book went to press, $225 per day was about average for a machine and operator. The price may seem excessive, but remember: A good operator with good equipment can do hundreds of times the work you can do in the same amount of time. If you expect to have excess soil to dispose of or require fill dirt delivered, find out exactly how much each truckload will cost. Once you choose your subcontractor, have him visit the site. Then have him put in writing everything discussed, including total price and when it is to be paid.

Establishing Grade Lines

Whether you hire an excavation subcontractor or not, establishing the grade lines yourself can result in a substantial saving.

From this point until the surface application, the most important requirement is that you want the excavation dug and the low areas filled to grade—within ¾ inch—and one that will follow the contour or slope of the finished court. To do this properly, you should work with a transit. One can do a fairly decent job using a line level, but using a transit is less time consuming and the results are more accurate.

If you've never used a transit, don't hesitate to either rent or buy one and use it. Your tool rental agency probably has one on display right now. Most likely it will be a basic simple-to-use model, practical enough for you to do any survey job required around the home, including laying out a tennis court.

Reliable land surveys dealing with benchmarks and other surveyor's lingo are still for the professionals, who need transits as expensive and complicated as some astronomical telescopes. But you need neither extensive training nor an expensive instrument to take accurate measurements to lay out a court.

If you want to extend your surveying knowledge beyond the techniques illustrated here, I suggest the purchase of a booklet, "How to Use Transits and Levels for Faster, More Accurate Building," published by Berger Instruments, 37 Williams Street, Boston, Massachusetts 02119. An instrument such as the 190A, found in many rental agencies, is as good as you need.

Slope for Proper Drainage

Here's some preliminary information you'll need before using a transit: Refer to it as often as necessary until all construction operations are complete. Is your court going to be porous or nonporous? There's a difference in slope requirements.

Slope a porous court surface one inch in 20 feet on a true plane from end-to-end, side-to-side, or corner-to-corner. The court should never drain to or from the net or center line: Such drainage would raise or lower net height. Draining from end-to-end gives the players on the high side a little advantage because they have a slightly lower net to clear. However, this is compensated for if they alternate, playing the same number of games on each side of the net. Ideally, it is better to drain from side-to-side where practical. On the other hand, sloping the court in accordance with the slope of the site can save dollars in excavation and fill costs. So you may be tempted to favor idealism over practicality. The high side of a porous court dries faster than the lower side, thereby forming a few birdbaths or more moisture, causing a slower ball bounce.

Slope a nonporous court one-half as much as a porous court—one inch in 10 feet. All other specifications for a porous court apply here.

Using a Transit

A transit has three basic uses:

1. To determine the difference in height or elevation between a known surface and an unknown surface.
2. To establish 90° corners and parallel sides of a square or rectangular area by using a given corner and side.
3. To determine if an object (stake, building) is plumb or tilted by using crosshair and swinging the transit.

A transit isn't complicated at all once you're familiar with the parts and their uses. Take a look at each part on your transit as it is discussed. The transit itself is an instrument containing a high-powered telescope with built-in crosshairs. Like any magnifying lens, you can read numbers, see marks, or see small objects, such as a nail head, at a distance not identifiable with the unaided eye. The crosshairs make it possible to relate

4-10

ing on wheel, level scope in a single plane with a bubble and four adjusting screws provided for making accurate adjustments.

4-11.   The rod (also called a story rod, leveling rod, or stadja rod) is a light pole marked with gradations, held upright by a helper, and read by the surveyor through the transit scope. If you purchase a transit, you can save around $30 by substituting a folding rule, as shown by the young man in the picture.

Before establishing grade stakes for excavation and/or fill, give consideration to the area immediately adjoining the court. Most of us have witnessed what heavy rain damage can do to them and sometimes to the fences as well, especially when the ground just outside the fence drops quickly.

During heavy rains literally tons of water flow toward the low end of the court, exerting tremendous force against everything in its path. Usually, the court proper can take it, but not so with the adjoining ground, particularly if there is a steep grade. It is here that washouts begin.

Now is the time to do some serious thinking and make provisions for a wide shoulder or apron on the side that will receive the runoff. Extend the shoulder about 5 feet beyond the court edge, with a grade no greater than ½ inch to the foot, to help slow the speed of oncoming

these small objects accurately. As you observe, the scope mounts on a round table containing degree markings completely around the circle or 360°. The table is fastened to a tripod.

4-10.   With scope set at proper degree mark-

4-11

water. Even if your ground is almost level, washing will occur unless it is well sodded.

What if you're crowded for space and simply don't have room for a wide apron? Don't give up. There are a couple of solutions. If the falloff is sudden, plan to pour a concrete trough or a runway to carry the water to lower ground.

Although somewhat more expensive, you can pour a retaining wall, especially if the court drainoff takes a sudden drop.

If you're building a porous-type court, don't hold too much faith in its ability to absorb excess water. During extremely heavy rains, the quantity of water flowing over any court can cause severe damage.

Here's how the washout culprit works. It begins with little rivulets forming on the shoulder; then the base begins to wash out from underneath the edge of the court. Unless a correction is made immediately, the court proper begins to break off. Final stages are noted when the court itself sinks into the void underneath caused by the erosion. If this happens you're in big trouble.

4-12. Assuming your north–south axis for one side of the court is located as described, determine the actual court outline, including the apron, with leveling stakes. Some 2 x 2 stakes, 3 feet long, driven about 12 inches into the ground, will be fine. Begin by driving *stake 1* at one corner of the north–south axis line. Placing a piece of scrap lumber on top of a stake, when driving, reduces chances of splitting or distorting it. Then center transit over stake with its plumb bob. Next level the table precisely on two axes 90° apart. To do this, use the four screw legs and the bubble level built into the transit for the purpose of leveling. When the scope is absolutely level, the horizontal crosshair is a mark in space at the same height no matter in what direction scope is pointed, and the vertical crosshair is a mark in space absolutely plumb.

Now measure 78 feet (length of court) along the north–south axis, at which point you drive the second corner *stake 2*. With your helper holding the rod plumb on stake 2, sight on it. Then set the angle scale at 0°. (Use a 100-foot steel tape to locate distances of remaining sides.)

Carefully swing the transit 90°, having your helper locate the rod so it is centered on the vertical crosshair of the scope. Then drive *stake 3* into the ground after measuring 36 feet from stake 1. Locate *stake 4* by repeating transit and rod operation from stake 2.

Here's the way to check the layout. Start at stake 4 and work back, using same operations as described in preceding paragraph. Distances between stakes 1 and 2 and stakes 3 and 4 are 78 feet. Distances between stakes 2 and 4 and stakes 1 and 3 are 36 feet. For layout to be perfectly rectangular, distances between stakes 1 and 4 and stakes 2 and 3 (diagonal measurements) must be of equal length.

At this point, move transit far enough from excavation area so it will be clear of large equipment operations. Then level transit as before.

4-13. Now locate a line of sight from transit to a mark on a fixed object, such as a tree or building, to keep check on a true level throughout the building operation. If a fixed object is not within 50 feet of the working area, substitute a tall stake extending about 6 feet above ground. Drive a small nail partway into fixed object at a point where the horizontal crosshair cuts it. Now

4-12

4-13

position rod on the ground next to nail in fixed object, adjusting 0 marking to coincide with center of nail head. In other words, center of marking on fixed object and 0 marking on rod or selected marking on folded rule must be at exactly the same height. Do not remove nail until court is complete, as you will want to use the nail as a checkpoint from time to time when using the transit. Also, use the nail to establish a level line each time transit is set up at the beginning of a new workday.

Rather than using a nail, you can use the center of a cross marked on cardboard and taped to a fixed object, such as a tree, as shown.

4-14. With nail driven into a fixed object, you now have a permanent means of establishing grade stakes. Locate height of corner stakes first. Begin by driving the corner stake located on the highest part of the site. If site seems almost level, use transit and rod to locate highest corner. Then drive intermediate stakes, about 20 feet apart, to proper height between corner stakes.

Either wood or metal stakes are acceptable. A piece of metal reinforcement rod is shown. There are two ways to show grades. One way is to drive a stake into the ground until top is on grade. (How to locate grade is explained in the next paragraph.) Another way is to drive all stakes "plenty high." Then show grade with a crayon

mark at proper height on each stake. If large equipment is coming to the site, tie a strip of rag on each stake; this helps keep operator from running over stakes.

Keeping in mind proper slope, as previously described, have helper hold rod or folding rule vertically on top of each stake around perimeter of court as you check elevation with transit. Sighting of plus inch marks indicates top of stake is X number of inches above true grade while minus inch marks indicate top of stake is X number of inches below true grade..For example, suppose a stake shows +4 and the slope at this point is one inch below grade. True grade is then 5 inches below top of stake.

If you plan to build a wide shoulder or apron, drive leveling stakes to correct grade to show excavator that slope decreases in this area.

Excavation

There's always a thrill in store as the mammoth piece of earth-moving equipment is unloaded on your site.

After the exchange of pleasantries, tell the operator the actual elevation of the stakes. Then he can see by the arrangement of them where to backfill over low areas and cut back the soil on the high areas to provide the finished grade according to your plans. Also instruct him to push the topsoil, approximately 6 inches thick, over to the side of your court area away from the subsoil pile. You can use it again in bringing the ground up to the elevation of the finished court. Have him go as far as he can in backfilling the low areas with subsoil.

Dirt isn't dirt cheap by any means. For instance, topsoil 6 inches thick on a site measuring 50 x 100 feet contains slightly more than 92 cubic yards. Costs of delivering topsoil vary the country over, but in any area it pays dividends to save as much topsoil as possible. Here's another point to consider when figuring the amount (and replacement value) of topsoil required. Soil packs over the years, so 6 inches of compacted soil is equivalent to more than 6 inches of loose soil. Take the 50 x 100 foot area mentioned here, for example: 5000 square feet times 6 inches yields 2500 cubic feet. Since soil is sold by the cubic yard, 2500 feet divided by 27 (27 cubic feet equal one cubic yard) equal approximately 92½ cubic yards. But this is packed soil. When you pur-

4-14

4-15

chase topsoil, loose soil is delivered. It is reduced to approximately 75 percent of its bulk when spread and packed, which increases the value of your topsoil moved to the pile. Since this is also true of fill dirt, always increase your order approximately 25 percent over the calculated volume required.

Between the time the excavation is finished and the starting of the base, you will likely have rain, which can leave you with a duck pond. To prevent the excavated area from standing in water, lead water away by digging a small trench from the lower end to a lower ground level. (If you require drain pipes for the finished court, read ahead so they can be installed at the most opportune time.)

Fill Material and Drainage

The removal of soil and the bringing in of fill dirt should provide the finished grade on which the base is constructed. Place the fill material to required grade in layers not exceeding 6 inches. Drainage pipes or systems are not required in the sub-base where normal drainage is good. However, if water flows underground, it may erupt near or inside the court area. If you suspect this problem, install a drainage system outside and adjacent to the court. Use drain tile with open joints or perforated rubber styrene plastic sewer and draining pipes laid in granular material as part of the sub-base around the perimeter of the court. The lines should be pitched not less than 6 inches per 100 linear feet and directed to outlet drains or open ditches. If drainage is extremely poor, install additional drain lines 10 feet apart underneath the court, connecting them to the perimeter drain lines to form one large drainage system. If drainage is reasonably good but you want to play it safe, install one 4-inch line through the center of the court each way, connecting them to the perimeter drain lines. (Instructions on the installation of drain pipes and systems are described in Ch. 9.)

4-15. Operator is shown completing grading in one direction. Now he is moving grader to end of court where he will cross grade. You and a helper can assist operator to bring grade to plus or minus ½ inch. Following passing of grader, stretch a line between grade marks of two stakes at a time. This clearly indicates where and how much fill or cut is necessary.

When grading is complete, cross section with roller weighing not less than 5 tons to pack fill and cut areas alike. Probably your equipment operator has such a roller available. If there's going to be a drop between the edges of your apron and the ground below, between 1 and 4 feet, build a retaining wall to prevent heavy rains from damaging the apron and possibly damaging the court surface as well.

First check the building code. Most likely you will need a permit and discover retaining wall heights are limited to 4 feet unless the design is drawn up by a qualified engineer.

Here's the way surface water works: It seeps into the ground until it strikes a layer of clay. Then it flows along the top of it, forming a most slippery surface. If a retaining wall is placed on a clay surface supplied by an abundance of water, it's possible for the wall to slide away, much like a sled over snow or ice. For this reason, soil adjoining such walls should be provided with a means of draining excess water away.

4-16. Begin building the retaining wall

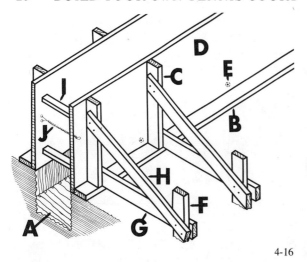

4-16

(maximum height 4 feet) by digging trench *A* a minimum of 12 inches wide and to a depth below the frost zone. Be sure to square the bottom. Where freezing is not a problem, dig the trench a minimum of 18 inches deep. The 2 x 4s (*B*) serve as straightedges to bottom of form. Next cut enough 2 x 4 studs (*C*) so they can be spaced 12 to 16 inches along the outside of each panel *D*. Then locate stud markings on shoes *B* every 12 or 16 inches (12 inches is better). Using two 16-penny box nails for each fastening, nail through shoes *B* into end grain of studs *C*. Next cut ⅝ or ¾-inch-thick exterior plywood *D* to proper widths and fasten to shoes *B* and studs *C* with 6-penny box nails spaced about 8 inches apart. To minimize pressure on retaining wall, use a hacksaw to cut pieces of 2-inch plastic pipe *E* exact distance between panels *D* (exact thickness of retaining wall) to serve later as through-the-wall drains. Space them every 6 feet horizontally on the inside, near bottom of form. Next drive one 8-penny box nail per pipe from outside of each form wall into pipe openings to form supports for holding pipes in position during concrete-pouring operation. Close ends of forms with ⅝- or ¾-inch plywood.

Now cut as many 2 x 4 stakes *F*, about 2 feet long (length depends upon solidity of earth into which they are driven), as you have studs *C*. Use a saw or an ax to point one end of each. Then drive them into the ground a minimum of 3 feet from stud location. Next cut bottom braces *G* and angle braces *H* to properly brace studs *C*, fastening in place as shown with two 16-penny box nails at each joint. Next cut enough spreaders *I* from scrap lumber to hold forms proper

distance apart until the concrete is poured. Locate them about 2 feet apart vertically and 8 feet apart horizontally.

Make tie wires *J* by cutting 12-gauge wire so as to pull plywood panels *D* against spreaders *I* during the pouring operation. Cut each wire about 6 inches longer than twice the width of form. Then run wires through panels, twisting tightly with a piece of wood or a large nail; if wires break, you're twisting them too tightly.

When form is complete, order concrete (*see* Appendix, Table I, for mixture and figuring correct amount) from a ready-mix firm. It's a good idea to place the order several days prior to delivery time. In case of unfavorable weather, find out how much time, prior to delivery, is required for cancellation. When the truck arrives, have the driver pour the concrete in layers of approximately 8 inches thick. Use a flat hoe to work the pliable concrete up and down panels *D* as it is being poured. This operation also helps the concrete to move better horizontally along *D* sides. While you're working the flat hoe on the inside of the form, have a helper use a carpenter's hammer to tap up and down outside edge of studs *C*. Also, have him tap panels *D* between studs below the level of concrete as it is being poured. The working of the flat hoe and the tapping of the hammer will work cement next to the outside panels, making for a professionally smooth retaining wall. As the concrete begins to set up, use a cement finisher's trowel to smooth the top and an edging tool to form a neat rounded top edge.

After 48 hours carefully remove the boards. Actually, about 30 days are required for concrete to cure and reach its ultimate strength. If you find a few pit holes along the outer retaining wall, trowel in some pancake-like batter made by mixing two parts Portland cement with one part of clean, strained sand and just enough water to make the mixture workable. If it doesn't want to trowel into the holes, moisten (do not saturate) the voids with water prior to applying the mixture.

4-17.   Before backfilling the back side of the retaining wall, place a layer of coarse gravel *A* all along bottom of retaining wall, as shown. This allows excess water to flow toward weep holes *B* formed by the through-the-wall drains installed while building the form. If approach to your retaining wall is a steep grade, build gutter *C* to lead excess water to lower ground. For easy cleaning, form gutter about the width of a shovel.

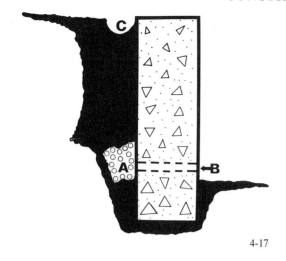

4-17

pearance. Also, you can smooth the gutter by substituting a round quart bottle or a round gallon glass jug, pulled back and forth over the length of the gutter. Use of bottle or jug depends upon gutter width. In either case, be sure to maintain about 4 inches of concrete on each side and bottom of form.

If you have backfilled to build your court on the side of a steep hill, use a series of close-set terraced retaining walls with gutters, rather than one high wall, to keep the soil from eroding. Several low retaining walls, say a maximum of 4 feet each, are more pleasing to the eye, easier to sod, plant shrubs or vines, and much more likely to remain in a vertical position.

Here's another solution to a drainage problem. If the grade, beginning with edge of apron, is steep but with no appreciable vertical drop, all you need for protection from erosion is a gutter sized to suit.

4-18. You can join clay tile (secured from a local lumberyard) of the half-hexagonal type with a mixture of one part Portland cement to two parts of clean sand with just enough water to make a workable mixture. There is a disadvantage, however: the gutter may crack at the angles.

The drawing shows how to make a more substantial gutter. Use 2 x 6 forms X, held in place to desired width with 2 x 4 stakes Y driven firmly into the ground. Cut pieces of 6 x 6-inch #10 reinforcement wire Z and bend them to gutter shape. As you pour in the concrete, (*see* Appendix, Table I, for mixture) place them in the form as shown. Next use a cement finisher's trowel to first shape the gutter, then to work it side-to-side as you give the gutter a professional smooth ap-

Perimeter Curbing

4-19. If you plan to build a surface requiring a curb, you can lay single bricks around the court as an edging. This is all that some contractors recommend. It is called a floating curb, designed to give with freezes and thaws in the coldest part of the country. With reasonable care, it should last the life of the court. Where the base will be thicker than 5 inches, lay the bricks on end for additional height.

For better construction, I recommend standard bricks set in concrete and joined together with masonry mortar, as shown in Figure 4-19: A, sub-base; B, concrete; C, finished surface; D, stone base. (For ingredients and proper mixtures, *see* Appendix, Tables I and II.)

Make finished curb of an elevation that will allow outside edge to be ½ inch below the finished surface. Also, be sure water can drain from under the curb on the low side of the court. Common practice calls for laying the curb following the fine grading. Omit sections so trucks and heavy equipment can enter and leave the court area. Sections should be in multiples of brick

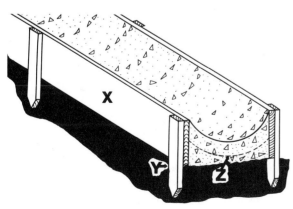

4-18

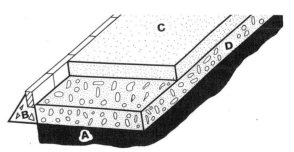

4-19

4-20

lengths, so when the sections are filled later, X number of bricks will fill the spaces exactly. (If you set bricks in mortar, this step is not necessary since a variation in joint widths can make full-size bricks come out exactly right.)

If you prefer a concrete curb over one made of bricks, all you need are some 2 x 4s held in place with stakes (see previous section for making gutter forms). There is only one difference between the two operations. Here, instead of finishing gutter style, you simply strike off the wet concrete with a short piece of 2 x 4. Then smooth the surface with a cement finisher's trowel.

INSTALLING THE BASE COURSE

If the ground adjoining the court was not properly sterilized during the grading operation, do it before proceeding. Apply weed killer to the width of the apron along the perimeter of the court. Handling growth problems now can prevent killing nearby shrubbery and lawns, as well as harming the surface, once the court is in operation.

As court surfaces vary, so do some of their base requirements. Start by checking recom-

mendations for your chosen surface in Chapter 5. (The base described here is designed for a non-porous surface. If you're building one of the porous types, see Ch. 5 for base preparation for your particular court.)

4-20.   To assure a stabilized mixture, install a base course made of crusher-run stone with a top size of ¾ inch in diameter and mixed sizes down to dust. Substitute slag, washed shell, or cinders only if crusher-run rock is unavailable.

Although some tennis court builders limit the thickness of the base to 4 inches, I recommend 5 inches as a minimum.

The truck shown in Figure 4-20 is spreading rock brought to the site wet. If there is too much delay between spreading and rolling, water must be added to pack properly.

4-21.   Spread rock with grader in one direction. Then cross grade, being careful not to overwork. Be sure that enough grade stakes are in place to assure uniform thickness and accurate grade, with no more than ⅜ inch deviation above or below base elevation.

Almost everyone knows that crushed stone is the ideal material for building a tennis court base, but not too many people realize that it can be overworked. Overworking crushed stone causes

4-21

the fine material to sift to the bottom, leaving the larger stones on top. This makes for a poor bond throughout the base, not allowing it to pack as solidly as it should.

4-22. Rolling with a roller of not less than 5 tons is the next operation. Rolling is of utmost importance, but it can be overdone. When this happens the base will crack, allowing erosion to take place. A qualified operator knows just when to roll for the last time. If you're building an asphalt base or later building an asphalt surface, overworking does the same thing, allowing water to seep into the cracks to create damage in years to come.

Complete base by alternately grading and rolling, adding rock if required, until court is packed solid to grade marks.

4-22

5

Building the Surface

Just as modern medical practice recognizes the value of preventive medicine, qualified tennis court builders recognize the value of preventive maintenance. For example, such problems as surface cracking, bubbling, and forming of depressions may result from faulty base construction.

To avoid such problems, which add tremendously to maintenance costs, be certain your base is properly dried, cured, and contains no additives unless specified by the manufacturer. Otherwise, the surface may not bond properly to it.

To put preventive maintenance into practice, start now! Be sure the base is installed with uniform thickness and that no cracks or depressions are in evidence. If such conditions exist, make corrections before applying the surface. It's best to make them now, rather than to put down an expensive surface and later have to re-do the whole job.

Regardless of the type surface you choose, be sure it has proper drainage for the court for which it is designed. (How to build a peripheral drainage system is described in Chapter 4.) Since it is necessary to drain either surface water or subsurface water that would otherwise drain over or under the court, do not proceed with construction until you are certain the court area will drain satisfactorily following the heaviest rains experienced in your locality.

Follow the construction procedures for clearing the site, making the excavation, constructing the base, and building the curb (where specified) as recommended in Chapter 4.

POROUS TENNIS COURTS

"I agree that synthetic tennis courts are making older varieties of porous courts obsolete, but I am building a grit court anyway," said a homeowner who had a new court under construction in his backyard. He went on to say, "Recently, I played on the Washington Hilton Tennis Club fast-dry court, and if a fast-dry court is good enough for Hilton, a grit court is good enough for me."

This was the only way for the homeowner to go. Inflation left no money in his budget for ordinary recreation, let alone money for building an expensive court. There were two things in his favor, however: He lived near natural deposits of good clay and clean sand, and they were both free except for the hauling; labor for building and maintaining the court amounted to zero. His two teenage sons, along with a large utility trailer, gave him advantages seldom equaled by the average tennis court builder.

If your job schedule calls for long hours and you don't have youngsters at the right age to carry out some of the maintenance, probably a porous court is not for you. Most of them are "dirt" cheap if you do all or most of the construction yourself, but if you must hire all of the maintenance, your saving on construction costs soon vanishes. And the maintenance costs continue to pile up.

On the other hand, if you have a fair amount of time available, you can build one of the finest courts money can buy. All it takes is a small investment—compared to a synthetic court—

Courtesy of Marco Beach Hotel and Villas   5-1
(photograph by Robert Caisse)

some muscle power, and a few garden tools, including a lawn roller. Of course, a riding lawn mower or a small tractor with a water-ballast-type lawn roller attachment really takes the drudgery out of both building and maintaining any of the porous courts you choose to build.

Follow the procedures for clearing the site, making the excavation (the slope for porous courts should be approximately 1 inch in 20 feet), constructing the base, and building the curb (where specified) as recommended in Chapter 4.

Fast-dry Courts

There are two essentials to consider when building fast-dry tennis courts. The first depends upon a correct, specially prepared surface mixture. The second depends upon having a proper surface slope. The slope should be within 1 inch in 30 feet to 1 inch in 20 feet. Most reliable contractors use 1 inch in 24 feet. As indicated previously, slope only in one plane and always in the shortest dimension. You can slope side-to-side, end-to-end, diagonally corner-to-corner, but never from middle to end. From a practical point of view, only careful workmen should try building a complete court by themselves. Others

should engage a reputable contractor to install it, especially the finish surface.

5-1.   Fast-dry courts are in wide use. For instance, batteries of fast-dry courts are conspicuous at the Marco Beach Hotel, Marco Island, Naples, Florida. Because of its granular surface, players can slide while hitting the ball. There's ball stain, and the dark color absorbs much of the light rays, thereby reducing glare. It the court is maintained properly, ball bounce is uniform. Keeping the court damp results in a slow ball bounce, which is desirable in that it allows a player a slight second longer to get to the ball and return it.

Some tennis players are critical of fast-dry courts because of ball deflection, tripping, or slipping. That was a valid criticism with old-fashioned lines. Lines are greatly improved in the last two years. Now they are made of synthetic material, lie flat, and will not buckle, eliminating the tripping aspect.

Base Construction

When the site is prepared and compacted to plus or minus ½ inch in 10 feet at any given area, build the aggregate base (for construction details, *see* Chapter 4). Here are some special considerations for building a base for a fast-dry court. Build it, after compaction, 3½ to not more than 4 inches thick; actually, bases over 3½ inches are not recommended. Second, it must be stable enough to support the leveling course and surface layer and, at the same time, porous enough to absorb excess water from the surface following a rain so play can resume. Also, the absorbed water must later feed back to the surface to keep it moist for best playing conditions. To accomplish this, use crushed stone or gravel ranging from ¾ inch in diameter down to limestone dust, with varying sizes. This will assure a stabilized mixture which provides maximum surface area for proper water retention. Set enough grade stakes to assure uniform thickness and accurate grade to within ⅜ inch above or below base elevation.

Since finished surface grade should be 3½ to 4½ inches above adjacent grade, drainage pipes are not usually required. However, if drainage is a problem, install a peripheral drainage system as described in Chapter 4.

Build the curb with enough of it extending above the aggregate base to compensate for the leveling and surfacing courses to follow. This curbing should be ¼ to ½ inch below the finished court to allow sufficient water to run off. Figure 4-19 shows the layered construction of an acceptable new fast-dry court, including a brick curbing set in concrete mortar.

Leveling Course

5-2. Install a leveling course of crushed stone or gravel screenings over the base. Using screeds set according to grade (as described later in this chapter for building Portland cement courts) and a straightedge as shown in the picture, level the crushed stone to correct slope. Gradations of the screening should meet the following specifications:

Size	Percent Passing through Screen
#100	10–35
#4	85–100
⅜ inch	100

Spread the screenings and compact them with a tandem roller to a thickness of about one inch.

Courtesy of Robert Lee Co.   5-2

The surface should not be more than ⅛ inch above or below leveling course elevation. If uneven areas exist, drag and cross drag with some screenings always in front, as explained for leveling dirt courts. Do not proceed without rolling the surface and rechecking the grade.

Surface Course

Install a surface course 1¼ inches thick, before compaction, of natural green stone, screened and blended with a chemical binder. A builder I know uses crushed red brick chips instead of crushed stone. Both are satisfactory.

5-3. Place fast-dry mixture between the screeds and level with a straightedge as shown in the picture. (Handles made of water pipe are shaped and fastened to a 2 x 6 straightedge for ease of manipulation. For building a single court, however, a 2 x 6 alone is quite satisfactory.) Next water thoroughly and, after about 15 to 25 minutes, roll with a roller weighing approximately 500 pounds. A water contained drum-type roller manufactured as a riding lawn mower accessory is satisfactory. However, if you plan

Courtesy of Robert Lee Co.   5-3

to purchase a roller especially for tennis court maintenance work, I recommend the Pro roller, shown in Figure 13-3.

As each bay is completed, remove the screeds and stakes. Next fill and level the voids left by the stakes and screeds. Then water and compact evenly with a roller.

If you do not wish to install screeds over the entire court, you can install several screeds, spread finish surface, water, and compact the bays, then remove the screeds for use farther down the court. When finish surface is completed, thoroughly water, roll and crossroll the court three or four times. The finish surface should not vary from the established elevation more than ⅛ inch in 10 feet when measured in any direction on any part of the court.

Workmen in the pictures are demonstrating how to use fast-dry materials supplied by Robert Lee Company.

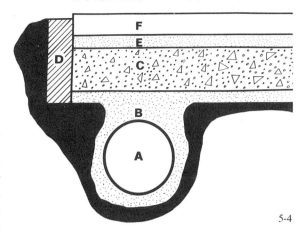

5-4

Clay Courts

Clay courts are made to order for the do-it-yourselfer. The materials for construction are available almost everywhere in the country. If the court is well constructed, maintenance and repairs are relatively inexpensive. Even then, surface replacement isn't necessary for 5 years on the average. The ball spin is effective, and there's no abrasive surface to wear shoes, balls, and rackets prematurely. First-aid treatments are kept to a bare minimum because players can slide on the surface. Also, clay surfaces are popular with many people because they are easy on feet and legs.

Drying time depends much upon the nature of the drainage system and the quality of the clay. Some courts take a day to dry out well enough for play following a heavy rain, and you can expect some ball stain, too. If you want regular ball bounce at all times, use painted lines. Some players claim that tape lines are responsible for considerable tripping during the game. This is true if old-fashioned tapes are used. However, where synthetic tapes are properly installed, tripping is almost nonexistent.

Base Layers

5-4. Peripheral drainage system *A* includes 4 or 6-inch drain pipes laid 10 feet apart, located 2

feet 6 inches, below finished grade. The drain pipes are in filter beds of ¼ to 1/16-inch sand *B* as shown (not drawn to scale). Over this, spread layer of same-size sand 1 inch thick. Then construct 4-inch base *C* as described in Chapter 4.

Curb *D* can be a floating brick curb (*see* Figure 4-19) because it gives with freezing and thawing and, under ordinary conditions, will last the lifetime of the court. Position the bricks on end for necessary height to accommodate part of *B* and *C, E,* and *F*. It's not necessary to use cement mortar between the joints, but it is preferred by many tennis court builders. Be sure to leave out enough bricks to permit trucks and heavy equipment free access to the court area.

Over base *C* spread 1-inch filter bed *E*, consisting of ¼ to 1/16-inch sand.

Clay Surface

Complete court proper by constructing clay surface course *F*, 2 inches thick. You can use clay prepared by mother nature, or you can use one that is mixed, crushed, screened, and blended. Here are some guidelines to assure a clay of satisfactory quality:

1. Clay content should consist of approximately 30 percent. Divide remaining percentage equally between sand and silt.

2. Before using, screen clay through a ¼-inch-mesh screen, such as hardware cloth, which you can purchase from a hardware store.

3. When selecting clay, be sure it has a plasticity index of between 12 and 20 percent.

4. Spread the clay over the area. Then lightly sprinkle to bring it to a puttylike material. After the water has evaporated, but while clay is still moist, cross roll surface once or twice in each

direction to compact it. Use a roller weighing between 1 and 3 tons.

5. Use a garden rake or a rake with iron teeth to loosen the clay to a depth of ½ to ¾ inch. Follow with another raking. This time use a bamboo broom-rake to remove small stones.

6. If birdbaths and voids are left by removing small stones, fill them with screened clay.

7. Smooth the surface by dragging a mat or running a grader over the surface for further refinement. Then roll and cross roll again, as before.

8. Repeat, spreading fine layers of clay, followed by dragging and rolling. Usually two or three applications does the job. The final surface should not vary from intended grade more than ⅛ inch in 10 feet when measured on any area of the court. Use transit and rod to check grade as described in Chapter 4.

Grit Courts

Grit courts are less expensive to build than clay courts. Also, grit courts cost about one-third as much to build as concrete courts.

Grit courts are easy on the feet and legs, have effective ball spin, and ball bounce is uniform on a well-maintained surface. Ball skid is controllable, since it is long on a dry court and short on a damp court.

Grit courts require daily maintenance, are slow to dry, and there's a possibility of glare if the surfaces aren't treated.

5-5. Although daily maintenance is required, a good cross rolling is about the extent necessary to keep the courts in A-1 condition during hot dry weather. Rolling is a lot of fun if you invest in a drum-type roller (amount of water in drum controls its weight) and hitch it behind a riding lawn mower as shown, or a small tractor. You can

Courtesy of Montgomery Ward and Co.   5-5

practice water conservation by applying calcium chloride (approximately 300 pounds per court) to reduce the amount of watering required to improve playing qualities.

Base Construction

Construction details of grit courts are almost identical to those recommended for clay courts. However, no drainage system is required unless the subsoil is not fairly porous and well drained. You'll save money on the aggregate base, because none is required.

Begin by leveling the site with a slope of 1 inch in 20 feet. Then use a heavy roller to compact and even the surface.

Build the curb next, allowing 2 inches to extend above grade. Fewer bricks are needed, because they can be laid end-to-end to form the curb (*see* Ch. 4 for details).

Surface Application

Next spread the surface material in three separate, equal courses. Use equal parts of clay and sharp sand thoroughly mixed together. Spread in three successive equal courses, each approximately ½ to ¾ inch thick, to make a total surface thickness of 2 inches. Sprinkle the first two courses well and follow by rolling.

After the third coat is spread and wet down, roll and cross roll. Then drag and reroll. Dragging tends to even the surface, especially if you cross drag. Use a straightedge at least 10 feet long and a level to check for uneven areas and birdbaths. On occasion you may need to spread some of the clay-sand mixture over the low areas, then drag, sprinkle, roll, and cross roll until the court is compacted and level.

Wet and roll the court daily for a couple of months following completion. Always keep loose sand swept off the court.

Line a grit court in the same manner as a clay court, described in Chapter 6.

Grass Courts

It's conceivable to erect a couple of net posts, stretch a net, lay out the playing lines on almost any large lawn, get a partner and play tennis! Of course, ball bounce would be anything but uniform, and you might not be able to play for days following a heavy rain. Friends of mine who have done just that to have a cheap court got exactly what they paid for—practically nothing.

Characteristics

The fact is that when a well-constructed grass court is worked into a landscape plan judiciously, it can relieve severity of line and add a softening tone of cool color to homesite. When properly constructed, it provides one of the most luxurious of all court surfaces. As most tennis players know, both the U.S. Championships and Wimbledon matches are held on grass courts. Grass surfaces provide a moderately long ball skid and stain the ball. There is no excessive wear on shoes, balls, and rackets, since the surfaces are nonabrasive. From a safety standpoint it is one of the safest, since players can slide without being subject to skin burns.

Lack of uniform ball bounce, unless the court is in perfect condition, is one of the reasons why more grass courts are not built. On the other hand, it's a cool clean surface free of excess heat, glare, and dust. However, due to climate, it cannot be grown everywhere with any degree of success.

Construction

Over a peripheral drainage system, including drain pipes laid in between, construct a 6-inch porous base. Construction of both the drainage system and the base are described in Chapter 4.

Here are the essential ingredients of an acceptable grass court.

Since certain species of grass grow better in some areas than in others, and subsoils and topsoils vary as to fertility, seek help for information on local situations from the county farm agent, college or high school agriculture teacher, state experiment station, or state department of agriculture. As far as testing the soil, you can do it yourself with a soil-testing kit, purchased locally or from a mail order firm. Kits are accompanied by easy-to-follow instructions.

Evenly spread a 6-inch layer of subsoil over the aggregate base. Since a successful grass court begins with the subsoil, have it tested or test it yourself. If needed, harrow or spade into the subsoil—to a depth of 3 or 4 inches—25

pounds of superphosphate and 25 pounds of lime per 1000 square feet.

If your topsoil was pushed aside during excavation and is worth saving, spread evenly a 6-inch minimum layer of it over the subsoil to proper grade. Purchase additional topsoil and have it delivered to the site if there's not enough of your own in the pile.

Construct a gentle slope away from the court to carry off excess rain water.

If you are excavating, filling, and leveling the surface around trees or evergreens near the court, build shallow walls of brick or stonework around them to allow air to reach the roots. Amount of space between trunks and walls depends upon size of plants and their future growth. Deep soil placed directly around trunks may kill them.

5-6. Incorporate lime, fertilizer, and other soil additives, such as organic matter—compost, peat, manure—into the topsoil before the finish grade is established. Don't overlook application of a balanced commercial fertilizer of 5-10-5 analysis. The amount of soil treatment depends upon the results of your topsoil test discussed at the beginning of this section.

Courtesy of Montgomery Ward and Co.   5-6

Next smooth the surface by raking and rolling with a lawn roller.

Now you're ready to seed or sod. Since sodding is quite expensive, I recommend it only if urgency requires rapid cover. If you do plan to sod, check installation costs with your local nurseries.

Seeding in the autumn is best, contrary to what some people may advise you. In cool weather the seeds sprout faster and the grass grows faster, too. Consequently, the grass requires frequent

Courtesy of Montgomery Ward and Co.   5-7

mowing, and every time a grass blade is cut off, a new growth is forced to form lower on the stem. The results are a multiplication of blades and the roots moving out faster.

5-7. You can use a broadcast or hopper spreader behind a riding lawn mower or pushed by hand to sow the seed or you can sow it by hand quite satisfactorily. First, dilute the seed by mixing it with soil or fertilizer. Second, divide the seed into two lots. Broadcast one lot by walking up and down the length of the court and the other lot while walking back and forth across the court, or at right angles to the first sowing. When the seed is evenly spread, cover lightly by raking. Be sure not to rake the seed in piles. For even distribution, select a calm day with no wind blowing.

Going over the court with a light lawn roller, weighing about 90 pounds, will press the seed into the soil for the shortest possible time to germinate.

Spread a bale of straw over each 1000 square feet of court to conserve moisture, reduce erosion during heavy rains, and prevent wild birds from eating the seed and green shoots when they form. Generally, it is not necessary to ever remove the straw mulch. However, if there's enough left come playing time, light raking will remove it easily.

Finally, don't hesitate to mow as soon as top growth reaches proper height for the species of grass planted. Be sure mower blades are sharp. Set height of mower to suit species of grass on the court. Stotoniferous (creeping or spreading) grasses—bent, Zoysia, Bermuda, St. Augustine, and centipede—will withstand close mowing of ½ to 1 inch if they are kept fertilized. Mow bluegrass, fescues, and other grasses that do not produce stolons to a minimum height of 1½ inches.

Usually, it takes a year or two to get the grass court in its best condition. However, with proper maintenance, explained in Chapter 13, you can play tennis, relax, and watch it thrive for years to come.

NONPOROUS, NONCUSHIONED COURTS

Nonporous, noncushioned tennis courts are more popular than ever. Even though the initial cost is high, the low upkeep, durable surface, uniform bounce, lack of glare on the surface, no discoloration of balls, and quick draining following a rain are some of the practical advantages responsible for their popularity. However, some players like a porous surface better, because it is not as hard underfoot. Then there are those who argue, "Once you become accustomed to a nonporous court, it's no longer hard on the feet."

Those who consider aesthetics may object to a nonporous court because, when a patch is needed to repair a surface defect, the appearance isn't attractive (new and used colored surfaces are hard to match).

Unless you are experienced, it's best to farm out the surface job for any court in this section to a qualified professional who provides the lowest bid.

Concrete Courts

Because of the two large, continuous pouring operations required to build a Portland cement concrete court, the amateur should refrain from building the slab and farm it out to professionals. Since each half of the court must be poured in a continuous operation to help prevent cracking, it's no one-man job, even for a pro. If you have had some experience in working with concrete, there's a way to save some money, however: Do your own contracting. Hire a qualified concrete finisher, laborers he recommends, and include yourself to make up the crew. Keep in mind that there is no place for mistakes in building a concrete court. Errors are both costly and difficult to correct.

The grade is the same as other nonporous courts, namely 1 inch in 10 feet.

Because concrete is difficult to cut through when seasoned, prepare concrete forms in preparation for installing permanent equipment, such as net posts and center strap locations, as indicated in Chapter 6.

Base Construction

One of the major problems when constructing a concrete court is to build it in such a way as to prevent the concrete from cracking. The problem is magnified many times over where heavy freezes followed by quick thaws are repetitious during the winter season.

Begin by laying a peripheral drainage system as described in Chapter 5. Place fill over pipes, then compact court area with a heavy roller.

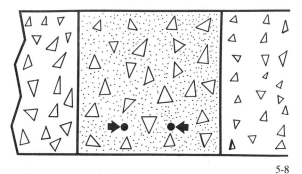

5-8

5-8. The base is constructed as indicated in Chapter 4, with this exception: Since the only joint permissible in the concrete slab comes at the net line location, you'll need solid support underneath the concrete edges of the surface that face each other. Build concrete beam (center, Fig. 5-8) so it lies in between aggregate base. Most likely, you can dig a trench in the base the width of a shovel (roughly 12 inches) and about 12 inches deep. If base wants to cave in, make a wood form with 2 x 12 boards spaced 12 inches apart, blocked at the ends, and held in place by 2-inch stakes driven firmly into the ground every 2 or 3 feet. Tops of the stakes should conform to the base grade (use transit and rod for this purpose, as described in Chapter 4). Be sure to locate form so it is centered directly underneath future net location. Position two #4 reinforcement rods as shown by arrows in Figure 5-8. For strength of concrete and how to figure the amount, *see* Appendix, Table 1.

When the ready-mix truck arrives, have the operator pour the concrete slowly as you guide it into the form with a shovel. Be sure to keep reinforcement rods properly located during the pouring operation. When the form is full of concrete, strike off excess from the top with a scrap 2 x 4 or a cement finisher's trowel. You can pour the beam before or after building the aggregate base. I prefer building it first, then doing my best to keep workmen from driving heavy equipment directly across it during the application and compaction of the base.

After 48 hours, remove form lumber if used. Then coat top of beam with an asphalt material to prevent concrete slab from bonding with it.

Note: Building a cross way with 2-inch scrap lumber on each side of concrete beam, similar to that described above for protecting the curb from heavy equipment, is well worth the effort.

Surface Preparations

If you are building in an area not subject to freeze and thaw, a 4-inch slab is satisfactory. Otherwise, pour nothing less than one 5 inches thick. Some contractors use wire mesh for reinforcing the concrete regardless of location. Where the temperature is above freezing the year round, 6 x 6 #10 reinforcement wire gives satisfactory results (the first two numbers refer to the inches the wires are apart, while the third number refers to the gauge of the wire). For localities subject to freezing weather, I recommend Hi-Bond steel reinforcing rods positioned at mid-depth in both directions and wired together with soft iron wire. Use a steel brush to clean rods of loose rust, films, or other coatings prior to pouring concrete. Otherwise rods will not bond properly to the concrete. Support either rods or wire with 2-inch limestone rocks to prevent them from sinking to bottom of slab during the concrete-pouring operation. Terminate either the wire or the rods 2 inches away from edges and expansion joint. Use a hacksaw for cutting rods to proper lengths. Use wire cutters to cut reinforcement wire. The table on p. 40 gives sizes and distance apart of rods recommended for different slab thicknesses and size of reinforcement wire.

The best reinforcement job will not be an absolute guarantee against cracks forming in the slab, but it will prevent parts of it from heaving if cracking does occur.

Slab thickness	Size of reinforcement materials	Positioned in both directions
4 inches	No. 5 rods or 6 x 6 #10 reinforcement wire	20 inches on center
5 inches	No. 4 rods	16 inches on center

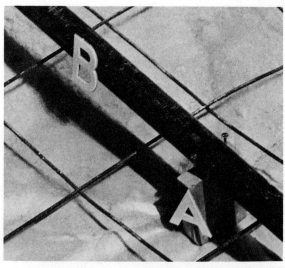

5-9

The following table gives specifications for concrete, based on one cubic yard, designed for tennis court slabs. Be sure the ready-mix company adheres to it in every detail. (*See* Appendix, Table I, for formula on how to estimate cubic yards of concrete required for the job.) *Do not* have coloring mixed with the concrete. It is difficult to keep it uniformly distributed over the surface. Instead, add color of your choice later to provide uniform color and ball bounce if you follow manufacturer's instructions.

Given six-bag mix per cubic yard of concrete and required concrete strength, your ready-mix company will proportion the crushed rock and sand accordingly.

5-9. Because pipe screeds require less filling in the voids with concrete when they are removed, I prefer them over 2-inch lumber.

Start at middle or net location of court. Begin with 2-inch form boards set perfectly straight and held in place with 1 x 2 stakes driven firmly into the aggregate base. Continue building 2-inch form square to proper dimensions around remaining three sides of the half-court. Width of boards depends upon thickness of slab. Be sure top of form conforms to correct elevation.

Next locate the screeds to the lines and grade a

maximum of 10 feet apart, beginning measurement at the 2-inch wide form board. Drive 1 x 3-inch stakes *A* firmly into the aggregate base at intervals of about 5 feet, allowing enough to remain exposed plus thickness of pipe to form proper lines and grade.

Position 1½-inch pipe (outside measurement) *B* on top of stakes *A*. Keep pipes in place by driving two 6-penny box nails into top of each stake flush with top of pipe *B*, as shown in Figure 5-9.

Check with your finisher to see how many screeds he recommends constructing at one time. As you move along and finish concrete down half of the court, the first pipes can be removed and set up again for receiving concrete. Plan to pour each half of court in one continuous operation without any construction joints. Pour second half of court a minimum of 48 hours later. At that time, remove the 2-inch form boards.

Concrete Specifications for Tennis Court Slabs*

Slab thickness	Cement	Aggregate size	Water	Air entrainment
4 inches	6-bag mix	¾ inch maximum	6 gallons maximum	Between 4 and 7 percent of total concrete volume
5 inches	6-bag mix	1 inch maximum	6 gallons maximum	Between 4 and 7 percent of total concrete volume

*On the twenty-eighth day after pouring, concrete shall have a minimum compressive strength of 3,500 pounds per square inch.

You can reuse some of them, after cleaning, to form the three sides of the second half court. Since the expansion joint material and first half-court edge serve as a form at net location, no form boards should be placed here.

Pouring the Slab

5-10. Since you will walk around in the concrete as you spread and level it with a shovel or garden rake between the screeds, wear rubber boots. The idea here is to keep the preliminary leveling job and the concrete coming from the ready-mix trucks on an even keel.

When about 8 feet of concrete are roughly leveled between two screeds or strike-off places, refine the leveling with a 2 x 4 slightly longer than the distance between them. This is a two-man job, whereby the 2 x 4 is slowly sawed edgewise, back and forth across the screeds, until a level finish is obtained, as shown in Figure 5-10. Don't overwork the concrete. With careful practice, always keeping a "ripple" of concrete in front of the moving 2 x 4, two to three operations over the same area should have the leveling process ready for the finisher.

5-10

When the concrete begins to stiffen, and before the finisher takes over, begin removing the pipe screeds for further use down the court. Drive the stakes flush with aggregate base and fill remaining voids left by stakes and pipes with concrete, leveling it to uniform grade with adjoining concrete surfaces.

5-11

5-11. Now the finisher takes over with a float to help push down coarse rocks and to bring fine material, mostly mortar, to the surface. In the picture, the finisher is using a long-handled float. He should neither overwork the concrete nor work ahead until the leveling is plus or minus ⅛ inch, as indicated by a straightedge placed across the screeds.

This is your last chance to remove any obstacles from the concrete that may cause accidents when players run off the court. The arrow in Figure 5-11 points to an electrical outlet placed too near the tennis court on a multipurpose playing area.

5-12. When the concrete has taken initial set sufficient to bear the weight of the finisher, he should finish the surface to the texture recommended by the surface coloring manufacturer.

5-12

Also, an extremely slick finish can cause players to slip and fall needlessly.

Figure 5-12 shows a troweling machine, which gives faster results than a finisher using a hand trowel.

The secret of pouring a large concrete slab is to work as a team. The pouring job must always be ahead of the 2 x 4 leveling operation and the finisher, but never far enough to allow the concrete to set too hard for the oncoming men to do their jobs properly.

When the slab is poured, cure it for seven days by covering with continuously wet burlap or polyethylene. Use of polyethylene requires no wetting of concrete. *Do not* use curing compounds or other chemicals supposed to aid the curing process.

After 48 hours, remove the 2-inch form boards, being careful not to chip the surface near the edge.

Place expansion joint material next to the slab face. Use material, such as prepared felt, supplied by your ready-mix company, building it up to a thickness of 1 inch.

Drive enough temporary stakes a few inches into the base to hold expansion joint material firmly against slab face. Since you will use slab edge adjoining expansion joint as one concrete strike-off point, build 2-inch-wide form boards to proper elevation around the three remaining sides of second half of court. Position reinforcement materials, set up screeds, and pour and finish second half of court in the same manner as the first half. As concrete is poured and leveled with a 2 x 4 between slab and first screed, remove temporary stakes holding expansion joint material in place. After 48 hours remove form boards and cure concrete for seven days as before. Then you can use the surface as it is or you can color it as described in the following sections.

Color Finishes

Finishing all-weather courts with a color surfacing is no longer in the experimental stage. Here are three sound reasons for using it: Better playability provided by a uniform nonstaining surface; better protection for the surface from elements of weather; more pleasing color on the playing surface.

The acrylic color system is gaining in popularity today. It has the tough and durable characteristics of acrylics, coupled with filling properties that produce uniformity in color and texture. Uniformity is provided because it is compounded at the factory. Two filler coats of acrylic followed by one finish coat of acrylic are applied directly over the asphalt. Because each coating consists of exactly the same color, the resultant surface is colored evenly in depth.

With an acrylic surface, you can expect four to eight years use following application before a recoating job is needed. Following the original coating or when recoating, be sure to paint the lines with acrylic court line paint.

Sometimes aesthetic considerations win out over practical considerations at the expense of the players. This is unfortunate, but often true. A good example is found in the widely accepted two-color tennis court painting design. Here one color is used for the court itself, while another color is used for the area surrounding the court. Beautiful, yes! Practical, no! Let's look at the situation from an ophthalmologist's point of view. First, it's most difficult for the player's eye to readily adjust to two contrasting colors when attempting to focus on a fast-moving ball. Second, since nine players out of ten have some degree of color blindness, they find it difficult to see the ball as it moves in a split second from one color background to another. Actually, they may have the advantage here, because players who are not color blind might experience even more difficulty following the ball under these conditions. In short, a two-color surface may be more pleasing to those on the sidelines, but it has exactly the opposite effect on those playing the game.

Make a final inspection before applying the color finish material. Begin by flooding the court with water. Following drainage, look for birdbaths. Those holding water deeper than 1/16 inch must be patched and leveled in accordance with recommendations for the particular color finish material used. The manufacturer will be glad to provide such information if it is not available locally.

There are numerous color finishes on the market (*see* Sources of Supply). Plexipave is one of the color systems used for coloring asphalt and concrete surfaces. It is manufactured by the California Products Corporation. You have a right to expect a guarantee for at least one year (following application) against fading, chalking, discoloration, or other undesirable effects from the sun, temperatures, or moisture. Be sure these terms are covered in your contract.

Apply color finish in multiple applications and only on a dry surface. Do not apply when rain is imminent or when the temperature is below 50° F or above 140° F unless so directed by the manufacturer. When finish surface is dry, it should have a uniform color over the entire court.

Begin by preparing the surface. Thoroughly remove all dirt, dust, and foreign materials by sweeping, scrubbing and/or vacuum cleaning; scrape or grind off any paint residue. Check for spalling and remove any loose concrete. Sandblast residue of asphalt coating, coatings, color treatments or extremely smooth finish.

After removing loose or spalled concrete, blow off all dust and material down to sound, hard surface. Repair with latex cement, which can be obtained from a concrete supplier. Apply a prime coat of latex as a penetrating primer, then trowel on latex cement mix using suitable aggregates to fill to surrounding area and feather to same texture. Then etch with a 10-percent solution of muriatic acid. Follow by flushing clean with water.

Now apply a penetrating prime coat of California Products' Lacrylic by brush or short-nape roller at the rate of 300 to 400 square feet per gallon. Allow to dry thoroughly. For indoor courts, insure adequate ventilation when using.

Next flood court with water. After twenty minutes, work perimeters of all areas where water is standing over 1/16 inch. Using Plexipave as it comes from container, undiluted, trowel or screed material to bring to proper level. If more than ⅛ inch is required, apply in multiple coats and add 20 percent by volume of coarse aggregate. Allow to thoroughly dry.

Repair hairline cracks and other minor cracks by squeegeeing Plexipave Crack Filler into voids, using a bricklayer's trowel or putty knife. (*See* Chapter 8 for repairing structure cracks and slab settlement if you have these problems.)

Do not leave ridges. Also, make certain that all edges are feathered to avoid patched appearance and different texture.

Apply two coats of Plexipave 100-percent acrylic filler coat at a rate of not less than 0.08 gallon per square yard for the two coats (60 gallons for an 800-square-yard court). If surface texture is not uniform, make necessary corrections. Apply the first coat lengthwise of court and the second coat, crosswise to the first. Dilute Plexipave at the ratio of 15 to 20 gallons of water per 30 gallons of Plexipave, allowing no puddles.

Prior to applying finish coat, make a final, careful inspection, removing any ridges and loose or foreign particles.

Apply a third finish coat of Plexichrome at a rate of not less than 0.04 gallons of materials (30 gallons of Plexichrome per 800-square-yard court). Make the application parallel to the net line; the color should be uniform throughout when viewed at a distance of 25 feet from any edge of the court at midday. Mix equal parts of Plexichrome and clean water in a mechanical mixer. Use Fortified Plexipave instead of Plexichrome for slower play. The following illustrations show how professionals apply a binder, if required, and Plexipave color surface to concrete or asphalt courts:

Applying Binder Coat

The binder coat described and illustrated here is called Plexibinder; it is used for concrete or asphalt courts and is manufactured by the California Products Corporation. It is an acrylic material and, if necessary, is applied prior to the color application of Plexipave.

5-13. Using a mechanical mixer, the workmen mix Plexibinder and clean water together to a smooth-flowing consistency. Then they spread it as evenly as possible.

Courtesy of California Products Corp. 5-13

Courtesy of California Products Corp.   5-14

5-14. Here the workman wheels a load of Plexibinder to edge of court. Slightly tilting the wheelbarrow, he slowly backs away from the spill, leaving a thin layer of Plexibinder.

5-15. Finally, using squeegees, workmen smooth the coat to a uniform thickness.

Courtesy of California Products Corp.   5-15

Courtesy of California Products Corp.   5-16

water to bring filler material to a smooth flowing consistency.

5-17. Figure 5-17 shows a workman spreading the material as he is backing away from beginning of a pour so as not to spread more than 0.08 gallons per square yard (a total of 60 gallons for 800 square yards) for both coats. He is applying the first coat lengthwise on the court and will apply the second coat crosswise on the court.

Applying Color Surface

Plexipave (available in eight selected colors) is described and illustrated by professionals to show how a color system is applied over a concrete or asphalt surface. Prior to application, the net sleeves and fencing for outdoor courts should be installed. Then allow asphalt to cure at least one week before color application.

This is a three-coat application and, in normal summer drying weather, the job can often be made over a properly prepared surface in one day.

5-16. The workmen begin by applying two coats of Plexipave Acrylic Filler Coat. For small jobs, pour estimated amount from a 5-gallon pail into a wheelbarrow. Then pour in enough clean

Courtesy of California Products Corp.   5-17

Courtesy of California Products Corp.   5-18

5-18. He levels each of the two courses with a squeegee to fill slight depressions and voids, providing uniform surface texture. No roller is required.

Note: If the asphaltic surface course is not covered to a uniform, even texture, free of all porosity, a third filler coat should be applied to obtain uniformity.

A final finish coat of Plexipave (Plexichrome if you want a faster playing surface texture) is applied at a rate of not less than 0.04 gallons of material (30 gallons per 800 square yards). Using a mechanical mixer, combine equal parts of water and finish coat. If you want slower play, make the application lengthwise along the court with a wide hair-type push-broom. When done correctly, it produces a uniform color throughout when viewed at a distance of 25 feet from any edge of the court at midday.

If increased wear resistance is desired for heavy foot-traffic areas, the workmen apply one coat of Clear-Glo (also manufactured by the California Products Corporation) over the Plexipave system.

Asphalt Noncushioned Courts

In general, you can figure that an asphalt court will cost anywhere from 150 to 200 percent more than a clay court. However, many tennis players feel the advantages are well worth the cost.

Characteristics

Generally, resurfacing is necessary only once in about five years, and maintenance is negligible. Since most of the light striking the court is absorbed, glare doesn't bother the players at all. If the finish is gritty, you can expect effective ball spin, while a glossy finish does produce some adverse ball spins. Also, a gritty finish produces a medium ball skid, while a glossy finish causes long ball skids.

By coloring the surface, you cut down on ball wear. Some other desirable points are uniform ball bounce, no ball stain, and fast drying after a rain, if surface isn't full of birdbaths. Asphalt also provides an excellent surface for multipurpose playing areas.

A Job for Pros

Although many do-it-yourselfers can perform the preliminary work, including building a crushed stone base, I recommend farming out asphalt surfaces to the professionals. A satisfactory job calls for large equipment and operators who have the know-how to use it.

Four valuable publications on asphalt court construction, *Guide Specifications,* may be had upon request and without cost from the U.S. Tennis Court and Track Builders Association, 1201 Waukegan Road, Glenview, Illinois 60025. There is a publication covering specifications for Hot Plant Mix, Emulsified Asphalt Mix, Combination Hot Plant and Emulsified Asphalt Mix, and Penetration Macadam.

Although the publications do not show you how to build the surfaces, they do tell you how they should be built. I find them most valuable in helping do-it-yourselfers prepare specifications for letting contracts. Also, they are helpful guides to check out construction steps, a reference to assure getting your money's worth as the surface is being built.

The Association also publishes free for the asking, a membership directory. Among other things, it lists qualified tennis court builder members and their addresses.

NONPOROUS, CUSHIONED COURTS

When it comes right down to the bottom line, there is a dichotomy as to which is the finest of the asphalt tennis courts. There are those experts who claim that cushioned-type asphalt bound courts are the best available. Also, they are quick to point out, cushioned-type courts are used for championship play. Other experts disagree: They argue that a cushioned court doesn't have the same feel as a noncushioned court. Thus, when a player moves about, playing on one court, then the other, he's really uncomfortable making the adjustment. Furthermore, they claim that it requires only a short time for the legs to become accustomed to playing on a noncushioned court, so why bother with the added expense of building one that is cushioned? Many agree with their counterparts if one is building a commercial court, but only if it is going to be in competition with other courts that are cushioned. Which group is right? Perhaps both believe they can substantiate their arguments. The fact of matter is this: All criteria for making judgments is subjective, since, as of this writing, there are no objective measurements available on deflection, recovery, resiliency, and durability of the various cushion course materials on the market. Your best answer will come from playing on both types of courts before you build; then make your own decision.

Cushion Courses

A cushion course is substituted for the surface course used in a noncushioned court. There are several types of cushioned courts available under different brand names (*see* Sources of Supply). At this writing, available brands include the following types:

1. Rubber particles compounded in a resinous binder, are overlaid with a urethane resin. It comes from the factory as 5/16-inch surface sheets, which are attached to the asphalt surface.

2. An additive of rubber granules is blended with an emulsified asphalt mixture on the job site to produce this course. It is spread to a maximum thickness of ½ inch.

3. An additive of rubber granules and vermiculite is blended with an asphalt mix in an asphalt plant. Then the cushioned material is delivered to the site, where it is spread one inch thick, either by hand screeding or by ordinary mechanical paving equipment.

4. Some manufacturers mix cork with asphalt at the factory and then package it in containers to be delivered to the site; it is spread to a maximum thickness of ½ inch.

5. Other manufacturers recommend mixing cork with an asphalt mix in an asphalt plant. Then it is delivered to the site, where it is spread one inch thick by hand screeding or by ordinary mechanical paving equipment.

6. A shredded cane fiber, with or without rubber granules, is mixed with emulsified asphalt at the factory. Then it is packaged in drums, delivered to the site, and spread to a maximum thickness of ⅜ inch.

Caution: Whichever cushioned surface you choose, beware of installing more than the maximum thickness recommended by the manufacturer. Sometimes this happens where there are low and high spots on the previous surface. The low areas could become "dead," causing ball bounce to be lower than in areas spread according to recommendations. If a careless workman spreads the cushioned course too thick all over the court, it could be disastrous, since conditions couldn't be much worse than playing on a "dead" court.

Installing Plexicushion

Here's the way the California Products Corporation details the installation of its cushioned material. Plexicushion is a unique, breathing plastic composition containing rubber particles. It imparts a shock-absorbing characteristic below the Plexipave to give added safety and comfort for restful, playing, indoors and outside. It can be applied over all types of asphalt and Portland cement surfaces.

Begin by checking and obtaining maximum leveling (including surface free of birdbaths) and "tight" surface density of asphalt leveling course to ensure maximum performance and economy. Also, clean surface of dust, dirt, greases, and oils. (For making such corrections, see techniques described in this chapter for asphalt courts.)

If areas on the surface show excessive porosity or lap marks, squeegee on a coat of Plexipave prepared and applied as described and illustrated earlier in this chapter.

Here are some points regarding Plexicushion application: Apply it only when the temperature is between 50° F and 140° F; store so it is exposed to neither freezing temperature nor hot sun; asphalt must cure at least seven days, concrete at least 28 days, prior to application.

For minimum standard application, apply three squeegee coats of Plexicushion prior to the complete Plexipave Color Finish System, described earlier in this chapter. Plexicushion I and II require additional coats to provide thicknesses of ⅛ and ¼ inch, respectively. Do not allow Plexicushion to run or drip on adjacent areas. Remove any drips immediately with water before drying occurs. Apply with 24 to 36-inch-long flexible rubber squeegees obtained from California Products Corporation. Do not allow ridges to form between passes of the squeegee, as they will cause an unsightly appearance unless extensive corrective action is taken prior to the application of the Plexipave Finish System. Be sure to wait at least six hours of good drying time before applying Plexipave.

Asphalt Bound Cushion Courts

The same suggestions apply to the construction of an asphalt bound cushion court as to an asphalt noncushioned court: Construction of the surface should be done by pros.

Here again, the U.S. Tennis Court and Track Builders Association offers three publications upon request and without charge. There is one publication each on Hot Leveling Course and Hot Cushion Course, Hot Leveling Course and Cold Cushion Course, and Cold Leveling Course and Cold Cushion Course.

Synthetic Courts

As the history of tennis courts goes, artificial court surfaces are relatively new. There are a number of synthetic materials currently on the market, such as poured-in-place materials, sheet plastics, grasslike surfaces, carpetlike materials, and so on.

The prerequisite for all these surfaces is a well-constructed base. Frequently, the blame for a synthetic court literally falling apart at the seams is attributed to the synthetic surface, when a poorly constructed base is the real culprit. As pointed out before, this is the most expensive court on the market. Therefore, construction—from clearing the site to building the base—must follow, to the letter, the highest construction standards, or you're wasting your money and time by installing any of the synthetics.

There is a silver lining in the clouds, however: You can reduce the cost by approximately half if you surface only the playing area with a synthetic surface, bounded by 5 feet outside the alley lines and 10 feet behind the base lines.

You will hear all kinds of rumors about synthetic surfaces. Some will say, "Synthetic courts are okay indoors, but not outdoors." Others will proclaim, "Synthetic courts don't dry out quickly; the surface is too fast; the surface is too slow." Actually, no criticism applies to *all* synthetic courts. True, several firms have withdrawn their products from the market, and that's as it should be when products don't prove to be satisfactory. On the bright side, however, there are a number of reputable manufacturers who guarantee their surfaces in writing to the customer. Of course, they also require certain court construction standards before they will honor their guarantee.

Installing Plexicarpet

Plexicarpet is an excellent synthetic-composition cushion system manufactured by the California Products Corporation. This resilient surface consists of prefabricated polyurethane-rubber mats suitably bonded to a prepared base and then treated to receive the long wearing, uniform surface texture of three coats of the Plexipave Color Finish System described earlier. The surface provides uniform resilience and total recovery after heavy impact.

Plexicarpet is recommended for *indoor use only*, but application is definitely not intended for the do-it-yourselfer. Installation is to be made only by trained or factory-supervised applicators. The subsurface to which Plexicarpet is applied shall be plant-mix asphalt or Portland cement concrete acceptable to the applicator. All concrete on-or-below grade shall have an adequate moisture preventative membrane, such as polyethylene. No subsurface shall be installed in conditions of high table water or excessive moisture.

Mateflex, A Relatively New Surface

The Mateflex tennis court surface is made of interlocking polyethylene modules, roughly ¾ x 13 inches square and available in either red or green. Its flexibility prevents leg fatigue. It is uniform in resiliency and ball bounce. The playing speed is ideal. Its "flow through" design provides instant drainage, which makes play possible following a heavy rain. It can be used all year round, either indoors or outdoors. It looks great and, most important, it requires no maintenance or repair.

The Mateflex tennis court surface should be installed on a hard, durable substructure. An existing or newly cast subsurface of concrete, asphalt, or comparable composition makes an ideal support for the Mateflex surface.

An entire Mateflex tennis court surface can be assembled or disassembled in a matter of hours. And, if you should move, the entire court can be picked up, packed, and moved right along with your furniture.

At this printing, the cost of the Mateflex tennis court surface is $1.25 per square foot. The cost for an entire single court runs about $900, including a three-year guarantee.

More than 300 courts are used at present in France and in other European countries, owned by tennis clubs, public authorities, and private owners. Although more Mateflex surfaces will find their way to many American courts in the future, a court can be seen and used at the new Abercrombie and Fitch Rooftop Sport Facility located in New York City. For more specific information on putting in your own court, write to Mateflex (*see* Sources of Supply).

Other Synthetics

The same suggestions apply to the application of any synthetic surfaces as to the construction of asphalt noncushioned courts. Installation should be done by experienced technicians. Here again, the U.S. Tennis Court and Track Builders Association offers two publications upon request and without charge. There are publications on Elastomer and Textile synthetic surfaces.

6

Completing the Basics

Having finished the playing area, it's time to accurately lay out the court—or courts, as your case might be—install permanent fixtures, and put down the playing lines.

Begin with the layout. Some of you will have only a single tennis court to lay out, while others will lay out a multipurpose game area. Since the techniques are the same, only the tennis court layout is explained here.

LAYING OUT TENNIS COURTS

Use of a transit is the easiest, quickest, most accurate way to determine angles to form perfect right angles or corners in laying out the court (review use of the transit in Ch. 4). However, with care, an accurate job can be done without such an instrument. What is required, though, are two 50-foot nonstretch metal tapes.

6-1. Unless you have built a playing area only large enough for a singles court, make the layout for both singles and doubles. Start by laying out one-half of a singles tennis court as shown in Figure 6-1. Then use similar techniques to determine second half, and here's why: Because the same lines (except sidelines extensions for doubles play) are required for both singles and doubles, it's the most logical approach.

Establish the north–south axis line as explained in Chapter 4. Next establish the net or centerline *VV* at a right angle to the axis line, making points *1* and *2* exactly 27 feet apart when point *2* is set in 4 feet, 6 inches, from the axis line.

Now locate point *4*. It is properly located when it is set in 4 feet, 6 inches, from the axis line (same distance as point *2*) and its distance on the first tape measure is 47 feet, 5¼ inches, from point *1* as it intersects the second tape measure, when stretched from point *2*, at the 39-foot mark.

Be sure tapes are pulled tight when measurements are taken. Complete layout for the four corners *1, 2, 4* and *5* by establishing point *5* in a similar manner, being sure distance from *4* to *5* is 27 feet. To have accurately squared corners, the diagonal measurements must be equal in length. In this case each diagonal must measure 47 feet, 5¼ inches.

The next step is to establish service line *WW* by locating point *6*: it should be 21 feet from point *1* and 18 feet from point *5*. Similarly, locate point *3* exactly 21 feet from point *2* and 18 feet from point *4*.

Locating centerline *XX* completes one half of the singles court layout. Locate point *7* an equal distance—13 feet, 6 inches—between points *1* and *2*. Next locate point *8* exactly between points *3* and *6* in a similar manner. Complete boundaries

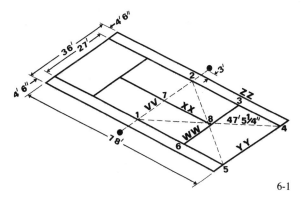

6-1

49

for the singles court by marking off second half in a similar manner.

Now complete doubles court boundaries by extending net line *VV*, 4 feet, 6 inches, in each direction from points *1* and *2*. Similarly, extend baseline *YY* from points *4* and *5*, as well as the baseline for the second half. Establish sidelines *ZZ* for the doubles court by connecting the four new points, making them parallel to those of the singles court sidelines. (Actually, dimensions for a singles court are the same as for a doubles, with one exception: The doubles court is 9 feet wider—4 feet, 6 inches on each side.)

Black dots in Figure 6-1 indicate net posts whose inside faces are 3 feet outside doubles sideline *ZZ*. For best playing conditions, keep space between baseline *YY* and fence a minimum distance of 21 feet; space between sidelines *ZZ* and fence should be a minimum distance of 12 feet. Generally, make lines 2 inches wide, with the exception of baselines *YY*. They may vary between 2 and 4 inches in width.

When using doubles court for singles match, position net sticks exactly 3 feet outside service lines. Net should be supported 3 feet, 6 inches, above court.

ESTABLISHING MULTIPURPOSE COURTS

There's little doubt that by now your decision to lay out only a tennis court or to create a multipurpose playing area, including several different kinds of courts. And most likely your decision was influenced by friends or family. I'd recommend that you reconsider the idea of laying out two or more courts with permanent lines overlapping, if this is what is uppermost in your mind. You might just discover the whole playing concept turning sour, with neither friends nor family enjoying playing any game where a series of unrelated playing lines create a constant state of confusion. Of course, the ideal situation is to have plenty of playing area, with ample space between courts. But if you do not have a large enough area to separate the courts, consider the tennis court first. Lay it out with permanent playing lines, if possible, using removable playing lines to designate other overlapping courts.

Figures 6-2 through 6-5 show the dimensions for several popular playing courts. Basically, you lay them out using the same procedures you did for the tennis court in the preceding section.

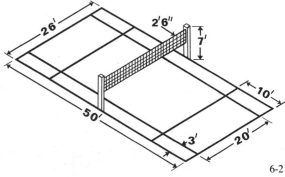

Aerial Tennis

6-2. Follow the simple layout provided in Figure 6-2. The singles game area is 20 feet wide; for doubles, the area expands to 26 feet. The net for aerial tennis is 2 feet, 6 inches, wide.

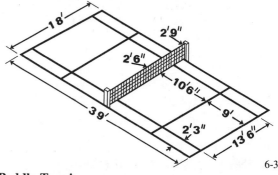

Paddle Tennis

6-3. Not to be confused with platform tennis, paddle tennis requires a court laid out to the dimensions shown in the diagram. Note that the net is 2 feet, 9 inches, at each post, but 2 feet, 6 inches, at the center.

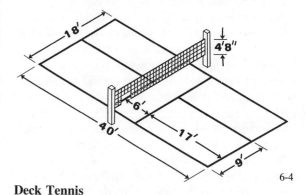

Deck Tennis

6-4. The doubles playing area for deck tennis is 18 feet wide; the singles area is 12 feet. The net, as shown, is 4 feet, 8 inches, wide.

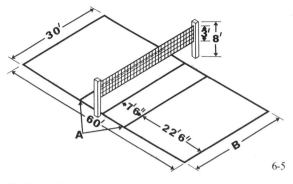

6-5

Volleyball

6-5. All lines on the volleyball court should be 2 inches wide. In Figure 6-5, *A* indicates the rear spiker's line; *B* marks the serving area. The net is 32 feet across when stretched tightly in position.

INSTALLING PERMANENT FIXTURES

The permanent equipment described in this section includes net posts, center net strap and anchor, and net sticks. Other auxiliary equipment is described in Chapter 10. Refer to Sources of Supply for manufacturers of these fixtures.

Net Posts

Net posts are manufactured from metal or wood and come in slightly different sizes. Some posts are 3 inches in outside diameter. Others vary slightly from this measurement. For instance, Rawlings sells two models constructed of 2⅞-inch steel pipe (outside diameter), complete with sleeves. One model is a conventional post with reel; the other a deluxe post with a jiffy net tightener. Wherever you purchase posts, be sure to check the locking devices. Some posts lock in wide-spaced positions without making allowances for fine tightening. This can result in net installations with incorrect tension, either too tight or too loose.

For a doubles court, locate two net posts positioned in their sleeves set in concrete 3 feet, 6 inches above the surface at the point of cable attachment. They should be 42 feet apart, with each post located exactly 3 feet outside the outer alley line.

Usually the court surface, base, and sub-base are firm enough that all you'll need for a form is a hole topped with a wood frame. Make it from four pieces of 2-inch-wide lumber, fastened together with 16-penny nails at each joint, to form a 2-foot square (inside measurement). Post foundations made of concrete should have minimum dimensions of 2 feet square by 2 feet, 6 inches, deep (deeper if frost line is deeper). *See* Appendix, Table 1, for proper mixture of ingredients. Be sure tops of frames are positioned flush with the surface for concrete courts. For porous-type courts, locate top of foundation forms below court level so that the surface layer covers the foundations when the court is completed. For asphalt-type courts, build foundations after pavement construction is completed. It's better to cut through the pavement to build the foundations than it is to build them first, then take a chance of having them damaged by large equipment. Position net posts in their sleeves—tops flush with surface and posts plumb—as the concrete is poured into the forms.

If you mix the concrete yourself rather than buy ready-mix, thoroughly mix dry Portland cement, sand, and rock. Then mix contents with just enough clean water to make the concrete work easily as you shovel it into the hole. It should be easy to work, but not soupy. Now level top of concrete with a scrap piece of 2 x 4, and finish surface with a cement finisher's trowel.

Center Net Strap and Anchor

Use an adjustable center net strap to maintain the top center of the net 3 feet above the surface by actual measurement with a yardstick or a metal tape. Fasten strap into metal anchor, installed where the centerline intersects the net line.

As you build the court, set the center strap anchor in the concrete surface as it is being poured. Be sure to keep it in the proper position completely through the finishing process. For porous and asphalt-type courts, drive the anchor firmly into the court at correct location after the surface is completed.

Net Sticks

If you are planning to hold tournaments, make a couple of net sticks to support the net at 3 feet, 6 inches, above the surface when positioned 3 feet outside the inner alley lines. Rip a straight piece of 1 x 2, making it 3 feet, 6 inches, long. Pencil mark one of the sticks 3 feet from one end to make a convenient measuring device for checking height of net at the strap anchor location.

Portable Tennis Post Standard

6-6.   If you are building a multipurpose playing area, perhaps you would rather have a portable tennis post standard than traditional posts. Figure 6-6 shows one sold by Century Sports, Inc. It is a free-standing tournament-type tennis standard of 2⅞-inch O.D. galvanized steel pipe, with postcaps and ratchet reel. No additional strap anchor is required. At time of printing, the price was $399, less net.

STRIPING THE COURT

Lay out and mark the court for lines, as described earlier in this chapter.

Porous Courts

Use white synthetic line tapes, 2 inches wide, either acrylic-coated or an equivalent secured from your tennis court material supplier. Use aluminum nails on courts with a stone base; copper nails with a cinder or slag base.

6-7.   Start by anchoring the tapes at corners with eight or ten nails driven through prepunched holes. Then nail down throughout length from midpoint to corner.

You can line grass, clay, and grit courts by using one of the mechanical hand-propelled markers, available in two styles. One style is a wet marker; the other, a dry powder marker.

Some owners of grit and clay courts use a two-shot method to apply painted lines. First, they use a paintbrush to apply a coat of linseed oil as a base. Second, following the drying of the linseed oil, which takes approximately 24 hours, they use a 2-inch paintbrush to paint the lines with white traffic paint. Some tennis buffs swear by this method, and they claim the lines hold up for a long time.

Nonporous Courts

It is general practice on nonporous courts to put the lines down with acrylic tennis court paint.

When selecting a paint, do *not* choose one with an oil base because it can cause peeling, crumbling, and cracking of asphalt surfaces and will probably require a prior treatment of diluted muriatic acid on concrete surfaces to prevent the

Courtesy of Century Sports, Inc.   6-6

Courtesy of Robert Lee Co.   6-7

Most line paints can be applied with a paintbrush, roller, spray and marking equipment, or an airless spray. Leave the latter two methods to the pros. However, you can do a job that looks just as neat with either a paintbrush or a roller, and if you carefully follow instructions on the container, one coat usually does the job.

Caution: Regardless of what anyone tells you, never use traffic line paint for lining asphalt-type courts.

Courtesy of California Products Corp.   6-8

line paint from peeling after it is applied. Rather, select only an acrylic line paint designed and guaranteed by the manufacturer for use on nonporous court surfaces. Be sure to follow accompanying instructions to the letter. For instance, surface curing of concrete courts generally requires a longer period of time than asphalt-type courts prior to the paint application. Also, the paint should fulfill three additional requirements: It should be reflective, nonglaring, and nonchalking.

6-8. Plexicolor line paint, manufactured by the California Products Corporation, is a highly reflective marking paint for use over any bituminous surface, color-coated and concrete surfaces. It contains no solvents to deteriorate asphalt. Nonglaring, highly resistant to climatic conditions, and fast drying, it can be applied (at temperatures between 50° F and 140° F) with brush, roller, spray and marking equipment, or an airless spray.

7

Building a Platform Court

Platform tennis is a relatively new game. It had its beginning in 1928 in Scarsdale, New York. The game evolved when a small group of men determined to start a year-round outdoor game especially suited to cold weather.

What unfolded was a new kind of tennis game, with the court laid out on a specially designed platform that would drain rain water and snow from the surface. It was supported on pillars, surrounded with wire fencing.

The game was originally designed for playing in cold weather with temperatures of 10° F to 50° F considered ideal: some rugged individuals played on the courts in sub-zero weather. This is not necessarily the objective today, since platform tennis courts are much in evidence from sunny California to Maine. Indeed, platform tennis courts are found on rooftops, marshy ground, hillsides, and backyards all over the U.S.A. In addition, increasingly popular on school grounds, condominiums, racquet complexes, and backyards are installations on concrete, asphaltic, and other traditional tennis court slabs constructed directly on the ground, minus the platform supported on piers.

The procedures in this chapter show how to build an outdoor platform tennis court within a limited space for playing day or night, in cold or warm weather. If you are not bothered with snow and prefer one of the traditional tennis court surfaces, dispense with building the platform, piers, and snow gates. In this case, use redwood, treated posts, or galvanized steel uprights, setting them in concrete (see Appendix, Table I, for proper mixture) to a minimum depth of 3 feet.

EQUIPMENT AND SUPPLIES

Tools

The following tools, usually found in most households, are all you need to build a platform tennis court:
Carpenter's hammer
Carpenter's level
Saw—power saw preferable
Framing square
Shovel
Brick mason's trowel—optional
Nail set
Paintbrushes—sizes to suit jobs.
Drill and set of bits

Materials

Use well-seasoned kiln-dried straight Douglas fir lumber of construction grade. Be sure it has been treated with pentachlorophenol, which can be purchased from any lumberyard. Treat only bottom and sides of decking. Do *not* use creosote as a method of treatment.

Use galvanized or other rust-resistant metal parts, such as nails, hinges, and door closures.

Parts	Quantity and Description
Piers	8 x 8 x 16-inch concrete blocks, or concrete and concrete forms; amount and number to suit
Reinforcement rods	#14, length and number to suit

54

Parts	Quantity and Description
Termite prevention	eighteen termite shields or termite treatment material in amount to suit
Build-up girders	twenty-one 2 x 12s x 12 feet long twelve 2 x 12s x 14 feet long two 2 x 12s x 16 feet long
Floor joists	one 2 x 6 x 10 feet long fifty-six 2 x 6s x 16 feet long eight 2 x 8s x 20 feet long
Solid bridging	five 2 x 8s x 12 feet long one 2 x 4 x 10 feet long
Cross bridging	ten 2 x 2s x 12 feet long
Headers	eight 2 x 8s x 12 feet long two 2 x 8s x 14 feet long
Flooring	one hundred thirty-two 2 x 6s x 24 feet sixty-six 2 x 6s x 14 feet
Posts	thirty 4 x 4s x 12 feet four 2 x 4s x 12 feet Corner posts require a 2 x 4 spiked to a 4 x 4
Line post top nailers	one 2 x 4 x 12 feet long one 2 x 4 x 10 feet long
Line post bottom nailers	one 2 x 4 x 16 feet long
Post braces	nine 2 x 4s x 12 feet long
Outrigger assembly	one 4 x 4 x 14 feet long ten 2 x 4s x 8 feet long
Middle rails	six 2 x 4s x 24 feet long two 2 x 4s x 14 feet long two 2 x 4s x 8 feet long
Top rails	six 2 x 6s x 24 feet long two 2 x 6s x 14 feet long two 2 x 6s x 8 feet long
Optional outrigger braces	five 2 x 4s x 12 feet long
Corner braces	two 2 x 4s x 16 feet long
Wood steps	2 x 8s, length to suit 2 x 10s, length to suit
Door frame	one 2 x 4 x 14 feet long one 2 x 4 x 3 feet long one 1 x 2 x 7 feet long
Post cleats	five 1 x 3s x 12 feet long
Snow boards	six 1 x 4s x 14 feet long thirty-nine 1 x 4s x 12 feet long five 1 x 3s x 16 feet long one 1 x 3 x 10 feet long

Parts	Quantity and Description
Door	two 1¼ x 3 inches x 7 feet long one 1¼ x 3 inches x 3 feet long one 1¼ x 5 inches x 3 feet long twelve 3-inch roundhead screws three door hinges, type to suit one lock set or one hasp set and padlock

TENSION BAR ASSEMBLY

Parts	Quantity and Description
Tension bars	two 2 x 4s x 16 feet long eleven 2 x 4s x 14 feet long
Wire screen	16-gauge, 1-inch mesh, 6 x 325 feet long
Wire screen connectors	325 feet of 20-gauge galvanized wire rope
Cap bars	six 2 x 2s x 24 feet long two 2 x 2s x 14 feet long two 2 x 2s x 8 feet long
Net post assemblies	one 4 x 4 x 7 feet long one 2 x 4 x 5 feet long
Strap iron	four ⅜ x 3 x 16 inches long
Reels	two, type to suit
Wood filler	Plastic wood or similar filler, amount to suit
Paint	Antirust primer, house paint, marine paint or an exterior porch and floor paint, white paint for marking playing lines, paint aggregate, amounts and types to suit
Coat hangers	Minimum of two
Threaded rods	twenty ½ x 30 inches long forty ½ x 24 inches long
Nails	25 lb. 16-penny box nails 45 lb. #16 galvanized casing nails 10 lb. 8-penny box nails 3½ lb. 6-penny box nails six #6 finish nails
Netting staples	1½ lb.
Carriage bolts	forty-six ½ x 4 inches long one-hundred thirty-two ½ x 6 inches long thirty-six ½ x 7 inches long ten ½ x 8 inches long eight ½ x 9 inches long
Washers	three-hundred forty for ½-inch bolts and threaded rods
Nuts	three-hundred forty for ½-inch bolts and threaded rods
Lag screws	six ¼ x 1½ inches long eight ¼ x 4 inches long

CONSTRUCTING THE PIERS

7-1. Begin by locating the eighteen foundation pier footing pads. Figure 7-1 shows location of piers, each one approximately 12 inches in diameter poured onto a concrete footing pad 24 inches square.

Use a transit, as shown in Chapter 4, to make the layout, or you can use a long straightedge, level, two steel tapes, and nylon cord as described in Chapter 6 for laying out the lawn tennis court. In either case, tops of footing pads and tops of piers must be on the same grade so that the platform will be perfectly square and level.

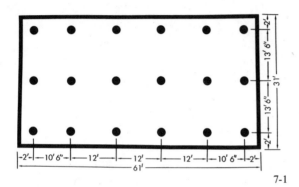

7-1

After the eighteen footing pad locations are made, remove dirt 24 inches square to a depth below the frost zone, being sure to maintain a minimum depth of 2 feet, 6 inches, with the bottom of each hole on the same grade. Then drive a wood stake in the center of each hole down to the level of the proposed footing: in this case, 8 inches. The earth walls serve as forms so no boards are required.

Using ready-mix concrete (*see* Appendix, Table I, for proper mixture), fill holes to top of stakes. Use a short piece of 2 x 4 or a brick mason's trowel to level concrete flush with tops of stakes. Allow concrete to set for 48 hours before proceeding.

There are a couple of ways to build the piers: namely, use concrete blocks or use concrete poured into prebuilt forms. In either case, bring the piers a minimum of 18 inches above grade. This provides room to pile snow in cold areas and provides a roomy crawl space for making underdeck inspections or repairs.

Construct block piers 16 inches square by using two 8 x 8 x 16-inch concrete blocks in each layer; blocks are actually 7½ inches thick with ½

inch of mortar in between making up the joints. Lumberyards supply a masonry mortar mix with only water added to make a workable mixture. Criss-cross the layers of blocks, using a brick mason's trowel to place the mortar. As the piers go up, use a level, keeping each block level and plumb. For added stability, place four #4 reinforcement rods inside the block openings. Also, fill the openings with concrete as each pier is constructed. Build the four corner piers first, being sure tops are on the same grade; each pier must be in perfect alignment.

7-2. If you decide to pour concrete piers, you can either purchase fiber tubes, such as those manufactured by Sonoco Products and stocked by large lumberyards, or you can build forms from 12-inch boards (actually 11¼ inches wide). By tapering the forms, bottoms slightly larger than tops, it is possible to build a few forms, slide them upward from the piers when the concrete has set, then reuse them over and over until the job is completed.

The form shown in Figure 7-2 is of proper construction for building piers a maximum of 5 feet in height. For piers extending more than 2 feet above grade, place four #4 reinforcement rods in the middle of each footing pad hole just before the concrete is poured. Position rods vertically about 4 inches apart, forming a square. To prevent rods falling out of alignment while concrete is setting, drive them into the earth a few inches below bottom of footing pad hole, being sure

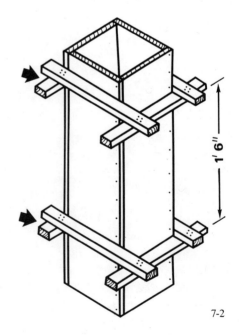

7-2

tops of rods reach almost to top of proposed height of form.

Construct the four sides of the pier forms from 12-inch lumber. Using a saw, taper the sides from 11¼ inches at the bottom to 9 inches at the top. For easy removal of forms, use a paint roller to coat boards with used crankcase oil, on one side only, prior to assembly.

Lap the edges as you fasten them together in the form of a square box with both ends open. Oiled faces of boards must be on the inside. Use 8-penny box nails spaced about 12 inches apart for the fastening job. Dots show location of nails. If lumber splits while nailing, predrill holes in face boards slightly smaller than shank of nail. In any case, always predrill holes near edges of face boards. Since fresh concrete has a way of bulging forms, use 2 x 4 yokes spaced 18 inches apart (arrows in Fig. 7-2) and fastened together with 16-penny box nails. The yokes hold the forms in shape while the concrete is setting up. If the yokes have a tendency to not remain in place, hold in position by toenailing a couple of 8-penny box nails through edges of 2 x 4s into sides of forms.

Next, center forms over concrete footing pads, checking to be certain sides and tops are in perfect alignment. After pouring the concrete (*see* Appendix, Table I, for correct mixture) and leveling the tops, allow to set 48 hours before removing forms. Tapping yokes with a hammer helps to break forms loose from the piers; then slide forms upward for use again. With forms removed, pack dirt around piers flush with grade.

If you're building piers taller than 5 feet, remember that height of piers should never exceed width of base by more than ten times. Also, use yokes of 4 x 4 material held together by bolts instead of nails. Because of the great weight of concrete at the bottom, place lower yokes a minimum of 12 inches apart, widening the distance to 18 inches near the top.

BUILDING THE FRAME AND PLATFORM

Since there are fifty-eight species of termites ready to chew wood of most varieties, some measure of protection is in order from these antlike devouring insects.

Termite shields placed over the piers, prior to putting down the built-up girders, is one means of protection, and your local tinner should know

how to make them. They must be larger than tops of piers and must be bent downward about 3 inches on their four sides. To do this, the tinner will make cuts which must be completely closed with solder, or the termites will crawl through to the wood. To do the job properly, noncorrosive metal should be used: 16-ounce copper is preferable, but #26-gauge galvanized copper bearing steel makes a reliable and cheaper substitute. If this preventive method is used, the steps (built later) will also need protection from termites.

Other than durable wood not bothered by termites, such as heart tidewater red cypress or heart redwood, wood stairs in contact with the ground should be pressure treated with zinc chloride. Your lumberyard can provide such treatment for the wood, or provide a source of treatment before the steps are constructed.

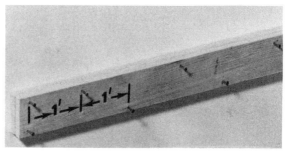

7-3

7-3. The illustration shows how 16-penny box nails are used in following steps to construct built-up girders or built-up joists, sometimes referred to as laminated girders and laminated joists. Note that two nails are used, one over the other, at the joint. Then nails are spaced 12 inches apart and staggered, one at the top and the next at the bottom, etc., until the boards making up the built-up piece are fastened together in a single unit.

7-4. Begin the platform framing operation by nailing up three sets of built-up girders. Built-up

7-4

girders are recommended because they won't warp as easily as solid-wood girders and are less likely to contain decayed wood. Here's the way to do it.

1. Length of side girders is a total of 61 feet each, consisting of a series of two sets of 2 x 12s with staggered joints located over the center of the side piers. For each set of side built-up girders, you will need four 2 x 12s x 14 feet long for making the ends, with six 2 x 12s x 12 feet long in between.

Length of the middle built-up girder is 61 feet plus 3 feet, 6 inches, on each end for the middle 2 x 12 *only*. This extension serves as part of the outrigger (Fig. 7-13). This built-up girder consists of a series of three sets of 2 x 12s with staggered joints located over middle of center piers. For the middle built-up girder, you will need four 2 x 12s x 14 feet long for the outside ends, two 2 x 12s x 16 feet long for the middle (including the extension of 3 feet, 6 inches, on each end), and nine 2 x 12s x 12 feet long in between. Be sure end of each board rests at least 4 inches on its respective pier.

2. Lay out the 2 x 12s, crown up, for one built-up girder at a time. Then cut 2 x 12s where necessary for making staggered joints. Next nail boards together as shown in Figure 7-3.

3. As each built-up girder is completed, center it over its respective pier. Check with a level. If not level, use small wood wedges at least 1½ inches wide to make it even.

There are two ways to correct crowns (convex curvatures on edges of some boards). One way is to plane or saw away the crown. The other way is to make small notches in built-up girder crown when installing the joists in a following step.

7-5. This picture shows how 16-penny nails are used in the next step where two joists butt together over a built-up girder.

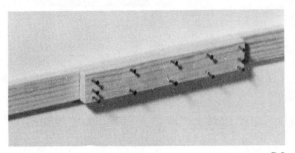

7-5

Position a board 2 x 8 x 4 feet long across the butt joint. Then use 16-penny box nails, spaced 12 inches apart, to fasten it in place.

Where joists lap, drive four 16-penny box nails through the lap joint.

Where joists are built up, fasten together as shown in Figure 7-3.

7-6. Floor joists are next, and here are some general principles that apply to their construction. Note that joists *A, B, C, D,* and *E* are given only for one half of the framing in Figure 7-6.

7-6

Length of joists is 31 feet, with joints falling directly over girders.

Beginning in the center (15 feet, 6 inches, from either end), mark locations on the built-up girders every 3 feet, since the joists are located on exactly 3-foot centers.

Next construct joists *A, B, C, D,* and *E* with crowns up. Note some of the joists are built up, others are not. When joists are correctly located, they are toenailed to their respective girders.

The following five steps explain in detail how to build each of the five different types of floor joists for half of the joist framing:

1. Begin by constructing two built-up flooring seam joists *A,* consisting of twelve 2 x 8s x 16 feet long, with staggered joints to fit over middle girder and fastened together with 16-penny box nails (Fig. 7-3). Make built-up joists *A* three boards thick. Also, the distance between centers of the two joists must be exactly 24 feet, since they must fall directly on center below the flooring seams as described later.

2. Next construct five joists *B,* each one consisting of two 2 x 8s x 16 feet long. A one-foot lap is fastened together with four 16-penny box nails driven through the lap joint. Unlettered joists are constructed the same as joists *B.*

3. Two built-up joists *C* are next in order, each one made up of two 2 x 8s x 16 feet long and

two 2 x 8s x 20 feet long. Saw 1 foot from one of the 16-foot pieces. Butt them together and butt the two 20-foot pieces together. Then fasten each pair together with 16-penny nails, as shown in Figure 7-3, being sure joints fall over middle built-up girder. The 20-foot boards must extend an equal distance on each end beyond the 31-foot built-up joist width. These extensions serve as a base for the side outriggers, shown in Figure 7-13.

4. Now make built-up joist *D* from four 2 x 8s x 16 feet long. Cut boards so joints are staggered and fall over middle girder. Then fasten boards to either with 16-penny box nails (Fig. 7-3).

5. Joist *E* consists of four 2 x 8s x 16 feet long, each pair butted together and fastened with a 2 x 8 x 4-foot board and 16-penny box nails as shown in Figure 7-5. To attain two 31-foot continuous joists, make cut from each board so joints fall over middle girder.

Now solid bridge the two joists together, with eight pieces of 2 x 4s x 7¼ inches long spaced approximately 5 feet apart. Fasten with 16-penny box nails, two nailed through the face of each of the two joists into the 2 x 4s. Begin the bridging operation about 5 feet from the joints. Be sure to leave ends of joists open so 4 x 6-inch posts can be installed between them later.

7-7. Next brace middle of joists with solid bridging. Cut pieces of 2 x 8 for snug fit, setting them at right angles to the joists. Check to be sure pieces are in a straight line directly over center of middle built-up girder. Then using eight 16-penny nails (four to each side), toenail bridging pieces to the joists as shown in Figure 7-7.

7-7

7-8. Now run two rows of 2 x 2 cross bridging *A* (sometimes called herringbone bridging) between the joists. Measure off 7 feet, 9 inches, from each end of both end joists, marking locations with a pencil. Follow by snapping a chalk

line between each pair of end marks. This provides two guidelines lengthwise for locating two rows of cross bridging between the joists.

Since spacing between the joists is not uniform, here's an easy and practical way to cut the bridging pieces. Hold a piece of 2 x 2 in bridging position over ends of two opposite joists. Mark piece at top and bottom along inside face of respective joists. This provides cutting lines, which must be parallel to each other. Then apply the same technique to second piece of 2 x 2 to locate angles of corresponding cross-bridging piece; check by fitting them in position at proper locations. Check other similar bridging locations to see how many pieces you can make from this pattern. Sound practice calls for the fitting of braces into position soon after they are cut. Otherwise, you may end up with much wasted material, as well as wasted time. Finish cross-bridging operation by cutting remaining pieces of different lengths, using the method just described.

Fasten cross-bridging pieces in place by first nailing to *top of joists only* with two 8-penny box nails. Do not drive them through cross bridging where thickness is more than ¾ inch.

Make a note to nail lower end of bridging pieces after the flooring is completed, as joists make certain adjustments when the flooring is laid. You will save time by starting the nails on the lower ends at the time of fastening top ends in place.

Complete platform framing by constructing and fastening joists to girders and installing both solid and cross bridging for second half of frame. The same number of 2 x 8s, 2 x 4s and 2 x 2s are required here, except for built-up joist *A*. Since center built-up joist *A* is already in place, only one more is required.

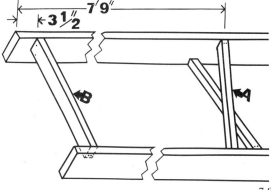

7-8

Next install cleats *B* for supporting tension bolts (Fig. 7-23) on both sides of platform. Begin by measuring in 3½ inches from ends of joists on both sides of framing, marking measurements on faces of joists near their top edges.

Next make cleats by cutting pieces of 2 x 4 to fit, edges up, snug between floor joists. With top edges of cleats set in 3½ inches and flush with top edges of joists, use four 16-penny box nails, one on each side near ends, to toenail them to faces of the joists, or drive them through faces of joists into end grain of the cleats. Cleats are *not* required between joists underneath door locations.

7-9

7-9. Close in floor joists on both sides of platform frame with headers, 2 x 8s x 12 feet. Drive three 16-penny box nails through face of header into end grain of joist. Use only three nails to the joist whether it is a single board or a built-up joist. For clarity, the 2 x 4 cleats are purposely omitted from Figure 7-9.

7-10

7-10. Locate and mark post positions on floor joists. Then follow nailing instructions below, being certain not to nail first board on each side of court and boards facing ends of court opposite post locations. Just place these boards loosely in place until posts are assembled. The reason for laying this much of the flooring at this stage of construction is to provide a platform to support workmen, ladders, tools, etc. Later, cut boards to fit in between posts.

Begin the 2 x 6 flooring operation from the center of the middle joist (seam joist) and from either side, laying the 24-foot lengths from the center joist to one of the opposite seam built-up joists. Position first flooring board flush with outside edge of header, but refrain from nailing. Use ¼-inch spacing between boards. (A short piece of ¼-inch plywood provides a quickly made gauge.) Use two 16-penny galvanized casing head nails at each joint to fasten flooring to the joists. Countersink nails ⅛ inch below surface. *Predrill* holes in ends of flooring boards. Otherwise, boards may split (if not now, later), causing earlier than normal maintenance problems.

7-11. Twenty-six line posts, 4 x 4s x 12 feet spaced approximately 6 feet apart, are required. You can substitute six posts, 4 x 4s x 20 feet long, if your plans call for lighting the court. Some light suppliers may recommend six metal posts 20 feet long instead of wood posts. In this case, anchor the metal posts directly to line posts as recommended by the supplier.

Begin by marking line post locations approximately 6 feet apart (every other floor joist) on both sides of the frame. Then locate line posts approximately 6 feet apart at each end of frame between the two end joists, bonded together with solid 2 x 4 bridging. Since middle and top rails in lengths of 14 and 24 feet are recommended later, be sure post locations are marked so joints of the attachments always fall on center of their respective line posts.

Line posts on both sides of frame require nailer *B*. Using five 16-penny box nails, fasten 12-inch piece of 2 x 4 *B* to each post 7 inches from the top, forming a notch. When posts are installed, nailers always face the floor.

Position side line posts *A* in corner of joist *C* and header on each side of frame and fasten to their respective joists with two ½-inch galvanized carriage bolts, washers, and nuts. Length of bolts vary between single-board joists and built-up joists. While installing, use a level to be certain posts are plumb on all sides.

Next position line posts approximately 6 feet apart between solid bridged joists on each end of frame. Then fasten each post with two ½ x 7-inch carriage bolts, washers, and nuts, being sure posts are plumb.

You will need a nailer on one side of posts located along sides of court on which to nail the flooring. So make nailers *D* by cutting pieces of 7¼-inch 2 x 4s, each spiked with four 16-penny box nails to bottom of posts—tops of nailers

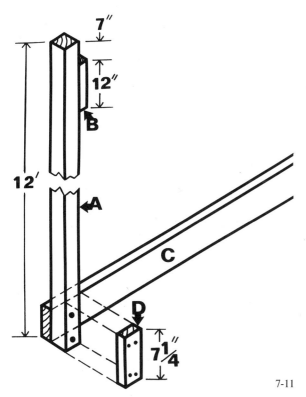

7-11

7-12

flush with joists—to bottom ends *only* of the line posts located on both sides of the frame.

The four corner posts are 4 x 6s x 12 feet, made in the same way as the line posts with one exception. Here you extend 2 x 4 nailer *B* for full length of the 4 x 4 post instead of 12 inches. Using 16-penny box nails staggered every 12 inches (similar to the built-up girder in Fig. 7-3), fasten 2 x 4 and 4 x 4 together, being sure of a 7-inch notch at the top.

Position 4 x 6 posts between solid-bridged joists, notches facing each other on the ends of the frame, then bolt in place with two 7-inch galvanized carriage bolts, washers, and nuts, being sure posts are plumb.

Check to be sure all posts are plumb and wrench tight. For clarity, girders, cleats, headers, and flooring are not shown in Figure 7-11.

Follow post installations by nailing loose ends of headers to line posts on each side of frame and nailing loose flooring boards in place, including nailing loose ends of flooring boards to nailers *D*.

COMPLETING THE STRUCTURE

7-12. Saw fifty-two 2 x 4 line post braces, 22 inches long, and cut at 45° angles. Using four 16-penny box nails, fasten in place as shown. By

now you should know where you want a door or doors located; line posts facing door frame have only one brace. The second brace is fastened to the door frame (Fig. 7-19) to serve as an outside track for sliding the short snow board (Fig. 7-21) in and out of position.

Next cut eight corner post braces at 45° angles, slightly longer than line post braces. Top ends of corner post braces should overlap to form a neat outside corner. Use four 16-penny nails to fasten each brace in place.

Outriggers

7-13. Next install 2 x 4 outrigger to each end of platform. Begin by using two ½ x 8-inch carriage bolts, washers, and nuts to fasten a piece of 4 x 4 to outside face of the two line posts (located opposite extended girder) 8 feet, 6 inches, above floor level.

After measuring and cutting a 2 x 4 outrigger to proper angle at each end, fasten in place with two ½-inch carriage bolts, washers, and nuts, with a 4-inch bolt at bottom end and an 8-inch bolt at the top end.

Next install four 2 x 4 outriggers on each side of platform. Here top ends of 2 x 4s are fastened directly to line posts with ½ x 8-inch carriage bolts, washers, and nuts. Fasten bottom ends of 2 x 4s to joist extensions with ½ x 4-inch carriage bolts, nuts, and washers.

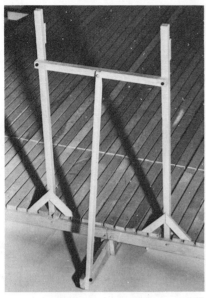

7-13

Use a ½ x 6-inch carriage bolt at each post (two at each joint, one for each board) with one exception: You'll need four ½ x 7-inch bolts at each corner where they go through the 2 x 4 fastened to the post.

Reinforce middle-rail joints with pieces of 2 x 4s x 2 feet long centered over joints, fastened in place with six 16-penny box nails staggered similarly to the way built-up girders are fastened together (Fig. 7-3).

7-15. Use 2 x 6s 14 and 24 feet long, for the top rails. After placing 2 x 6s on inside of posts and resting them on the 2 x 4 nailers, fasten to each post with a ½ x 6-inch carriage bolt, washer, and nut. Use two bolts at each joint, one for end of each board. There is one exception, however: The 2 x 6 on side of platform fits into the notch and is bolted onto the corner post, while the 2 x 6 on end of platform forms a butt joint against adjoining 2 x 6 and fastening is made with two ¼ x 4-inch lag screws.

Rails and Braces

7-14. Use 2 x 4s, 14 and 24 feet long, for the middle rails. After positioning them on the outside of the posts 6 feet, 10¼ inches, above the floor, fasten in place with ½-inch carriage bolts, washers, and nuts.

Note: The exact measurement above the floor is most important at door locations. Otherwise, you could encounter trouble later when installing the door frame.

7-15

7-14

7-16. This step is optional. Sometimes platform tennis court posts have a tendency to bend inward. If this is a problem in your locality, or if high winds prevail, add an outrigger brace to each of the ten outriggers.

Position a 2 x 4 x 6 feet long, as shown. Make top cut to angle of outrigger. Then hold in place with two ½ x 4-inch carriage bolts, washers, and nuts (one each at top and bottom).

7-17. Cut eight pieces of 2 x 4s x 4 feet long at a 45° angle at each end to serve as corner braces. Then position them as shown. Fasten to top rail with ½ x 4-inch carriage bolts, washers, and nuts. Fasten bottom ends of braces to posts with ½ x 9-inch carriage bolts, washers, and nuts.

Stairs

7-18. Perhaps steps, due to faulty construction, cause a greater number of accidents than the whole platform tennis court area.

You may want to have a set of precast concrete steps installed. If not, here's the way to make a solid set of wood stairs, which should be a minimum of 6 inches wider than the door entrance.

1. Measure distance between top of platform and ground level. Then divide the distance by 7 inches to give number of steps required. In Figure 7-18, the distance was 29 inches, making the steps 7¼ inches apart. (Include ground level as one step.)

2. Measure from a point on the ground, exactly plumb from edge of platform, outward 9¼ inches (width of steps) times number of steps required. In the diagram, this was 9¼ inches times 5, or 46¼ inches. Mark the measurement.

3. Use a nonstretch tape to measure distance from the mark to 1½ inches below top of platform. This gives length of side pieces, called *stringers*.

4. Use a piece of 1 x 2 with one end positioned on the mark while the remainder of the piece rests on top of platform. Either with a sliding T-bevel or by sight, determine angle of cut for the stringers. Remember top and bottom cuts of stringers must be parallel to each other, as well as parallel to top of platform and the ground. Now make the stringers by cutting two pieces of 2 x 8s to angle and length to suit.

5. Locate bottom edge of stairs by dividing number of steps required into length of stringers. Then fasten top edges of 1 x 3 cleats cut to fit to the marks. Be sure cleats are parallel to top and bottom edges of stringers. Use three 8-penny box nails to each cleat.

6. Saw a 2 x 10 for the top step, length to suit. Using six 16-penny box nails, fasten to top end of stringers. Next cut enough 2 x 10s to suit, each 3 inches shorter than top step. After positioning steps in place, fasten with six 16-penny box nails. Drive these nails at an angle so they fasten into

7-16

7-17

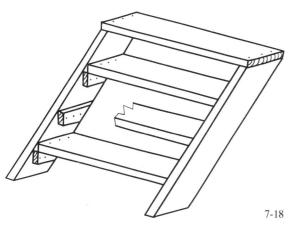

7-18

stringers, rather than directly down into the cleats.

Good construction practice calls for resting steps on a concrete slab. If this is out of the question for you, rest each stringer atop an 8 x 8 x 16-inch concrete block buried with its top surface flush with the ground.

Hold stairs in position by toenailing a 16-penny box nail through each outside edge of stringers into 2 x 8 header and three 16-penny box nails through top step into header.

If termites are a problem in your area, treat stair wood as described earlier in this chapter.

Door Frame

7-19. Make the door frame by cutting two side pieces of 2 x 4, 6 feet, 8¾, inches long and a top piece of 2 x 4, 35½ inches long. Using two 16-penny box nails at each end, fasten top piece onto the two side pieces as shown to complete the frame.

Next cut one piece of 1 x 3 x 6 feet, 8¾ inches, long to serve as a door stop. Plan to swing door *inside* to better protect players from falling off platform if they should accidentally run into the door. Then measure in 1¼ inches from door frame and fasten door stop in place with six 6-penny finish nails. Be sure to countersink heads.

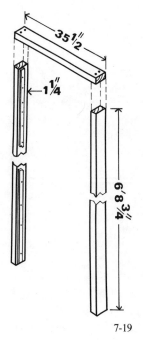

7-19

Using four 16-penny box nails, fasten one side of door frame to the post nearest door location. Then toenail bottom end of opposite door frame to the flooring, being sure frame is plumb and its clearance is 32½ inches between the two 2 x 4 door frame members.

Now fasten the leftover brace indicated in Figure 7-12 to the 2 x 4 door frame member.

Snow Boards

7-20. Next make sixty cleats 1 x 3 x 12 inches, shown by arrow. *X* indicates post, *Y*, flooring, and *Z*, header. For clarity, 2 x 4 post braces are not shown.

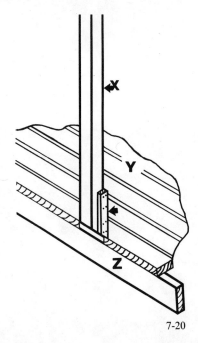

7-20

Using eight 8-penny box nails to the cleat, fasten two cleats above flooring to each post flush with faces of posts as shown. There is one exception, however: Do *not* fasten a cleat on post adjacent to the gate. Instead, fasten it to the 2 x 4 door frame member not fastened to a post. Then nail two cleats to each of the four corner posts.

As you work, remember cleats and the post braces form tracks for installing and removing snow boards. If you elect to hinge snow boards to bottom end of tension bars, omit this step, but do not omit the 2 x 4 post braces.

7-21. Length of 4-inch snow boards equals distance between posts, minus ½ inch.

Make each set of snow boards by fastening

7-21

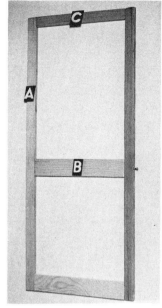

7-22

three pieces of 1 x 3 to three 1 x 4-inch snow boards spaced ½ inch apart, with bottom board to clear the floor by one inch. Use six 6-penny box nails for fastening each 1 x 3 (two nails to each 1 x 4 board).

For clarity, Figure 7-21 shows one set of snow boards (nails partly driven), in position ready for sliding down between 1 x 3 post cleats and 2 x 4 braces.

Door Installation

7-22. Make door frames from 5/4-inch clear stock. Begin by cutting two stiles *A* 3 inches wide x 6 feet, 8 inches, long. Next cut middle and lower rails *B* 5 x 26 inches long. Now cut top rail *C* 3 x 26 inches long.

Fasten stiles *A* to rails *B* with three 3-inch #10 roundhead wood screws at joints, with exception of lock location joint. Here use only two screws spaced far enough apart to allow for cutting lock mortise later if you plan to use a house-type lock.

Similarly, fasten top end of stiles *A* to rail *C*. Here use only two screws for each joint. Prepare stiles *A* for countersinking screws by drilling holes 1½ inches deep times diameter slightly larger than screw head. Figure 7-22 shows a screw positioned in hole before tightening. After tightening screws with screwdriver, fill holes either with dowel pins cut flush with edges and coated with waterproof glue or with your favorite brand of wood filler. Then sand edges smooth.

Some builders use a house-type lock set to hold door closed; others use a hasp and padlock. Complete instructions for installing house-type lock sets are found on the packing insert.

Use three hinges to hang the door. These may be either strap hinges or half-surface butt hinges, which are mortised into the inside face of the door frame and fastened to the surface of the door. Allow ½-inch clearance at bottom of door, ¼ inch on side of door at stop location, and ¼ inch over top of door.

Screen Assembly

7-23. The wire-screen assembly is next. The view in Figure 7-23 is from the platform facing the screen. For clarity, post braces, middle rails, outrigger assembly, snow boards, snow-board cleats, and corner braces are not shown.

Begin by cutting 2 x 4 tension bars *A* the distance between center of face of posts (parallel to the flooring), minus ½ inch. Lengths differ from job to job, but the distance is approximately 6 feet.

Drill two vertical holes ½ inch in diameter in tension bars *A*, 12 inches from each end. Then position side tension bars *A*, set in 5 inches (1½-inch header plus 3½ inches), on the floor. Next drill ½-inch holes through floor and 2 x 4 cleats *B* previously installed, using holes in tension bars as guide holes. Drill holes through floor on ends of platform in the same manner. Here, of course, you drill through one of the 2 x 8 floor joists. Utmost accuracy is important here. To drill per-

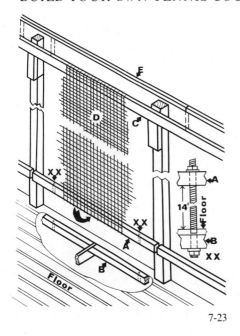

7-23

with 16-penny box nails spaced approximately 16 inches apart. For better strength, be sure joints are staggered between the top rails and the cap bars.

Keep wire screen adjusted tightly with ½-inch galvanized threaded rods through ends of bars *A*, flooring, and 2 x 4 cleats *B*, held in position with washers and nuts, as shown in detailed drawing *XX*. So that bottom nuts stay put, flatten threads on lower end of rods with a hammer. Use ½ x 24-inch threaded rods on the sides and ½ x 30-inch threaded rods on the ends of the platform.

Cut to size and staple a piece of leftover wire screen to the door.

Net Posts

7-24. Make each net post from a 4 x 4 x 3 feet, 1 inch, long with a notch cut on top to act as a guide for the net rope (exaggerated view of rope shown). Mount post to floor with two ⅜ x 3 x 16-inch pieces of strap iron bent at right angles and drilled so each piece can accept two ½ x 4-inch carriage bolts, washers, and nuts on the top end and three ¼ x 1½-inch lag screws on the bottom end.

Position net post. Then fasten carriage bolts, nuts, and washers, and screw lag screws in place. Further stabilize post by fastening a 30-inch piece of 2 x 4, cut at 45° angles, to post and floor with 16-penny box nails, as shown.

fectly vertical holes, first drill a ½-inch hole in a scrap piece of 2 x 4, using a drill press. Then use the hole in the scrap as a guide hole wherever accuracy is imperative.

Cut pieces of 16-gauge 1-inch galvanized wire screen so, when bent and stapled to bottom of tension bar *B* and brought up and bent and stapled over top rail *C*, the distance between bottom of tension bar *A* and floor is 14 inches.

Begin in the center of either end of platform, fastening one 6-foot section by using netting staples, spaced approximately 6 inches apart, to fasten wire screen *D* to bottom edge of tension bar *A*, indicated by arrow. Then bend wire over inside face of bar *A*, bringing wire screen upward over face of top rail *C*. Then bend down and staple onto the top edge.

Continue hanging sections, leaving ½-inch clearance between them as you work toward the corners. When end is completed, hang wire screen in the same manner on opposite end of platform.

Start installing wire screen on sides of platform from the corners, overlapping at midpoint. As you install the sections of wire screen, constantly check to be sure tension bars *A* clear the floor by 14 inches.

Use pieces of #20-gauge galvanized wire rope to lace adjacent widths of wire screen together. Follow by lacing corners together as true as possible.

Now fasten 2 x 2 cap bar *E* over top of rail *C*

7-24

Mount reel on opposite side of post onto which wood brace is attached so axle is 2 feet, 6 inches, from top of floor.

Finishing Touches

Give exposed iron metal parts, such as pieces of strap iron fastened to net posts, a coat of anti-rust primer paint if not already done. Touching up exposed nail heads with antirust primer is always a good idea. When paint is dry, give two coats of green or dark brown quality house paint (according to instructions on container) to all exposed materials with exception of the floor.

7-25. Paint the floor with three coats of marine paint or an exterior porch and floor paint, following instructions on the container. To add friction between the floor and the players' feet, add an aggregate to the second coat, such as Har-tru granules, walnut chips, or purified sand. Lay out the court as shown in Figure 7-25; follow

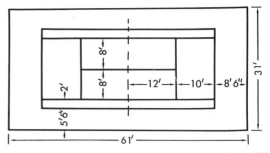

7-25

procedures given in Chapter 6. Use green paint inside the white line area and brown paint outside the white lines for the remainder of the floor. Paint all lines 2 inches wide.

If your schedule calls for playing during cold weather, install a couple of screw-type coat hangers (secured from a hardware store) to a couple of posts near one of the gates. For safety's sake make installations above head height if made inside the fence.

8

Electrical Installations

Electricity is fascinating. And almost everyone wants to get into the act, whether it's making an extension cord for the living room lamp or installing a lighting system for the tennis court. But before you get carried away with it all, find out if you can do the work yourself or if you must hire professionals to do it.

Sometimes, local or state code requirements supersede those of the National Electric Code. For instance, nonmetallic cable, which meets the National Electric Code, is illustrated in this chapter. For communities not accepting use of nonmetallic cable, thin-wall conduit is suggested. Also, check with your local power company and your fire-insurance agent. Usually, their only requirement is for the completed installation to be approved by a licensed electrician. Certain regulations may seem odd to you, but they are to safeguard you and other people since faulty electrical work is particularly dangerous.

Electricity for homes begins in power houses of utility companies. Many power houses contain water boilers heated by gas, oil or coal to form steam at high pressure, which is directed against huge blades mounted on turbines coupled to electric generators, which in turn produce electricity. The latest power houses contain the same generating equipment as traditional ones. However, here water is changed to steam at high pressure by nuclear reactors.

You don't have to be an electrical engineer to understand how electricity works and to make and maintain basic electrical installations for your tennis court. But a knowledge of terminology and the understanding of basic principles of electricity are necessary for making safe and workable installations.

Does the very mention of an electrical vocabulary—alternating current, cycle, amperes, ohms, watts—sound like words from a far-removed civilization? If so, let's see how they sound with simple, everyday English definitions. Here's what they're all about.

THE NATURE OF POWER

Most likely the electricity supplied by your utility company is called alternating current (commonly referred to as AC). It is so named because it travels one way over the utility wires (*conductors*) 1/120th of a second, then reverses itself for another 1/120th, continuing this pattern as long as the power is "on." Each of these patterns is simply called, as you would expect, an *alternation*. Two complete alternations are called a *cycle*. The word *hertz* is now accepted as the international term for cycle. You may run across it in your readings, instead of alternation. *Frequency* is defined as the number of alternations the electrical current makes each second; hence, the current supplied to your home is labeled as 60 cycles or frequencies.

Much is said and written about current, but exactly what is it? You don't see it, but it's there, much to the chagrin of those who have eagerly picked up an electric wire without first checking to see if it was "dead."

You really don't need to know *what* current is to respect its power and to work with it safely, but it does help to improve your understanding of electricity itself. An *electrical current* consists of a physical agency consisting of a moving stream of electrons and other charged particles, all of which are much, much too small to see with the naked eye.

UNITS OF ELECTRICITY

Before discussing safety and making workable installations, let's talk about circuits. Then let's take a look at some of the units of electricity that sooner or later will face you.

Perhaps you have heard electricians speak about circuits. There are low-voltage circuits, high-voltage circuits, 115-volt circuits, 230-volt circuits, etc. What does all of this mean? A *circuit* is the complete path taken by an electric current as it makes its journey from its source through a series of wires to the device of electrical consumption, such as an electric light, motor, or whatever. Some circuits are called low-voltage because the wires carry, say, 6 or 12 volts of electricity; others, high voltage because the wires carry, 115, 230, 460, or more volts of electricity.

To understand how circuits actually work, let's take a look at what it is that actually goes through them. Water, corn, potatoes, etc., can be poured into a measuring unit or weighed on a scale. Electric power cannot be poured into a measure or weighed. However, it can be measured, not in ounces, pounds, quarts, or pecks, but in terms of how much of it flows past any given point at any given moment. The total amount over a given period of time is the way electricity is measured and a charge is then made to the customer, following the reading of an electric meter.

Just as air, water, and other substances can be measured in pounds per square inch, electric power pressure can be measured in volts, which indicates the speed at which electrons pass through the circuits. The power coming into your home, for example, is most likely 115 and 230 volts, while the voltage at which power is transmitted long distances is as high as 345,000 volts and sometimes even more. Since 115 volts travel at a rather slow pace, they're not as dangerous as 230 or higher voltage. Saying it another way, touching a "hot" wire in a 115-volt circuit sometimes may cause death; coming in contact with a 230-volt circuit can cause death and, at the very least, a severe burn; bringing any part of your body in contact with a 345,000-volt circuit—for instance, when installing a TV tower, it accidentally topples across a high-tension wire—spells sudden death. The difference in speed or power in each case is due to the difference in the speed or power of the electricity.

Liquids are measured in units. Electricity, too, can be measured. The unit for measuring the rate of flow of electric power is called an *ampere*. An electrical engineer would likely say *coulomb*.

To understand better the word *ampere*, let's take a look at the word *ohm*. As electric power travels through wires, it meets a certain amount of resistance. The *ohm* is a unit for measuring such resistance. An *ampere* is the electrical current that flows for one second through a resistance of one ohm with a pressure of one volt. This formula provides the *rate* of flow, *not* the amount of current.

A specific number of volts and amperes by themselves don't describe the specific amount of electric power flowing through a circuit, any more than X number of gallons of water flowing through a pipe per minute describes the actual amount of work being accomplished. Together, volts times amperage equals watts. A *watt* is a unit of electric power equal to one ampere in a one-volt circuit. (This rule holds with alternating-current electric devices, such as lights, dish washers, toasters, and the like. However, it is not true with motors. Here the watts are considerably less than volts times amperes.) As you probably know, the word "power" is the *rate* at which work is done. Since number of watts equal volts times amperes, a watt is the accepted electrical power unit.

Students of electricity are quick to point out that the ampere separately is only a *rate*. Furthermore, they say the watt is more correctly stated as the *watt-second*. Logically, it follows that the *watt-minute* and *watt-hour* represent slightly larger amounts of electrical work. For instance, one watt hour equals one watt of electricity used for one hour. Watts times number of hours of usage equals *watt-hours*. For example, using a 1,000-watt electric iron for three hours consumes 1,000 times 3, or 3,000, watt-hours of electricity. However, the unit of work most widely accepted for figuring the cost of electric power is the *kilowatt-hour*, or 1,000 watts consumed during a period of one hour. The electric meter in your home measures the kilowatt-hours of electric power flowing through it. For instance, if the electric iron mentioned above was the only consuming device used for the three-hour period mentioned, your meter would register three kilowatt hours (kw-hr). Three times your utility company's rate per kw-hr gives the cost of ironing.

SAFETY GUIDELINES

1. Much mechanized equipment, including large air conditioners, operate on 230-volt power. If you plan to install such equipment, include a 230-volt supply, as well as the common 115-volt supply

2. If you are installing a service panel, use one requiring reset-type circuit breakers instead of one requiring replacement fuses.

3. Plan the lighting circuits separate from those used for motors, including those for air conditioning and heating.

4. If yours is an indoor court, install enough double service outlets to meet your needs. For convenience, locate them about waist high on the walls.

5. Place switches in convenient locations to control lights and other equipment. If you plan to have motor-operated equipment, make sure the switches are either on or near its location.

6. Never locate switches or outlets near areas that might come in contact with water. For example, a service outlet too near a hose bibb may be splashed with water. If an outlet must be located in such an area, use an outdoor, weatherproof receptacle. Of course, all outlets located outdoors must be of the weatherproof variety.

7. Ground all metal objects. This includes switch, outlet, and light boxes if metal, fans, heaters, and air conditioners.

8. If you plan to use power tools, be sure they are equipped with a grounding plug or are double-insulated to eliminate the need for grounding.

TOOLS AND MATERIALS

You'll need the following basic tools for making installations, in addition to a long-handled shovel if underground installations are in your plans: regular pliers; long-nose pliers; multipurpose wiring tool; pocketknife; screwdriver; drill with bits to suit.

The following list serves as a guide to materials required for making electrical installations. Since your job may not require all of them, order only those items necessary from the electric supply house.

Optional 115/230-Volt Service Installation

Material	Description
Service panel or branch service panel	Amperage to satisfy total amperage required, such as 100-, 150-, 200-ampere capacity
Service wire	To run between meter box and service panel, size approved by utility company
Service wire conduit and fittings	To cover and hold service wire in place between meter box and service panel; sizes as approved by utility company
Ground rod	Copper rod placed in the earth to serve as the ground for the electrical system; size as approved by utility company
Ground wire	To run between meter box and ground rod; size as approved by the utility company
Ground wire conduit and fittings	To cover and hold ground wire in place between meter box and ground rod; sizes as approved by the utility company
Ground wire clamp	Used to connect ground wire to ground rod

115-Volt Installation

Material	Description
Rectangular metal boxes	Switch and service outlet boxes. Purchase type designed for kind of wiring used, such as non-metallic sheathed cable (shown in this chapter)
Octagonal metal boxes	Lighting and junction boxes. Purchase type designed for kind of wiring used, such as nonmetallic sheathed cable or conduit
Metal hangers	Fastened between 2-inch wood members for the purpose of supporting metal boxes; sometimes two 16-penny nails are used through holes in metal boxes to fasten them directly to structural wood members
Nails	1½-inch galvanized nails, used for fastening service boxes and their hangers to structural wood members
Wire	Three-wire (two wires plus bare ground wire), nonmetallic sheathed cable unless conduit is required by local code; size determined by your electrical plan

Optional 115/230-Volt Service Installation

Material	Description
Plastic cable	Covered, nonmetallic cable designed to run underground, code permitting; if not permitted, use the cable run through conduit
Staples	Designed and used to hold non-metallic cable in place on wood framing members; if conduit is used, fasten in place with straps designed for it
Weatherproof receptacles	Designed for mounting outdoors, should be used inside also if water might splash on receptacle
Switches	Single-pole, three or four-way types, number, kind, and color (brown or yellow) in accordance with lighting plan
Switchplates	Fastened to switch boxes; number and color in accordance with lighting plan
Service outlets	Number and color in accordance with lighting plan
Service outlet plates	Fastened to outlet boxes; number and color in accordance with lighting plan
Electrician's plastic tape	Used as insulation to cover splices, taps, and wire connections if non-solderless connectors are not used

230-Volt Installation

Material	Description
Service outlets and outlet boxes	Designed for 230-volt nonmetallic cable unless conduit is required; outlet boxes are the same kind as those used for 115-volt outlets; sometimes, however, two boxes joined together are required to accommodate a single outlet
Three-wire cable	Nonmetallic sheathed cable with each wire insulated or conduit sizes as called for in your electrical plan; (do not confuse this cable with three-wire non-metallic cable designed to carry 115-volt current)

Optional Installations for Indoor Courts

Material	Description
Electric motors	To run ventilating, cooling, and heating systems
Thermostat	Used to control temperature automatically
Temperature alarm with bell	Used to call attention when high or low temperature is reached

SERVICE PANEL AND ACCESSORIES

A separate electric meter and service panel for the tennis court is optional. If your home service panel does not contain enough unused circuits to supply the electrical requirements, you can install a branch service panel in the tennis court. Connect it to the takeoff lugs on the main switch in your home service panel. Make the connection with the correct size plastic cable designed for underground use. If you do supply the tennis court with electricity in this manner, the cable must be inside plastic pipe buried at least 3 feet underground and to a point at least 6 inches above ground level where it enters and comes out of the ground (*see* Ch. 9 for plastic pipe installation).

Caution: Before making installation, check local electric code. If weatherproof plastic cable encased in plastic pipe is not permitted underground, run the cable through conduit, making bends with a conduit bender, which you can rent. Also, see copper wire size tables, presented later in this chapter.

In order to carry the additional amperage, your original service wires from the electric line to the meter and from the meter to the service panel, as well as the ground wire, must be sized large enough to deliver the total wattage required for both your home and the tennis court. This is not the problem it appears. Your local power company will be glad to examine your present wiring system and advise you whether it will be cheaper to rewire between your home service panel and the electric line or to install a separate meter and service panel in the tennis court.

If you elect to have the power company bring service wires to the tennis court, be sure to request an underground installation from the electric line to the meter box. The small additional cost difference between underground installation and overhead installation of service wires is well worth the price. Not only does an underground installation mean that the natural look of your property will be unspoiled, but high winds or ice storms can never damage the service wires.

8-1. If you elect to install a separate meter and service panel for the tennis court, first check with your local power company for its recommendation of the best meter location. At this time find out how much of the outside wiring, including conduit and fittings, is your responsibility, and whether you or the power company fur-

8-1

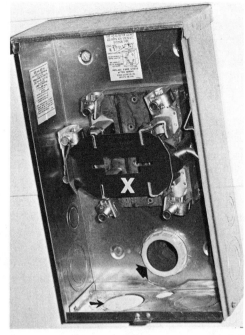

8-2

nish the meter box. Also, obtain their recommendation on the best size of service panel, 100, 150, or 200 amperes, to meet your electrical requirements.

Use round-head screws to fasten service panel approximately 5 feet above the floor to a solid support, such as wall framing members or a post. Arrow in Figure 8-1 points to breakers in electric power from the meter. The breakers serve as a main switch, disconnecting power from meter to all circuits. *X* indicates a 115-volt circuit breaker mounted in place with a two-wire (one "hot" wire and one ground wire) circuit cable to be connected to it. (Ground wires are always white; black or red wires are always "hot" wires unless otherwise noted.)

Wires to the top left show circuit wires to be connected to proper breakers later.

8-2. When you obtain the meter box, usually supplied by the utility company, one of the electricians will gladly show you the proper lugs on which to connect the three-wire cable leading from the box to your panel and the ground wire leading to a ground rod below the meter. (Some utility companies require the ground wire to lead from the box to a water pipe inside the building.)

Figure 8-2 shows a meter box mounted to a wall (5 feet above grade) with ¼-inch round-head screws. Two knockouts were removed from the bottom of the box: the larger one (small arrow),

for admitting the utility company's service wire brought in underground; the smaller one nearby for admitting ground rod connector to box. Since knockouts are constructed so holes of various sizes can be made, be sure to find out exactly the correct sizes required. If in doubt, let the utility company remove the one for admitting their service wires at time of installation. Large arrow points to conduit connector fastened in place after removing knockout and cutting hole in wall, later to lead conduit and service wires from meter to service panel.

X indicates meter mounting bracket and lugs for mounting the utility company's meter, service wires, and your wires leading to the service panel. Remove about ½ inch of insulation from the cable wires to run from meter to service panel. Then remove clamps from the three lay-in terminals of meter box and connect the two "hot" (black and red) wires and the ground wire as recommended by the utility company's electrician. Then replace clamps and tighten terminals to 21 foot-pounds. (You save a little time if ground clamp is tightened later when ground wire from ground rod is also attached.)

Next connect one end of service wire conduit to conduit connector (shown by arrow) in rear of box and connect opposite end to a conduit connector installed in top of service panel, following removal of knockout. If conduit run is long, do the following step along with conduit assembly. Wires are easier to string this way. (*See* Wiring with Thin-Wall Conduit, near end of this chapter.) Now work the three service wires through conduit connector, then through conduit, until they come through conduit connector in top of service panel.

To complete your part of outside installation, work is continued outside. Next, jab ground rod into the earth directly below conduit connector located in bottom of meter box. Do this by using a shovel to dig a shallow hole about 8 inches deep. Then fill with water. Holding ground rod with both hands, gently push it into the mud. Then raise it, allowing water to seep into hole. Repeat this operation over and over. Soon you will be surprised how easy it is to sink an 8-foot ground rod completely into the ground. Once you are underway, it is not necessary to bring bottom end completely out of the ground as you lift the rod. Raise it only far enough to allow water to fill the hole. Easy does it! Do not try to drive rod into the ground with a hammer or sledge. You could end up with the rod half out and half in, with no way possible to remove it—short of mechanical power.

When top of ground rod is below surface to a depth recommended by the utility company, cut a piece of conduit to fit between it and conduit connector; using conduit straps every 4 feet, fasten conduit to wall. In most cases only one conduit strap is required.

Fasten and tighten one end of ground wire with 21 foot-pounds of pressure—ground wire does not require insulation—to solidly grounded neutral connection in meter box.

8-3. Now run ground wire through conduit

8-3

connector in bottom of box, on through conduit, and out to ground rod. Using a special ground-rod clamp, fasten ground wire securely to ground-rod as shown in Figure 8-3. The black plastic pipe to the left of the ground rod and ground rod clamp contains three service wires brought in by the power company.

If you have not yet divided the lighting, service outlets, and motor equipment requirements into branch circuits, do so now. The number of branch circuits required depends upon the total number of watts possible from your electrical system. It is considered good practice to place lights, service outlets, and motor equipment on separate circuits. To do this, total the anticipated wattage for the lights, then for service outlets, as well as for the motors, if your plans call for them.

Caution: Use number of amperes required to *start* a motor rather than number of amperes required once the motor is underway. If you find electrical equipment indicates amperes but not watts, find the wattage by multiplying voltage times amperes. Unless you plan to use equipment, such as an air conditioner, that requires more than 2300 watts, I recommend limiting branch circuits to 20 amperes each. The following table shows the relationship of maximum watts permitted in a branch circuit to copper wire size and size of circuit breaker.

115-Volt Branch Circuit Requirements*

Maximum watts	Copper wire size	Circuit breaker in amperes
1625	14	15
2300	12	20
3450	10	30
4600	8	40
6900	6	60

*Double maximum watts for same wire size and circuit breaker to figure 230-volt branch circuit requirements.

The copper wire sizes indicated in the table are based on the assumption that length of wires is kept within required limits, allowing for a maximum voltage drop of 2 percent or less.

While installing main or branch circuits, make sure the wire sizes as given in the table are not undersize for the distance they are to carry electricity. Undersize wires should not be used for two good reasons: More than normal heat is created, resulting in wasted power; more than normal voltage drop (a drop of 2 percent is considered acceptable) takes place, so that less than the required electrical capacity reaches the equipment. For example, a cable containing two #12 wires plus ground will carry electricity a distance of 35 feet (one way) with only a 2-percent voltage drop. Run that same cable 90 feet (one way), and the voltage drops 5 percent. Rather than delve into electrical technicalities, the following tables are given for selecting cables with proper size wires for the *one-way distances* they are to carry electricity.

Copper Wire Sizes: 115 Volts

		One-Way Distance						
Amperes	Watts	#14	#12	#10	#8	#6	#4	#2
10	1,150	45'	70'	110'	180'	280'	450'	700'
15	1,725	30'	45'	70'	120'	180'	300'	475'
20	2,300	22'	35'	55'	90'	140'	225'	350'
25	2,375	18'	28'	45'	70'	110'	180'	280'
30	3,450	15'	25'	35'	60'	90'	150'	235'

Copper Wire Sizes: 230 Volts

		One-Way Distance						
Amperes	Watts	#14	#12	#10	#8	#6	#4	#2
10	2,300	90'	140'	220'	360'	560'	900'	1400'
15	3,450	60'	90'	140'	240'	360'	600'	950'
20	4,600	45'	70'	110'	180'	280'	450'	700'
25	5,750	35'	55'	90'	140'	220'	360'	560'
30	6,900	30'	50'	70'	120'	180'	300'	470'

Aluminum Wire

Although the Code approves the use of aluminum wire, I recommend you use it sparingly. Aluminum is a poor conductor of electricity compared to copper; therefore, it requires a larger wire to deliver the same voltage. Generally, electricians, if they use it, select an aluminum wire two sizes larger than copper wire. Although receptacles and switches with screw terminals, where the wire is wrapped around the screw, are suitable for making good connections, never fasten aluminum wire to friction-type or push-in terminals. Since aluminum oxidizes readily, soldered connections should be left to the expert.

Aluminum wire has one point in its favor; when a large electric cable is required for a long distance, it is considerably cheaper to use one containing aluminum wires two sizes larger than that required for copper wires. Take the example of the tennis court owner who wanted to install a stand-by generator to supply electric power to home and tennis court during brownouts. A cable of three #8 copper wires would cost $124.86. For $32.25 he bought a cable with three #4 aluminum wires; this delivered the same voltage as the copper wire cable.

OUTLETS, LIGHTS AND SWITCHES IN 115-VOLT CIRCUIT

Here are instructions on connecting service outlets, lights, and switches with nonmetallic cable. Be sure operations do not violate local or state codes. Some codes require all junctions be made inside a junction box. This is especially true where conduit is required. If nonmetallic cable is banned in your area, the use of conduit and its accessories is described at the end of this chapter. The following instructions apply to either.

8-4

8-4. The three steps in making a splice are shown in Figure 8-4. Remove about 3 inches of insulation from each wire with a pocketknife or a multipurpose wiring tool. Next cross wires at midpoint as you use pliers and fingers to wrap them tightly in opposite directions. Stagger joints. Do not make joints on parallel wires opposite each other. Using soldering paste designed for soldering copper, lightly coat joint area of bare wires. Now heat with a torch as you apply a thin coat of solder. Finish job by wrapping joint with electrician's tape.

8-5. Here is how to make a tap. When you have removed the insulation, as shown, and wrapped the bare end of one wire several times around the bare area of the tapped wire, solder and wrap the joint with electrician's plastic tape, similar to above instructions for wrapping the splice.

8-6. Make connection at screw terminals by removing ¾ inch of insulation from end of wire. With long-nose pliers, bend bare end of wire

8-5

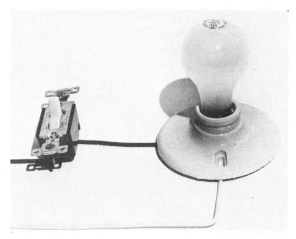

8-7

clockwise to fit around screw. Tightening screw tends to hold end of wire firmly against screw; wires bent counterclockwise tend to pull away from screw as it is tightened.

Keep these 5 principles in mind as you install the circuits.

1. Attach "hot" wires (black or red) directly to switches.

2. Attach neutral wires (white) to current-consuming devices, such as lights and motors.

3. Attach ground wire (bare or covered green) to metal, such as outlet, switch, or light metal box.

4. Attach "hot" wires to brass-colored terminals; neutral wires to light or silver-colored terminals.

5. Join black wires to black wires, red wires to red wires, and white wires to white wires continuously throughout the circuits. The only exception is at switch loops, where ends of white wires are taped or painted black to denote hot lines.

8-7. A single-pole switch is used to control one or more fixtures from a single point.

8-8

8-8. Two three-way switches are used to control one or more fixtures from two different points.

8-6

8-9

8-9. A four-way switch is used between two three-way switches to control one or more fixtures from three different points. You can control one or more fixtures from as many different points as you please by connecting as many additional four-way switches as you have control points between the four-way switch (just described) and either one of the three-way switches. Suppose you want to control a fixture from ten different points. Your hookup would require eight four-way switches installed between two three-way switches.

Install service outlet boxes next. *Caution*: Never permit service boxes, connected to electric cables, to hang free. This is not only a sign of poor workmanship, it is also an indicator of disaster. Sooner or later one can expect a short inside a box itself or along its run of free-hanging cable. Contrary to sound electrical practice, such installations do exist in some tennis court building installations.

Always fasten service boxes to a sound support. Some tennis court structures have wood supports spaced periodically around the walls. If yours is such a building, use two 1-inch roundhead screws or 1½-inch corrugated nails to fasten boxes, flush with supports, about waist high, directly to the wood supports. Temporarily removing one side plate of box makes installation a breeze.

Next install switch outlet boxes, 48 inches above the court surface, in the same manner as the service outlet boxes.

"Grip-tight" boxes are also available. If your building has finished walls, it is necessary to wire the circuits first but without making connections to the switches and service outlets. Next install finish walls, cutting holes properly at required box locations and sized to accept the boxes. Then connect cables to proper boxes, push them through the prepared holes cut in the walls, and tighten side screws to bring side plates of boxes up tightly against walls.

Manufacturers of tennis court lighting systems usually recommend hanging their ceiling lights from strong metal supports. Sometimes, however, rooms adjoining the tennis court, such as an office or sauna room, require ceiling lights as found in homes. If you have rooms requiring traditional lights, secure ceiling light boxes and hangers from your electric supplier. Then, using 1½-inch galvanized nails and a hammer, fasten ends of hangers to ceiling joists. Then use hanger attachment to hold boxes firmly in place.

Next install the junction boxes if required.

They, too, can be fastened to hangers if wood supports are not too far apart. Also, they can be fastened to the side of a wood support in the same manner as described for nailing service boxes to wood supports. (These boxes are the same as those used for ceiling lights.) Later, when bare ends of wires inside are twisted together and insulated, either with solderless connectors or electrician's plastic tape, use screw to fasten flat metal cover (made for the purpose) onto open end of box.

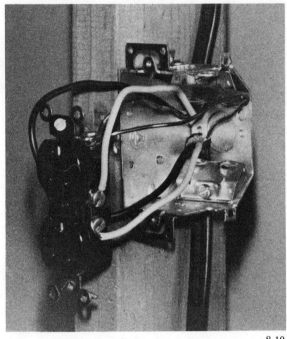

8-10

8-10. Now you are ready to wire the 115-volt service outlet circuits.

Caution: Be sure power is not connected to service panel. Remove ½ inch of insulation from black and white wires, as well as enough cable covering to make panel connections. Fasten white wire and bare ground wire to neutral strip in service panel. Then fasten black wire to a single circuit breaker—after snapping in place on service panel—of correct amperage for circuit. If cable has not been previously brought to outlet box, do it now. Bring cable to approximately 1 foot beyond first outlet box. Then make cut, forming two cable ends. Trim about 8 inches of cover from each of the two cables with a sharp pocketknife. Be sure not to damage insulation on wires. Then string each cable through a knockout hole after removing two knockouts from box.

Each outlet box—with exception of last box in circuit—has an incoming and outgoing cable. Tighten clamps inside box with a screwdriver, holding cables firmly in place. Fasten ground wire from each cable with screw to an unused hole in box.

Strip about ¾ inch of insulation from each of the four wires with a multipurpose tool or pocketknife. Then connect black wires to copper-colored terminals, white wires to silver-colored terminals, on the service outlet. Now position outlet to box with wires pushed inside. Then using the two screws packaged with outlet, fasten it securely to box.

8-11. If you've installed traditional ceiling light boxes to form one of the circuits, string the cable wires next. Fasten them at service panel, stringing and fastening cable to each light outlet box, and extending, cutting, and fastening cable wires to box as described above for wiring the service outlets circuit, with this exception: *A* shows the hot line or incoming feed cable. *B* shows control cable running from light outlet box to single-pole switch. *C* shows outgoing feed cable from outlet box to next light outlet box in the circuit. Twist together black wire from feed cable *A*, black wire from switch cable *B*, and black wire from feed cable *C*. Paint black or tape end of white wire in switch cable, as well as end of white wire at the switch location. *Always* blacken both ends of switch wires if not already black. This denotes line is hot and not neutral. Now twist together white wires of incoming feed cable *A* and outgoing feed cable *C*. Also, use a screw to fasten the three ground wires to the metal box.

Wire remaining boxes in light circuit. Then mount light fixtures of your choice to each box, after twisting bare end of black wire (switch wire) to bare end of single black wire in box, bare end of white wire to twisted white wires in box,

and green wire (ground) to previously fastened ground wires inside box. Insulate bare ends of insulated wires in box, either with solderless connectors or plastic electrician's tape.

Wiring of light circuit is complete after you connect the two black ends of switch cable wires to a single-pole switch and ground wire to inside of metal switch box. With wires pushed back into the box, use the two screws packaged with switch to fasten it to box. With the single-pole switch you can turn the light on and off from only one point. If you wish to control a light from more than one location, use three and four-way switches, as illustrated in Figures 8-7 through 8-9.

Complete service outlet and light circuits by fastening proper cover plates onto service outlets and switches. Use screws packaged with the plates.

INSTALLING LOW-VOLTAGE CIRCUITS

Some of the equipment, such as heaters and air conditioners, may show low-voltage circuits of 24 volts. Generally, instructions accompanying such equipment include wiring diagrams and one or more transformers, which are used in reducing a 115-volt circuit to 24 volts. One side of a transformer contains terminals for making connections to a 115-volt circuit, while the opposite side contains terminals for connecting to low-voltage devices, such as timers and electric water valves. Here, different-colored bell wire is used for making the connections, while wire previously recommended for 115-volt circuits is used for connecting the transformer to the 115-volt circuit.

INSTALLING ELECTRIC MOTORS

Provide separate circuits for any electric motor equipment you plan to use, such as air conditioners, electric heating devices, etc. Be sure to follow information on the electric motor nameplate, where you will also find the model and serial numbers. These are required when contacting the manufacturer for replacement, repairs, or general information.

The nameplate also shows the current necessary for safe operation. Sixty-cycle alternating current (AC) is required for most motors. Without going into technical details, motors with a

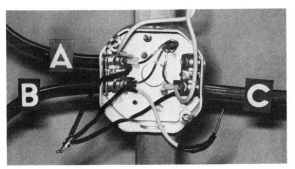

8-11

smaller capacity are manufactured to use one-phase current; some require 115 volts, while others require 230 volts. Generally, larger motors use 230 volts and may be either one-phase or three-phase. These differences in design should not cause problems in wiring. Circuits—with the exception of low-voltage circuits—previously described are on single-phase current. This is the common current found in most home and farm wiring; only single-phase motors should be connected to it.

Three-phase circuits are commonly found in industrial wiring, such as in factories, and three-phase motors are designed to be connected to them. Incidentally, three-phase motors are smaller, less expensive to manufacture, and much simpler in design than single-phase motors. It is unlikely that the average residence can be supplied with three-phase power, but be sure to use three-phase motors of large capacity if it is available. To be on the safe side, always follow the wiring diagrams included on the motor nameplate and/or the instruction leaflet. Double check that you receive the instruction leaflet from your supplier, because it also contains maintenance suggestions for the motor, including whether to oil or *not*. All motors require free air circulation around them.

Most motors today use V belts and pulleys to transmit power to electrical equipment. Belts and pulleys have a way of wearing out, but the replacement data will be on them. Even though the numbers may be obliterated come replacement time, take the worn pieces to your electric supplier, who can offer duplicates. When you make the replacements, be sure pulleys are tight on the shafts; the belt between pulleys must be tight enough not to slip, but not tight enough to smoke when the motor is in operation. In short, belts need only be tight enough to furnish the right amount of friction between them and the pulleys so that the motor operates freely without being under strain.

Once the motor specifications are understood, use the following table to determine maximum amperage to be carried by the motor cable wires.

Now that you have the total amperage required for the motor, 115 and 230 volts, determine correct wire size for the circuits from wire size in this chapter. Selecting wire size for motors is different from selecting wire size for other electrical devices, such as lights, for example. Motors consume more amperage in the process of reaching full speed than they do when full

Amperage Requirements of Motors

Motor horsepower	115-volt amperes required	230-volt amperes required
¼	6	3
⅓	7	3½
½	10	5
¾	14	7
1	16	8
1½	20	10
2	24	12

speed is reached. Therefore, select wires large enough to supply required voltage for both starting the motor and running it at full speed. Generally, if wires are selected to supply required voltage when motor is running at full speed only, there will be a drop of voltage during the starting period of approximately 3 to 7 percent, depending on such factors as type of motor and how hard the load is to get underway.

As mentioned before, many smaller motors operate on 115 volts. However, if you have a motor or other equipment operating on 230 volts, install a 230-volt circuit breaker, amperage size to match wire size, in service panel. Connect black and red wires to circuit breaker and ground wire to neutral strip in service panel.

Then run cable from service panel to outlet box, where you install a 230-volt service outlet, mounted to a metal service box, to accept the 230-volt male plug on end of cord from the motor. Sometimes, the terminals are located on the motor for accepting the cable wires directly. In this case, service outlet box and service outlet are not required. (For safety, ground *all* electric motors, no matter how small.)

WIRING WITH THIN-WALL CONDUIT

The principles of wiring for laying out and installing the circuits for service outlets, switches, lights, and motors are the same whether you use nonmetallic cable, as described previously, or thin-wall conduit. Therefore, only the installation techniques applying specifically to thin-wall conduit follow.

8-12. The picture shows a hookup for a service outlet. Thin-wall conduit—also called electrical metal tubing or Type EMT—is used. (One side of service outlet box is removed in Fig. 8-12 for clarity.)

Begin by fitting threadless end of connector *A*

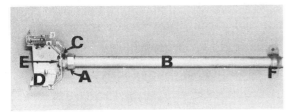

8-12

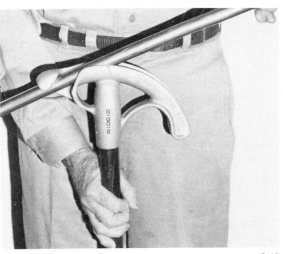

8-13

over conduit *B*, and tighten compression nut *C*. Now insert threaded end through knockout of box *D*. Then screw locknut *E* (tooth side faces box) tightly against box from inside. Support conduit with pipe straps *F*. Use a coupling to join two lengths of conduit together.

Keep in mind these eight cardinal principles as you install thin-wall conduit.

Thin-wall conduit can be placed indoors or outdoors. However, you should not use it either in cinder block construction, such as foundations, or buried in cinders.

Since metal conduit and metal boxes provide a continuous ground, no separate ground wires are required for them.

Select the correct size of conduit, which comes in 10-foot lengths, from the following table.

Conduit Size

| | Number of wires to be installed | | | | | |
| | 1 | 2 | 3 | 4 | 5 | 6 |
Wire size	Size of conduit in inches					
14	½	½	½	½	¾	¾
12	½	½	½	¾	¾	1
10	½	¾	¾	¾	1	1
8	½	¾	¾	1	1¼	1¼
6	½	1	1	1¼	1½	1½
4	½	1¼	1¼	1½	1½	2
2	¾	1¼	1¼	2	2	2
$1/_0$	1	1½	2	2	2½	2½
$2/_0$	1	2	2	2½	2½	3
$3/_0$	1	2	2	2½	2	2

Use a hacksaw (blade with 32 teeth per inch) to cut conduit, then ream inside, rough edge with a file.

8-13. Use a conduit bender as shown for bending conduit. This is an inexpensive tool that you can purchase from most hardware stores or electric shops. Also, you can rent one from a tool rental service. Bend gradually, keeping in mind that if bend continued to form a circle, it would

equal at least 12 times the inside diameter of the conduit. Use factory-bent elbows for bending large sizes. Unless you are experienced, I advise bending conduit first, then cutting. Also, fasten boxes temporarily in place so they can be moved slightly if cuts or bends are not quite up to measurements.

Anchor conduit to surface with a pipe strap, 3 feet from each metal box, 6 feet thereafter on exposed runs, and every 10 feet on concealed runs.

Make splices and taps inside metal boxes. Splice must never be inside conduit itself.

Following installation of conduit and boxes, pull wires through conduit into boxes. You can probably push a few small wires in at one end, on through to next outlet, if run is not too long. For long runs, especially if there are bends, use a fish wire. This is a steel tape approximately ⅛ inch wide, in lengths of either 50 or 100 feet. It is especially designed for pulling wires through conduit and may be purchased from your local electric supply house.

Note: Always use individual wires inside conduit. Never run cable, such as Romex, through it. Also, for outdoor conduit installations, make watertight connections for conduit end or box entry and exit. Your electrical supplier can furnish watertight connectors for whatever connections are required.

LIGHTING SYSTEMS

It's a far cry from lighting a lawn for lawn mowing at night and lighting a tennis court for night playing. For the former, the field of view is at ground level and, since movement is relatively slow, glare, shadows, and uneven illumination are of little importance in designing a lighting system.

But not so in the latter. For example, the field of view alternates between horizontal and above, sometimes referred to as an "aerial view." Movement of both players and the ball is fast enough among amateurs to give most lighting designers a headache, but the speed of the players and the ball increases as they become more accomplished. This further complicates the lighting problem. Then, too, age of players makes another difference. Older people require more illumination than younger ones. To further add to the problems of design are additional factors, such as glare, uneven illumination, contrast between objects, and blind spots.

The human eye is another wonderful part of God's creation; not perfect, but still wonderful. Everyone who sees has experienced going out of a building into bright sunlight. The eye muscles quickly close the iris in the eye to compensate for the sudden glare but not quickly enough to prevent squinting and often, spots before the eyes. If your light poles are not of correct height and the floodlights are not aimed properly, you will find glare a serious problem. Your eye muscles will constantly expand and contract as they attempt to adjust the iris for existing light. Ophthalmologists tell us such adjustments cause eye strain but not eye damage, but as almost everyone knows, it is a tiring experience, generally resulting in headaches. "All of this may be true," recently said an old tennis pro, but the spots do make it hard to follow the ball." Therefore, illumination with minimal glare is the primary test of a good lighting system. It must be designed with nonglare devices to minimize glare over the entire court.

Because of uneven illumination when lights are located either too far apart or too near the court, they create bright and dim areas. This causes an optical illusion. The ball seems to alternate between slow and fast speeds as it passes from dark through bright zones of light. So the second test of a good lighting system is to provide evenness of illumination over an area between 6 feet of the back walls and between 4 feet outside the sidelines.

A third test of a good lighting system is closely related to the player's line of sight. He must clearly see and follow the ball from the beginning of the serve for as long as the ball is in play, regardless of any erratic path it might follow as it is repeatedly hit. To do this, a good lighting system should provide for contrast.

8-14.   Part *a* shows how controlled direction and intensity of light enhance the ball when in flight so it's easily followed by the players as opposed to Figure 8-14*b*, where illumination is harsh, making it difficult to follow the ball. *Contrast* is the relative difference between dark and light areas. For example, good photographers demand some blacks, degrees of grays, and whites in their black and white pictures. They refer to these variations as *contrast*, and sometimes call it simply a *modeling* effect. The meaning of modeling is further clarified by examining any portrait printed by a professional photographer. White, variations of grays, shadows, and possibly jet black are much in evidence. The opposite effect is noticed in a photo made by an amateur photographer, where a flash gun or

8-14a

8-14b

other bright light is aligned directly into the subject's face. Such shooting produces a ''burned-out effect,'' as evidenced by a white face with no signs of gray or shadow areas. This is exactly the effect a tennis court lighting system should *not* produce.

A lighting system that produces a modeling effect is highly desirable. Such an effect on the players' faces and the ball is an indication of an effective lighting arrangement, which is produced by well-planned side lighting. What this does is to provide more illumination on each side of the ball and the players' faces, accentuating their features. This, of course, helps a player to better recognize the head movement of his opponent and the ball spin.

Caution: Over-illumination is undesireable. It can result in extreme contrast, causing the loss of shades of gray. This shows everything on the court in black and white.

Surrounding structures, including walls, affect contrast on the court. Generally speaking, more illumination is required for indoor courts than outdoor courts because light walls and ceilings reflect more light than a dark sky, thereby reducing contrast between them and the ball and the opponent's face. Sometimes, however, if a group of light-colored buildings surround an outdoor court, illumination will require stepping up. And the brighter the surroundings, the more illumination required.

By now you may be saying to yourself, ''How does all this affect me?'' To answer the question, first decide on your lighting objective. If recreation is the primary purpose, you might want to install an inexpensive lighting system, such as the economy model described later. However, if the players' proficiency is high, or if one or more of them are in training to break into the professional ranks, then plan to spend anywhere from $3,000 to $8,000 for a lighting system designed by a reputable manufacturer. A partial list of lighting system manufacturers is given in the Sources of Supply.

Here are some types of lighting you're likely to find, with an evaluation of their effectiveness and life expectancy. High-pressure sodium is excellent in effectiveness but only fair in life expectancy. Metal halide and 1500-MA fluorescent are both highly effective but only fair in life expectancy. Mercury and phosphor mercury are fair in effectiveness but high in life expectancy. Incandescent and tungsten halogen are both poor in

effectiveness and life expectancy. Take your pick after getting price quotations for each lighting system.

Outdoor

Because of lack of outdoor tennis court background for reflecting light downward, only direct lighting is considered here.

Other than the Economy Lighting System described in the next section, special considerations are in order for club play, tournament play, and for rank amateurs hoping to eventually break into the pro level. For these players the best in lighting is not too good. Therefore, it stands to reason that design is a job for the lighting engineer. Many manufacturers of tennis court lighting systems have spent a fortune in research to produce lighting systems to satisfy the most discriminating taste. So there's little for an individual to gain in an attempt to design his own lighting system.

The court owner's ultimate objective is to select a system of lights, the quality of which produces normal flesh tones. Incandescent fixtures, such as quartz, are chosen by many court owners for this very reason. On the other hand, some mercury vapor lights cast a cold bluish-toned light which does not show skin flesh tones as they actually appear. But don't give up on mercury vapor lights, because some manufacturers sell multivapor lamps or color-corrected mercury vapor lamps, both of which help to produce a warmer color, in turn showing skin tones near normal.

How much light is required? First purchase a light meter through your local electric supply house. You'll find much use for it long after the court has been completed. For instance, you can use it to see firsthand whether the contractor is providing the correct number of foot-candles of light. If you install your own lights, a meter is a must to be absolutely sure the correct amount of illumination is equally spread over the court area. Then, too, as days move into weeks and weeks into months, pollution will gradually build a shade over the light sources. Checking periodically with your light meter will show you exactly the loss of foot-candles of light long before you can tell it with your unaided eyes. Here's another thing to think about: As pollution builds up on the outside of the lights, the same amount of current as usual is being consumed on the inside. In short, you're paying the full amount for the electricity but receiving fewer foot-candles of light for your money.

As you may know, units of light are measured in foot-candles. With the light meter held approximately waist high, about 42 inches above the playing surface, light required ranges from 10 to 35 foot-candles as shown in the chart.

Light Requirements for Outdoor Courts

Type of play	Foot-candles	Distance above surface
Recreation	10–15	42 inches
Club play	20–25	42 inches
Tournament play	30–35	42 inches

Be sure light poles and fixtures are located parallel to the sidelines. In this way, the fixtures are easily adjusted so the light beams are aimed across the court, which can provide even distribution of light.

Poles must be of sufficient size and strength to withstand winds up to 100 miles per hour. This is one point to make absolutely clear to your supplier. Metal, steel, or aluminum poles 30 to 35 feet high are satisfactory, provided they are manufactured especially for supporting the fixtures in question. For instance, quartz fixtures weigh approximately 10 pounds each, while mercury vapor fixtures weigh in the neighborhood of 70 pounds each.

Install the system for easy maintenance by using poles fastened to a base; this works on the principle of a hinge, thereby allowing each pole to be bent down for relamping and general maintenance. This is especially important if quartz fixtures are used because their life is roughly 2,000 hours. On the other hand, mercury lamps normally provide 24,000 hours of service.

Caution: Quartz lamps must be installed to burn in a horizontal position, plus or minus 10 degrees. However, they can be angled to direct equal distribution of light over the entire playing surface.

To avoid glare, insist that no poles be located at the back corners or back sides of the court. This is especially true if two or more courts are located parallel to each other.

Another way to avoid undue contrast and glare is to prime and finish the metal poles with a dark color, nongloss paint. A dark green color will harmonize nicely with adjoining lawns, trees, and shrubbery.

Economy Lighting System

An economy system can provide good illumination (10–15 foot-candles) where tennis is played purely for recreation. When the fixtures are lighted, exciting new dimensions are revealed. Trees, shrubs, flowers, and gardens adjoining the court show up in all their splendor, as beams of light bounce over and through them, creating highlights and shadows against a dark sky.

The following text explains the mechanics of any lighting system, including an economy system. Although lighting the court for playing tennis at night is the primary objective, you can let your imagination go wild and create additional uses of light without much extra work. For instance, separate switches, including dimmer switches, can reduce the total light output for nighttime outdoor living or for discouraging intruders from lurking in the shadows while you are in the house unaware of their presence.

Here are six important questions to consider before you make the installation: Is the court located so that lights will be least annoying to the neighbors? Have you given due consideration to type of fixtures and qualities of illumination as previously discussed? Before choosing type of light poles, have you considered how they and the fixtures will look during the daytime?

Are all pieces of electrical equipment, including the wiring, waterproof—with no plans to use indoor wiring or indoor extension cords outdoors? Are extension cords and metal service boxes manufactured for outdoor use and are provisions made for grounding them? Are the electric wires in the circuits sized large enough to handle the total wattage proposed for them?

There are several ways to acquire the six poles with a minimum height of 12 feet above the surface. Telephone and electric utility companies frequently have discarded poles because of taller replacement requirements. The poles are treated, so they have many more years of useful life. They vary in length in 2-foot intervals, such as 14, 16, 18, and 20 feet, ranging from 4 to 6-inch diameters at the tops. Recently, a friend of mine purchased six used telephone poles for the sum of $15. Rather than dig the holes with a posthole digger, he hired an operator with a power auger to drill them 5 feet deep. (Bottom of holes must be at least 6 inches below the frost zone.) Then he positioned the poles in the holes plumb and tamped in dirt. He used an extension ladder to fasten the fixtures in place, bringing electric current to them through UF-type vinyl three-wire underground cable fastened every 4½ feet along the sides of the poles.

As shopping centers and other places of business continue to enlarge and remodel, they generally replace parking light poles and fixtures with bigger and better ones. Usually the contractor ends up with, among other things, the discarded poles and fixtures intact. Since the demand for such equipment is minimal, junkyard prices generally are all a customer is required to pay for it.

8-16

8-15

8-15. Dale Hampton got a real bargain from a local contractor by purchasing regulation metal poles for building an economy lighting system, including the electric fixtures shown in Figure 8-15. The six poles, working on the principle of a hinge for easy lamp replacement and other maintenance, cost a total of $30.

8-16. Here's what Hampton did to erect the poles. First he had an operator with a power auger dig a hole 4 feet deep and square, so an 18 x 18 x 12-inch-high open box-type form would fit flush with the sides of the hole. Then as he was

filling the hole and form with concrete (*see* Appendix, Table I, for proper mixture), he placed a piece of curved conduit for feeding the underground cable to the light fixture. Just before topping the form with concrete, he positioned four ¾ x 12-inch bolts extending above the concrete, running them through a piece of one-inch lumber with four holes drilled to match the dimensions of the light pole base. He completed the job by painting the poles, removing the piece of wood and form lumber from the concrete base, and positioning and fastening the bottom of the poles to the concrete base with four washers and bolts.

Indoor Systems

No matter whether you farm out the lighting installation to a contractor or do the work yourself, the responsibility for a successful system rests entirely upon your shoulders. Contractors, manufacturers, suppliers, local tennis players, and books and magazines on tennis courts can provide a good many useful pointers. But when it's all said and done, can you and your friends play the game in a comfortable, pleasing and distraction-free environment? No answer short of "yes" is good enough.

How much will the job cost? I've talked about general costs previously in this chapter. However, one pitfall to avoid is a temptation to purchase a system short of meeting your every need. Because you have quite an investment in building an indoor court, you may be tempted to shortchange the lighting system. If you're thinking of buying a system not quite up to your expectations but still don't like the idea, cheer up.

There's a better solution. Rather than purchasing an inferior system and trying to adjust to it, plan a long-term installation. Here's the way to do it. At the outset, install what your budget can stand. Then upgrade it, as you enjoy playing tennis, without having to replace or completely remodel the system later on. Any manufacturer, supplier, or contractor worth his weight in tennis balls can design a flexible system with future expansion taken care of step-by-step.

Basically, there are three different systems used in lighting indoor courts: direct, indirect, and semidirect. Direct is where the light shines downward; indirect where the light is aimed toward the roof, thence reflected downward; and the semidirect where the light shines downward through a lens, thereby diffusing the light.

Regardless of the system selected, an important facet is up-lighting. A rule of thumb in up-lighting is for the playing surface to receive 70 percent of the illumination with 30 percent, or the balance of the light, to shine upward. Such an arrangement makes for better contrast between the lighting above and below the fixtures which, in turn, makes it easy for the players to follow the ball when it is hit high into the air.

In addition to the previous general discussion on what makes a good lighting system, the following ten questions are presented for your further consideration. A positive answer to each denotes a well-planned lighting system that should provide the players with all the comforts of home.

If lenses are a part of the system, are the lamps located far enough away from them so as not to produce an abundance of glare? If louvers are installed to protect the eyes, do they provide a cutoff of about 45° when the players are looking parallel to the court and of roughly 35° at right angles to its length?

Is the illumination spread evenly without signs of high intensity in small areas throughout the surface? Since light beams are either reflected or absorbed to some degree as they strike objects, do you have dark colors for partial light absorption surrounding the court and to a height of approximately 8 feet to its side? Some players prefer an additional 2 feet added to these heights.

Are the areas above the dark levels surrounding the court and the ceiling painted white or a light even color, including all structural members? If you have indirect lighting, are the fixtures at least 4 feet below the ceiling? If not, you'll more than likely have a series of "hot spots." Are wire guards used to protect the lights from balls hit by the players? This applies to indirect as well as direct lighting.

Are the fixtures located above and behind the base line and above and outside the alley lines of the court, so as to cause minimal interference when the ball is in play? Lighting fixtures are fastened onto poles inside portable buildings, such as air structure systems (bubble buildings), rather than onto metal channels as usually found inside permanent buildings. Therefore, if you are erecting a portable building give special consideration to the pole design. If you take down the structure or move it to another location, you should be able to remove the light poles, along with all connections, without leaving hazardous obstructions on the site. (One manufacturer of such poles is Air-Tech Industries, Inc.)

Since light sources from various types of fixtures were previously rated, let's expand a bit on sources themselves.

Historically speaking, incandescent fixtures and lamps were the first used to light tennis courts. However, they are not as much in demand today because of their low life expectancy, fair lumen output, and general inability to perform as economically or efficiently as several newer lighting systems. However, I recommend incandescent light fixtures or, for that matter, any of the fixtures previously mentioned if they meet your standards and expectations.

Interestingly enough, indirect lighting is rapidly gaining in popularity. Usually, these fixtures are mounted on a metal channel, especially inside permanent buildings. When properly aimed at a white or light-colored ceiling, the light beams reflect or bounce back to the playing surface in a most pleasing manner.

Regardless of which system meets your fancy, first check with your supplier for the recommended voltage. The added cost of bringing in a higher voltage line than is now a part of your home wiring system may not be the most economical installation to meet your requirements. However, under some conditions, the cheapest operational cost over a period of years may dictate bringing higher voltage to the tennis court.

Inquiring into voltage requirements for several different lighting systems just may give you exactly what you want with a lower price tag.

When research is done right down to the bottom line, here's what you should demand in illumination. Indoor court lighting is considered good if it ranges between a minimum of 50 foot-candles and a maximum of 100 foot-candles when the light meter is held approximately 42 inches above the surface. It's a good idea to wear dark clothing and to hold the meter about an arm's length away from your body while taking readings. Light beams reflecting from white clothing can shoot the needle reading way above the actual foot-candles of light present. Most likely, accurate meter readings will vary as you move about an area bounded within 6 feet of the backstops behind the ends of the court and about the same distance outside the alley line. However, you should be proud of your system if the lowest reading is at least 65 percent of the highest reading, assuming there are no "hot spots" present.

9

Plumbing Installations

Primarily, a good plumbing installation is a system of pipes to deliver a water supply from a source to fixtures, then to drain waste materials away from them to a sanitary sewer, septic tank, or cesspool. Tennis court plumbing may be as simple as installing a water fountain or as complicated as installing hot-water tanks, toilets, sinks, water fountains, and saunas.

The answer to whether you should do your own plumbing depends entirely upon your assessment of your own ability and local plumbing codes. This chapter shows the principles of plumbing and how to apply them, but some building codes are so strict that only a licensed plumber is allowed to do the work. On the other hand, other codes are more tolerant, so all that is required is a job approval by a licensed plumber.

There are many smaller communities where no code exists at all. This in itself is not necessarily a healthy situation unless workmen adhere to good plumbing procedures in making installations. For example, a family of five was hospitalized because of contaminated drinking water. It seems the hot water furnace line was a branch of the cold water supply line without any means of cutoff in between. One day the city water pressure dropped to near zero for about an hour. This caused some of the furnace water to back its way into the drinking water line, since the hot-water pressure in the furnace line was momentarily greater than the cold-water supply. That evening at the dinner table contaminated water was part of the menu, resulting in five very sick people.

I'm not advocating that everyone do his own plumbing. However, if you are a do-it-yourselfer, a careful workman, and follow codes and the instructions given here, you should be able to do a successful plumbing job and save about 60 percent.

Now that you want to do the plumbing, begin by checking with your municipal building or county courthouse relative to the existence of a plumbing code. Here your local librarian can be of assistance. Generally, there's at least one book on the shelves that outlines the national code, even if a local code does not exist. Study it. Then make it a part of your installations.

I purposely do not discuss air conditioning and heating in this book as they apply to indoor tennis courts. Generally, these jobs are for the pros. However, installation is not the problem. In fact, much of the installation work makes use of the plumbing principles explained in this chapter and the electrical principles explained in Chapter 8. The catch lies in the layouts, figuring the right materials for the right place in terms of a particular tennis court building. For example, two major mail-order houses tell me they do not provide heating and air-conditioning systems and installation data for do-it-yourselfers for tennis court buildings, as they do for homes, because of the wide differences in construction layouts from building to building.

By purchasing your heating and air-conditioning equipment locally, it is possible the dealer will not only figure out what you need and where it goes, but will let you do much of the work, thereby saving you money. If you encounter difficulties, advice is close at hand.

MATERIALS AND TOOLS

9-1. The illustration literally brings the plumbing system out of hiding from under floors, between walls, and in the ground. Now you can see the relationship of each plumbing part to its counterpart. Study the illustrations carefully, first as you estimate the plumbing requirements, then again as you make the installation.

Supply System Parts

1. Stop and waste valves: Install at low point of cold and hot-water lines as they enter the building.
2. Cold-water main line: It serves two or more fixtures or pieces of equipment requiring cold water.
3. Hot-water main line: It serves two or more fixtures, if required.
4. Branch line to fixture: A line (hot or cold) designed to serve one fixture only.
5. Shutoff valves: One required on each branch line, and in all main lines if cutoff is required.
6. Antihammer: To prevent pipe banging, install one in each branch line where it is connected to a faucet.
7. Fixture supply line: A section of a branch line leading directly to one fixture only.

Sewage and Drainage System Parts

8. Fixture drain: A section of branch drain leading away from a specific fixture. For health reasons, each requires a trap (as shown in Figure 9-1) or has a built-in trap. The purpose of traps is to prevent gasses escaping into the tennis court.
9. Branch drain: A drain line leading away from one fixture only.
10. Soil stack: Vertical pipe, generally 3 or 4 inches in diameter, into which branch drains empty.
11. Vent increaser: Uppermost length of stack. It is larger in diameter than the stack proper and is required by some building codes, especially in extremely cold climates.
12. Vent: Top end of soil stack. It is from this end that gasses escape into the air.
13. Revent: A bypass for air and gasses between a branch drain and the vent part of the stack. This prevents fast-flowing liquids leaving fixtures from sucking all of the liquid from the trap, which would allow gasses to escape into the tennis court.
14. Cleanout: Install one at points where obstructions may appear. A good rule of thumb is to install a tee with a pipe plug in one opening instead of an elbow in all drain lines. By all means install one at the foot of the stack as shown in Figure 9-1.

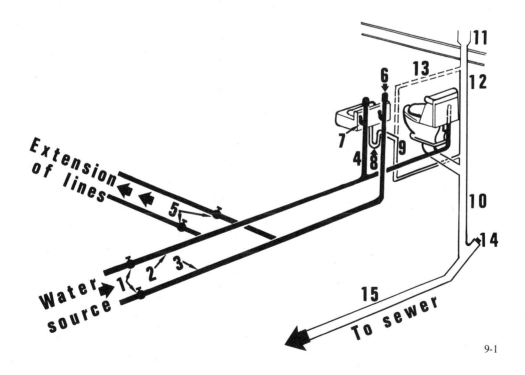

9-1

15. Drain: Be sure all wastes drain toward stack, thence through main drain to final destination, such as a sump or a sanitary sewer.

Tools

The only tools required for installing plastic water supply and drain pipes are hacksaw, wrench, pocketknife, and screwdriver.

WATER SUPPLY SYSTEMS

When laying out both the hot and cold-water lines, use no smaller supply pipe than ¾-inch ID for main lines and ½-inch ID for branch lines. Install a shutoff valve near source of water supply. This may be a continuation of your home water supply system or a special supply system located inside the building. Also, pitch the pipes slightly as they drain toward shutoff valve. This valve provides a means of draining the system for repairs; a drainable system prevents costly repairs in a cold climate. To avoid hammering noises when faucets are closed, install antihammers in hot and cold lines prior to their attachment to fixture.

9-2

9-2. If you use plastic supply pipes, be sure they are designed for the job you have in mind. Some plastic pipe is designed to carry only cold water. Other plastic pipe is designed only for indoor use. I recommend Chlorinated Polyvinyl Chloride (CPVC) water pipe because it is designed for indoor and outdoor use with hot and cold water. Be sure to use the solvent specifically recommended for the type of plastic pipe purchased. Figure 9-2 shows fittings used in making the connections:

1. Tee	5. Cap
2. 90° elbow	6. Reducer bushing
3. 45° elbow	7. Male IP adapter
4. Coupling	8. Strap

Begin by making a layout of your particular needs. Plan to use reducer bushings to connect larger pipes to smaller ones, such as a ¾-inch main line to a ½-inch branch line. Connect pipes of the same diameter with couplings. If you expect to extend the water line in the future, fasten a nipple (2- to 6-inch piece of water pipe) with a pipe cap cemented on one end and opposite end cemented to a coupling, which in turn is cemented to end of water pipe. Use 1-inch roofing nails for mounting pipes with straps.

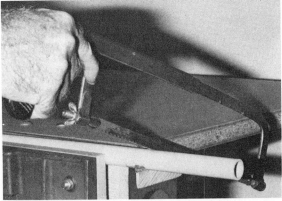

9-3

9-3. Use a hacksaw, or a tube cutter if you have one, to cut ends of pipe square.

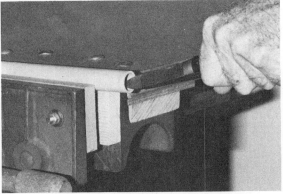

9-4

9-4. Using a pocketknife, carefully ream inside of pipe.

Caution: Never leave fragments in pipe; the obstruction prevents faucets and valves from closing.

9-7

9-7. Using either plastic or metal straps and 1-inch roofing nails, support both vertical and horizontal runs at 3-foot intervals, being sure straps are not located closer than 3 feet to a 45° or a 90° turn. This arrangement allows normal contraction and expansion to take place without damaging cemented joints.

Caution: When installing straps, be sure pipe can pass through them freely; this provides free movement during contraction and expansion.

9-8. Next connect faucets to cold and hot-water lines. Screw male adapter into shutoff

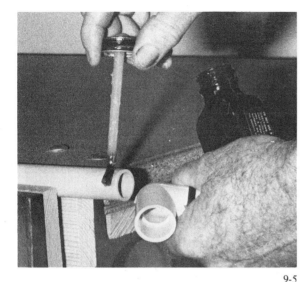

9-5

9-5. Use a nonsynthetic brush to apply solvent designed for your kind of pipe to inside of fitting socket and to outside surface of pipe to a distance equal to depth of socket.

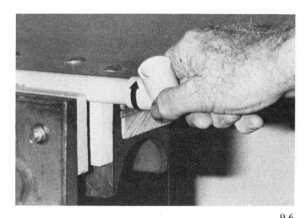

9-6

9-6. Give fitting a quarter turn as you push it over pipe. Fitting must be properly bottomed and aligned before solvent begins to set. Let assembly remain put until joint sets, otherwise fitting and pipe may pull apart. Follow setting time instructions on can of solvent. If excess solvent oozes around outside of fitting or pipe, wipe off before laying assembly down to set. Work on other pipes and fittings while waiting for previous ones to set.

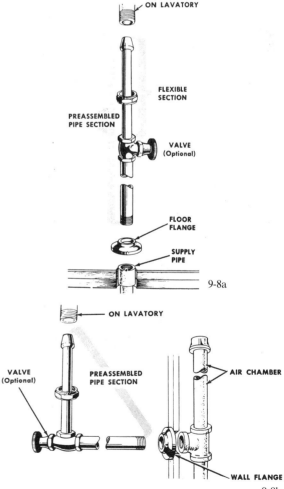

9-8a

9-8b

valve before cementing plastic supply pipe to socket. Generally, tightening with a wrench one turn past hand-tight is tight enough. Figure 9-8*a* shows a floor-type installation, while Figure 9-8*b* shows a wall-type installation.

9-9.   Although some builders do not include antihammers in water supply lines, I recommend their installation to prevent hammering noises when faucets are closed. Cement one end of short nipple *1* into tee *2*, and other end of nipple into small end of reducer *3*. Then cement a piece of 12-inch-long pipe *4*, one size larger than water supply pipe, into large end of reducer. Complete antihammer by capping 12-inch pipe with a pipe cap *5*. Be sure to cement all joints well. Arrows show direction of water supply.

Use a female adapter to connect to metal garden hose valves and shutoff valve.

If you connect to a hot-water tank, use a temperature relief valve set no higher than 212°F. Install valve into a galvanized tee so probe enters water in top of heater. Extend cold-water supply and hot-water discharge line in galvanized pipe a minimum of 12 inches from hot water heater. Connect plastic pipes to galvanized pipes with galvanized unions. Screw male adapter into union and tighten approximately one turn beyond hand-tight. Connect plastic pipe to male adapter, as previously described, to complete installation. For tight joints—and ones that are easily loosened if repairs are needed—always place pipe thread compound on threads of galvanized

pipe before attaching galvanized fittings. (Short pieces of threaded galvanized pipe and fittings, as well as pipe thread compound, can be secured from most hardware stores.)

9-10

9-10.   Sometimes pumps, underground sprinkler systems, and other pieces of equipment have threaded openings or discharge connections. In such cases, flexible polyethylene pipe can be used to make the connection by using an adapter and a screw-type clamp as shown in Figure 9-10. The threaded or male end is screwed into the threaded or female opening to complete the connection.

SAFE DRAINAGE SYSTEMS

A drainage system must provide complete and final disposal of waste water. Ask your supplier for plastic pipe especially designed for drainage use. I recommend Rubber Styrene (RS) plastic sewer and drainage pipe because it is designed for use indoors or underground. Pipes for drainage systems are not the same as those used for water supply lines, and *neither one should ever be substituted for the other*. Drainage pipes are larger because the flow is entirely by gravity. Therefore, they should be pitched ¼ inch per foot toward point of disposal. Water supply pipes, on the other hand, are smaller because their flow is under pressure. The purpose of their slope is to allow gravity to come into play when the water is shut off and the lines are drained for repairs.

The drainage system consists of three parts. All are required even if the only fixture is a lavatory. The three parts are: drainage lines, traps, and vent lines.

Drainage lines may be vertical or almost horizontal for the purpose of carrying waste water to the sanitary sewer or septic tank.

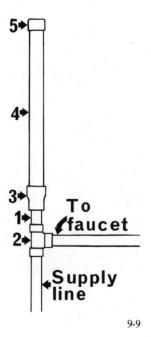

9-9

Traps may be separate parts, or they may be a part of the fixture itself. They should be located close to the fixture and should be accessible.

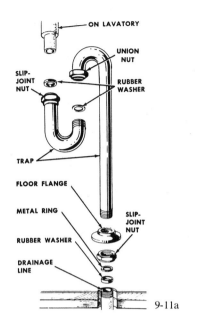

9-11a

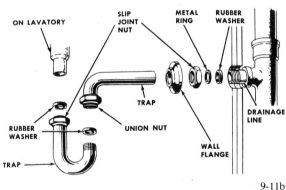

9-11b

9-11. A floor-type installation is shown in Figure 9-11a; a wall-type installation in Figure 9-11b. Connect a male adapter to trap. Then cement drain line into adapter socket. Tighten all parts together, as shown.

Vent lines, which extend upward through the roof, allow air to flow into or out of the drainage pipes, thus eliminating a partial vacuum by equalizing air pressure in the drainage system. This prevents the water from being sucked out of the traps, which would allow sewer gas to enter the building and become a health hazard by polluting the air.

9-12. In addition to the tools used to make the hot and cold-water installation, you will need a hand saw and shovel for making the drainage

9-12

installation. You might need a jig, if you have difficulty sawing the 4-inch plastic soil pipe square (main line to sewer). Here two boards are nailed to a 2 x 4, as shown in Figure 9-12. Next, a line is marked square on both sides. Then a hand saw is used to cut out the marks from top edge of boards to the 2 x 4. This makes it a simple operation to saw 1½-inch branch vent pipes, 3-inch drain pipes, and soil pipes square when placed in the jig. To attach fittings to pipe, be sure to use solvent specifically designed for the drain and vent pipes you are installing.

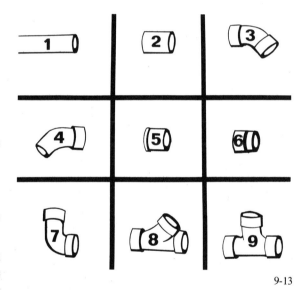

9-13

9-13. Pipe and fittings required for installing a safe drainage system are shown in Figure 9-13. To prepare the pipe, use solvent on the fittings and pipe as described for the supply system.

1. Solid pipe
2. Coupling
3. ⅛ bend
4. ⅛ street bend
5. Hub end adapter
6. Reducer
7. ¼ bend
8. Y
9. Tee

Here are guidelines for the drainage installation. Pitch or slope pipes ¼ inch per foot to establish desirable gravity flow from fixtures to final disposal into the sanitary sewer or septic tank line. Never slope drain pipes more than suggested. To do so can cause solids, such as paper, to clog the line. This happens when the water rushes away, leaving solids behind. The only exception is a 45° or 90° drop. In these cases, the pitch is great enough to carry both solids and waste water along their way at the same speed.

Exercise care to cement joints totally, so gasses cannot leak. Each fixture must have a vented trap to hold water. The trap acts as a seal, preventing sewer gasses from passing into the building.

WORKING WITH COPPER PIPE

Sometimes copper pipe is used to fulfill code requirements or for some other reason when making connections on heating, air conditioning, and other pieces of equipment. If this is your situation, you can use copper pipe or tubing for both supply and drainage lines, provided they are sized correctly for their purposes.

With flexible tubing, type K is used for underground and outdoor use, while type L is used for indoor piping.

With rigid tubing, type L is used for indoor piping, while type M is designed for general-purpose use and for forced-hot-water systems. Copper fittings are similar in appearance to the plastic fittings shown in Figure 9-2 through 9-7.

9-14. You can use a pipe bender to bend copper pipe. If you make only a few bends and do not have access to a pipe bender, carefully work the pipe around a wood wheel made from a scrap piece of 2 x 6, as shown in Figure 9-14. The trick here is to prevent the pipe from kinking. Wherever possible, I bend copper pipe of 45° and 90° turns rather than use fittings. Not only does this save both time and money, but the bends reduce friction between the pipe and water.

Before cutting pipe, be certain of the measurement. Begin by measuring the exact distance between faces of fittings, sometimes called *face-to-face* measurement. Then add the length of the depth of the *two* fittings.

Note: Tools and supplies mentioned in the following steps may be secured from any copper supply house.

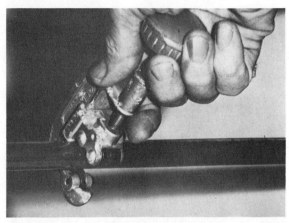

9-15

9-15. Use a tube cutter for making even, square cuts. You can also use a hacksaw fitted with a #24 blade. In either case, remove all burrs by reaming with the reamer attached to the tube cutter or with an old pocketknife.

9-16. Use a special wire brush for cleaning and brightening inside of fitting; use fine steel wool to clean end of tube.

9-14

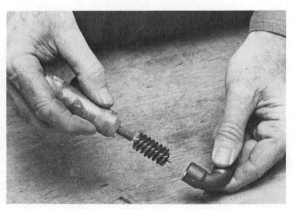

9-16

9-17

9-19

9-17. Apply a thin coat of noncorrosive flux or soldering paste to the inside of the cleaned fitting and the end of the tube. Next place tube as far as it will go into the fitting. With fitting held tight, rotate tube to evenly spread the flux.

9-19. As soon as possible after the line of solder forms, use a rag or small brush to remove surplus solder from around edge of fitting.

UNDERGROUND SPRINKLERS

9-20. One way to water your lawn, clay, or fast-dry tennis court surface is to install an underground sprinkling system. Since the major portion of the installation is in the labor, you can slash the cost immensely by doing the job yourself.

There are several different systems designed for the do-it-yourselfer, and your local hardware supplier may carry exactly what you need. If not, he will probably order a system for you, including an easy-to-follow instruction sheet. Coupled with the plumbing techniques found in this chapter, this should make your installation the envy of the neighborhood. Also, your supplier can acquaint you with various accessories, such as a mechanical timer, which takes the drudgery out of having to be at the right place at the right time to turn the water supply on and off. If a hardware store is not handy, several companies advertise their systems in the tennis magazines. For example, Uni-Spray is one such company (*see* Sources of Supply).

Since instruction sheets are generally clear and easy to follow, installation techniques here would be superfluous. However, there are three procedures I find most helpful that are not included on some instruction sheets. First is the question of having enough water pressure. Arrows in Figure 9-20 show how four heads can supply enough water to properly water a single court. Incidentally, the heads are adjustable. They can be set to spray either a quarter, half, or

9-18

9-18. Using a small, lighted propane torch, heat fitting evenly (apply flame to fitting, *not* to pipe). Heat until flux begins to bubble out of joint. Then apply wire solder (50–50) to edge of fitting. The melted solder will flow by capillary attraction, filling the joint. If the solder doesn't flow freely, the joint and pipe are not hot enough (pipe draws its heat from the fitting). In this case, apply more heat until solder does melt and flow freely. Watch for a line of solder to form completely around the joint. Then immediately remove the flame. To heat further causes the melted solder to flow out of the joint into the elbow of the fitting. If this happens, apply more flux and start over.

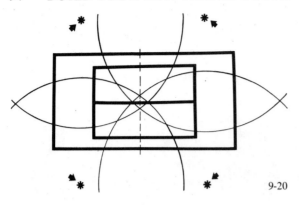

9-20

full circle. Check with your city or county public works department to find out if you have enough pressure to supply a spray to all parts of the court without having any of the heads on the playing area.

The second point has to do with good health practice. Be sure to install an antiback flow valve at the outset of the installation to prevent water from accidentally backing into the main supply line. Third, put the system together above ground. Then check it out to see if the whole court is being sprinkled. When there are no leaks and the sprinkling is effective, dig trenches to bury the system. Begin by laying aside the first 4 inches of turf for replacement later, as the ditches are filled with dirt. With the subsoil watered and tamped in place and the pieces of 4-inch turf replaced, signs of "ditching" are hardly noticeable.

10

Auxiliary Equipment

In letters to tennis magazines, in conversations with clerks, and with anyone else who will lend a friendly ear, the question is loud and clear: "I am about to buy tennis equipment. What do you advise?" And the inquiries are made in the best of faith; there are hundreds of tennis court equipment manufacturers, making everything from tennis rackets to tennis ball-throwing machines.

But, as every professional tennis player knows, it's a question that can best be answered by asking several courter-questions. To wit: What do you expect to do with the equipment? What do you want the equipment to do for you? Is the game of tennis just one more of your hobbies? Or do you strive to reach the professional ranks? Do you want a lot of frills, wherever they are available; or do you want practical equipment made to do the job for which it is intended?

Whatever your goal, the right equipment has the capacity to give you the satisfaction of eventually playing the game to your own expectations, but you must know what you want to do and how to do it. For satisfaction is anything but happenstance.

To help you completely answer your questions would require several volumes. So what I have done in this chapter is to present a random sampling of some of the many excellent pieces of equipment found in today's market. Hopefully, this and the Sources of Supply listing will provide some answers to your questions, thereby making it simpler to choose the kind of equipment that will best help you to improve your game. After all is said and done, final selection depends on you and your specific requirements.

RACKETS AND BAGS

Rackets used on courts today come in wood, metal composite, and graphite composite. And every player can give you ten good reasons why his racket is made from the best material. It is a somewhat personal matter; the "best" is found by trying them all until you find the one that improves your game the most.

Rawlings is one of the companies manufacturing an aluminum frame racket. Among other features, it is lightweight and the rounded edges eliminate court damage. It is designed so that racket vibration, yoke slippage, or cracking is almost impossible. The open design reduces wind resistance, which increases stroke velocity, accuracy, and power. Also, its shock-dampening qualities with shock-absorbent grip contribute to playing ease, comfort, and endurance.

Tennis isn't what it was in the old days, and neither is the equipment. Tennis bags are one good example of change. There are a number of good ones on the market, such as those manufactured by Bags of Leisure Ltd. They manufacture distinctive-looking bags made of water-repellent, mildew-resistant canvas duck. They may be had in colors of bright red, yellow, white, tan, or blue. The bags vary in size to meet the demands of the most discriminating player. Sizes vary from those just large enough to carry a single racket to those 18 x 6 x 14 inches, large enough to carry a complete change of attire, towels, and equipment. With the assortment offered by various manufacturers, you'll have no problem finding one to fill your needs.

Racket Stringers and Ball Refurbishers

If you've reached the place where your racket is never strung tight or loose enough to meet your every demand, why not invest in a racket stringer and do the job yourself? The Electro-Matic racket stringer manufactured by Court and Slope, Inc., is one of several machines on the market that should meet the requirements of the most discriminating player. With this machine, you can string your racket to the tension of your choice.

Are you throwing away balls long before they're worn out? If so, look into the possibility or refurbishing them. Several machines are available to do the job of extending ball life. Tensor Corporation is one of the manufacturers supplying a ball refurbisher.

PLATFORM TENNIS EQUIPMENT

When it comes to platform tennis, equipment is on the market to meet the player's every need. For instance, Semanco manufactures a moderately priced platform tennis racket consisting of a five-ply laminated head with a beveled edge and wood grip with leather cuff plus rawhide thong. Also, it produces a superior platform racket slightly higher in price. It's five-ply hard maple with mahogany finish. Features include a deluxe aluminum edge to protect racket, plus rawhide thong and leather grip.

Platform tennis balls are handled by most sporting goods stores, and they vary in quality and price. For instance, Semanco manufactures two different types: One is a 2½-inch orange-flecked sponge rubber ball; the other, a 2½-inch rubber ball, more durable, with better bounce, and slightly higher in price.

SAFETY PADDING

If you're planning an indoor court where beams, walls, and other obstructions are bound to present problems, think about covering them with safety padding. One product on the market is made by Ehmke Manufacturing Company, Inc. The material is made of tough vinyl-coated nylon. It is flame resistant and comes in any color to complement the curtains or decor of your building. The padding is tailored to the shape of the object and designed for easy installation and removal.

UMPIRE'S CHAIR

10-1. A much-needed accessory for any tennis court is a well-constructed umpire's chair. An outstanding one is manufactured by the J. E. Francis Company: 64 inches high, in accordance with USTA standards, this rugged tubular steel welded frame with durable enamel finish may be easily rolled on the standard casters to any convenient location. It is shipped knocked down, but this presents no problem. Using the clearly defined, exploded view assembly plans that accompany each unit, it can be assembled in less than 30 minutes with just a wrench and a hammer.

Courtesy of J. E. Francis Co.   10-1

BUILDING A BACKBOARD

10-2. Practice, anyone? Without a partner? There are several tennis backboards offered for sale, or you can build your own and do just that. It's the quickest, easiest way to improve your game.

Wilkinson Enterprises manufactures a backboard called Perma-Partner. It's a great aid to the tennis instructor, for it allows him to

Courtesy of Wilkinson Enterprises   10-2

create a number of teaching stations, thereby handling more students per session. Also, it's made to order for the tennis buff who wants to practice on his own.

Virtually all strokes can be practiced, even volleys and overheads. Simply adjust the angle of the playing surface.

Another good point is that you have time between each return of the ball to determine your next stroke, time to draw back your racket and make the stroke correctly. If the ground is uneven and deflects the ball, you can overcome this easily by using the optional bounce board. By consistently returning the ball at the same pace, to the same spot, a player can practice the basics over and over again. Also, it lets you practice up to 3,000 strokes an hour—equivalent to 5 or 6 hours on the court.

10-3 The adjustable backboard—Figure 10-3 is inexpensive, easy to make, and can be built as a one-evening project by any do-it-yourselfer. It is useful as a warmup device, in correcting poor habits, and as a valuable teaching aid since it permits an instructor to teach close to the student.

Because the angle of the backboard is adjustable, you can practice volleying to suit your needs. Then, too, several players can play in the same general area, each with his own backboard. Such an arrangement is ideal for close supervision by one instructor.

Because the ball rebounds to the player at a right angle to the board, players are not bothered by interference from other tennis balls.

When practice is over, or you expect a high wind, pick up the rear leg brace and roll the backboard to inside storage. With legs folded all you need is 7¼ inches of wall space.

Tools required for making the adjustable backboard are:

Carpenter's saw
Drill and bits
Screwdriver
Band saw or jigsaw
Adjustable wrench
Reamer or bit slightly smaller than head of a
   ³/₁₆-inch flat-head stove bolt.

10-3

Backboard Materials

Part	Quantity and Description
Backboard	one ⅝ x 4 x 7-foot exterior plywood
Rear legs	two 2 x 2s x 4 feet long
	one pair 4-inch light strap hinges
	six flat-head stove bolts $^3/_{16}$ x 1½ inches, washers, and nuts
	six flat-head stove bolts $^3/_{16}$ x 2 inches, washers, and nuts
Front legs	two 2 x 2s x 3 feet long
	six flat-head stove bolts $^3/_{16}$ x 2½ inches, washers, and nuts
Wheels	two 2 x 8-inch wood wheels or two discarded lawnmower wheels
	two round-head stove bolts ¼ x 3½ inches, washers, and nuts
Angle adjustment bars	two 1 x 2s x 3 feet long
	two round-head stove bolts $^3/_{16}$ x 2½ inches, washers, and nuts
	two round-head stove bolts $^3/_{16}$ x 2½ inches, washers, and wing nuts
Rear legs brace	one piece 1 x 4 x length to suit
	four round-head stove bolts $^3/_{16}$ x 2½ inches, washers, and nuts

10-4.   Make the board proper from 7 feet of ⅝-inch exterior plywood.

Using six $^3/_{16}$ x 2-inch flat-head stove bolts, washers, and nuts, fasten a 4-inch light strap hinge to each of two rear legs made from two pieces of 2 x 2-inch lumber 4 feet long. All parts of the backboard are assembled by first drilling holes through both adjoining pieces; then they are held together with bolts, washers, and nuts.

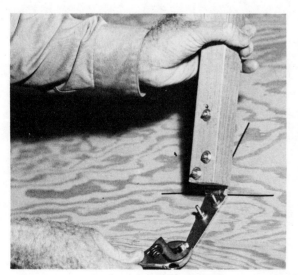

10-4

Next locate two cross marks on the rear side in the middle of the backboard, each vertical mark 20 inches from its respective edge.

Rear legs should extend 2 feet below bottom of backboard. Using six $^3/_{16}$ x 1½-inch flat-head stove bolts, washers, and nuts, fasten the two hinged legs to rear side of backboard shown in Figure 10-4. Be sure to ream holes on front side of backboard so when hinge bolts are tightened, heads on front side are flush with surface.

10-5.   Make front legs by cutting two pieces of 2 x 2-inch lumber 3 feet long. Using a band saw or jigsaw, cut two 7¼-inch wheels from 2 x 8-inch material. (You can substitute two discarded lawnmower wheels if you desire.) Fasten wood wheels 2 inches from bottom of front legs with two ¼ x 3½-inch round-head stove bolts, washers, and nuts. Make finger tight. If wheel nuts do not stay put, jam two or more bolt threads together with a cold chisel and hammer.

10-5

Using six $^3/_{16}$ x 2½-inch flat-head stove bolts, washers, and nuts, fasten the two front legs to rear side of backboard. Be sure to ream holes on front side of board. Position each leg 12 inches above bottom of backboard with centers located 22¼ inches from their respective edges of backboard. When folded, rear and front legs and angle adjustment bar (described in the following step) must lie side by side against rear of backboard.

10-6.   Make two angle adjustment bars *A* from 1 x 2-inch lumber 3 feet long. Then beginning at one end, drill ¼-inch holes every 6 inches as shown.

Using two $^3/_{16}$ x 2½-inch round-head stove bolts, washers, and nuts, fasten one end of bars to front legs. Tighten nuts finger tight.

Then using two $^3/_{16}$ x 2½-inch round-head stove bolts, washers, and wing nuts, fasten ad-

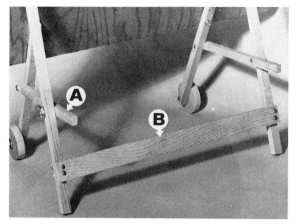

10-6

10-6

justment bars to rear legs, using holes of your choice. Tighten wing nuts finger tight.

Next make rear leg brace *B* by cutting a piece of 1 x 4-inch lumber to proper length, as shown.

Using four ³⁄₁₆ x 2½-inch round-head stove bolts, washers, and nuts, fasten brace 8 inches from lower end of rear legs.

Although the backboard is designed for either indoor or outdoor use, apply two coats of quality nonglossy exterior paint to it and its component parts if exposed to the weather.

BALL-THROWING MACHINE AND PICKUP BASKETS

10-7. All over America, amateurs, professionals, and teachers alike are making use of

Courtesy of Prince Manufacturing, Inc.   10-7

ball-throwing machines as if they're going out of style. Prince Manufacturing Company makes a machine designed by a court owner and a professional. It holds 250 balls for continuous play. It does more than simply toss the ball—invaluable though that is for grooving your strokes. It can be used to develop court coverage and court strategy. It gives you every shot in tennis from a toss or a lob to a baseline drive, and anything in between. With the server you can practice return of serve. You can set it for any stroke, any interval, and any trajectory in a matter of seconds, and you can go back to the same settings whenever you wish. There's an eight-page booklet included with every shipment and it reveals practice methods used by teaching pros around the country.

Courtesy of Hoag-Co.   10-8

10-8. Ball pickup equipment saves court time and effort in individual practice or tennis teaching.

Shown here are two Hoag-Co pickup baskets, the Rally-S (seventy-ball capacity, picks up one to nine balls at a time) and the Pro (ninety-five-ball capacity, picks up one to twelve balls at a time). Both feature a patented pickup mechanism which operates quickly and effortlessly. Handles are removable for storage and are instantly reversible to provide a hand-high stand for replay of the balls.

10-9. Ball Preserver, sold by Century Sports, Inc., is a new product (patents pending), whereby the manufacturer makes the following claims: The Ball Preserver extends the life of

Courtesy of Viking Sauna Co.　10-9

tennis balls to several hundred games while maintaining official USLTA bounce and weight specifications. Keeping balls pressurized properly prevents the rubber core from collapsing and separating from the flat cover, thus reducing cover wear. Extensive testing of tennis balls has shown that the cover will normally wear below USLTA specs in seven to twenty games (depending on the players). Balls stored in the Ball Preserver when not in use will meet USLTA wear specs (measured as loss of weight) for 200 to 300 games, and exhibit negligible wear for well over 300 games.

SAUNAS AND WHIRLPOOLS

Many Americans would become red faced if they were invited to "Come have a bath with us." Not so in Finland, for the greatest honor and pleasure a Finn can offer a guest is an invitation to a sauna. The Finns firmly believe the sauna is solely responsible for their physical and mental relaxation. In short, it's doing their thing.

Perhaps you have never seen a sauna room. It's a special heated, redwood-lined room where one sits and sweats profusely while meditating or practicing togetherness with family or friends.

"Not for me" might be your reaction. "I've been blinded by steam vapors before, with air so thick I could cut it with a knife. That's for the birds or for people who must lose fat in a hurry."

If you react this way, most likely you're thinking about a Turkish bath. To begin with, there's no steam in a sauna, and the humidity is purposely kept within a minimum range of 5–10 percent. With the air so dry, you perspire freely, even with a temperature of 175° F. There's no sweltering sensation, and you breathe freely. Although heavy perspiring melts away fat (some reports give as much as 3 pounds per session), the sauna isn't mainly a reducing device. Sweating clears the pores far more efficiently than scrubbing with soap and water. It is claimed the increase in body temperature reduces tension and increases blood circulation, but not to the point of exhaustion that comes from strenuous exercise. Manufacturers and distributors say little about the physical benefits of their saunas. It's not a lack of faith; rather, it is a regard for the Food and Drug Administration's position relative to certain medical principles.

Sauna baths are most beneficial shortly after a game of tennis, but they are more useful than that. Taken in the morning, they prepare you and your family for the day ahead. Because the heat inspires complete relaxation, the sauna room is great for holding family conferences.

10-10. Tight clothing is taboo in a sauna room. Although some people bathe in the nude, a loosely fitted garment or just a large bath towel

Courtesy of Viking Sauna Co.　10-10

loosely tucked around the body is acceptable attire.

Saunas are relatively safe. From a technical point of view, the sauna industry has been policed by the safety standards of Underwriter's Laboratories. This action has done much to bring safety standards to a high level that has resulted in greater protection to the users.

Where to place the sauna is not the problem it may seem at first. A sauna room can become a part of an indoor tennis court complex, be tucked away into a corner of the basement, or built as a separate structure in the backyard. No matter where you install it, the sauna is an ideal project for any do-it-yourselfer. Usually the installation takes no longer than a few weekends at most.

If you would like to unwind like the Finns do, why not contact a distributor who can put you in touch with people who are using saunas right in your own locality (*see* Sources of Supply). Better yet, try one out at your local tennis court club before you make the investment and spend time putting it together.

Cautions for Sauna Bathers

1. Exit the sauna when you no longer feel comfortable at the required temperature; return only after a brief rest period precluded with a cool shower.

2. If you are getting along in years, suspect a heart problem or have any other health problem, neither play a hard game of tennis nor take a sauna bath until you have consulted with your medical doctor.

Because the blood is busy helping with digestion and can't be in two places at the same time, wait at least an hour following a meal before taking a sauna bath.

3. Refrain from smoking or excercising in a sauna room.

4. To avoid burns, strip your body of anything metal (wristwatches, rings, earrings, etc.) before stepping into a sauna room.

5. Pets have no place in a sauna room because their cooling systems are different from yours.

6. If you must try for higher temperatures, be sure no small children remain in the sauna room. Their perspiration glands are underdeveloped.

7. Refrain from taking a sauna bath immediately following extreme physical exertion.

8. If you brought up the subject of cautions to a Finn, he would probably say, "Never violate the sanctity of a sauna!" And if you asked him to elaborate a bit, he would proclaim, "Don't be noisy, don't whistle or sing, don't swear, don't dance, don't watch TV or listen to a radio, don't read, don't worry, and, finally, don't even think. Just sit back, relax, and give yourself to a wonderful experience."

Assembling Your Own

A sauna bath may not improve your tennis score, but it'll sure make you feel better when you lose. The soothing desert heat of the sauna works like a massage on tired muscles, which is why so many tennis pros use saunas regularly.

You can spend a lot of time building your own sauna from plans advertised in numerous magazines, or you can assemble a prebuilt one shipped in a package and ready to assemble with nothing but an Allen wrench. They come in a variety of sizes, ranging from one the size of a phone booth to one big enough for the whole family. They are complete with heater controls and carpet. Oddly enough, there's one you can assemble in about an hour. And there's no plumbing installation to worry about.

You'll find several suppliers offering prepackaged saunas in the Sources of Supply listing. To give you a general idea of what's involved in assembling one, I'll use as an example one built by the Viking Sauna Company. It is free-standing and has self-contained rooms. The walls and ceilings consist of prebuilt redwood panels that lock together effortlessly and come apart just as easily if you decide to move and take your sauna with you.

The prepackaged sauna arrives knocked down in cartons complete in every detail, ready to assemble. Remove all panels and parts from cartons, checking for damage as well as checking all items against packing list. Do not overlook the instruction sheet, containing, among other things, helpful how-tos for your particular model.

Next, place floor in position on a level area. Then latch corner posts to wall panels and lock into place on metal retaining clips on floor. Install the thermal strips between the wall and ceiling panels. Then continue adding remainder of panels, preassembled door, and posts to complete the wall assembly.

Courtesy of Viking Whirl-Spa, Inc.   10-11

Bench installation comes next. Then install metal retaining clips to ceiling panels and carefully lower ceiling panels into place, checking to see that metal retaining clips are securely seated.

Caution: At this point, be certain wiring has not been connected to the electrical panel. Now carefully unpack sauna heater. Then install it to the electrical panel, being sure to follow installation instructions for connecting electric current to the room. (*See* Chapter 8, for additional help in making electrical connections.)

There are a number of luxuries you can add to your sauna. Handy is a hygrometer which shows you how quickly the percentage of relative humidity drops as the temperature rises. If you enjoy a steam shock, obtain a wooden ladle and bucket to use in sprinkling water on the sauna rocks. A timer that dings on a preset time is a handy gadget to own. And if you want the ultimate in status symbols for saunas, purchase an audio transducer, which you attach to the sauna exterior, producing a stereo effect inside.

Whirlpools

10-11. If you're a tennis buff who doesn't like or can't use a sauna, there's still another amenity that should interest you. It's a whirlpool.

Everyone enjoys warm water, and the relaxation and restful appeal of soaking in a tub is known to almost everyone. However, only a few people have followed a hot and heavy match on the courts with a whirlpool bath; the idea is catching on as more tennis players realize that the game just isn't complete without being relaxed, yet invigorated.

Figure 10-11 shows a Whirl-Spa unit called the "Norseman," manufactured by Viking Whirl-Spa, Inc. (For further information, *see* Sources of Supply). The unit sells for approximately $2,500, has six jets, and seats seven people. In addition, there are three smaller units, selling for as low a $700 each, and two of these are designed to seat one person each, which is plenty large for family use where turns are taken.

Think of a whirlpool as a small swimming pool. For instance, a 550-gallon whirlpool operates on the same principle and with similar equipment to a 40,000-gallon swimming pool. For example, a Viking Whirl-Spa package consists of six jets for maximum water action, 1½ hp bronze pump for filter and heater circulation, sand filter, and built-in skimmer to meet local health codes. The units are one-piece construction and factory installed piping that takes the guesswork out of the installation. They can be filled with a garden hose, once installed. The only maintenance is water treatment. It must be treated with chlorine and acid to keep it sparkling clear. There's no worry about installing recirculating pumps and filters. They are already correctly installed as part of the package. In addition, complete instructions are included in the package for making either an indoor or an outdoor installation in a matter of hours.

11

Fencing

If your plans call for fencing the tennis court, your own needs are the best determining factors for setting up specifications. However, there are three basic areas that every owner should consider: aesthetics, protection, and backstop.

BASIC REQUIREMENTS

Aesthetics

Making the most of your particular plot of land and each of its individual structures requires careful consideration, and your tennis court fence is no exception if it is to add its share, aesthetically speaking, to the total site. I have known owners who fenced in their tennis courts without giving any thought to the actual planning of type, quality, or construction details. All three are most important, and none should take a back seat to the others.

Soon such owners become unhappy with what they have and wonder why they didn't take just a little more time in planning before they built. Billy is one such person. He built a beautiful, well-constructed vinyl-clad chain-link fence at each end of his court. Because he was running short on cash, he installed a 6-foot welded wire fence fastened to wood posts along the sidelines. Not only did the cheap wire fence lower the property value by several hundred dollars, the game was interrupted time and again while players retrieved balls stuck in the wire mesh or outside the fence.

Protection

A tennis court is a sizeable investment and it deserves fencing, if for no other reason than the protection it offers. More insurance companies than ever before are asked to write vandalism clauses into tennis court insurance policies.

One owner recently told me that he was fencing in his court the very next week. Then he said, "I get a sick feeling in the pit of my stomach every time I harbor the thought of vandals pouring oil over my asphalt bound court."

Backstop

If you're more interested in chasing balls than in playing tennis, then you don't need a fence. But if you're like most players, you abhor running down balls.

Some people cut down on ball chasing by building a 10 or 12-foot fence at each end of the court to serve as a backstop. Others extend the fence 20 to 30 feet along the sidelines. Still others begin by fencing in the ends of the court. Then they add fencing little by little until the entire court is enclosed. Money comes in little by little, they reason, so why not go easy on the pocketbook by building the fence piecemeal.

MATERIALS AND SPECIFICATIONS

Which is best, a 10 or a 12-foot fence? The latter will cost approximately 20 percent more to build. However, if ready cash is available, the higher fence is recommended as it will stop a number of balls that would clear the lower fence.

"Perhaps there are more mistakes made in planning and constructing tennis court fences than in any other type of construction," says Dave Cox, fencing contractor with 20 years of experience. He points out two basic reasons for this: Frequently, tennis court owners insist on following inferior specifications in spite of the contractor's recommendations—apparently, they want to cut costs; at other times, uninformed contractors or careless do-it-yourselfers do not take the time to study and follow accepted practices, such as those clearly described in the *Guide Specifications for Construction of Tennis Court Fencing*, published by the U.S. Tennis Court and Track Builders Association. As a result, this contractor says, "Tennis court fencing is either practical, beautiful, and sturdy, or it is impractical, flimsy, and ugly."

Chain link is the most popular tennis court fencing but it is not all alike. There are four different kinds on the market: galvanized steel, vinyl-clad steel, aluminum-coated steel, and solid aluminum. Aluminum, of course, is the softest of the four, but it is used by many fence contractors and it provides satisfactory results. Aluminum and vinyl-clad are thought of as maintenance free. Aluminum coated steel and galvanized steel are both low-maintenance materials, but in time they do corrode and require painting.

Before making the actual purchase of materials, appraise your environmental situation carefully. Give consideration to wind exposure and its maximum velocity. What about windscreens? Remember that posts, rails, and windscreens are triple threats unless materials of proper size are used and sound construction employed.

Finally, consider special problems if they exist. For instance, salt air and some chemicals belched from industrial smokestacks might cause galvanized or aluminum wire to deteriorate. Otherwise, galvanized fencing can last a lifetime, if it is painted periodically shortly after the first signs of corrosion appear.

If galvanized fencing in your location is subject to deteriorating factors, fencing of aluminum should be used, aluminum-covered steel, or vinyl clad. Aluminum fencing and galvanized fencing cost about the same, but vinyl-clad fencing is more expensive. However, it is being used more often. It is used so much that some contractors

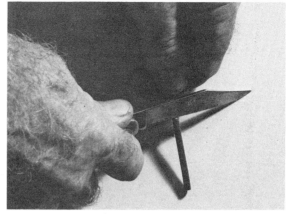

11-1

are saying it is undoubtedly the tennis court fence of the future.

11-1. Like all chain-link fence materials, vinyl-clad fences are not of the same quality. Therefore, it's best to buy only from reputable suppliers. Since vinyl-coated material can cover up its cheapness perhaps better than any other type, here's how you can tell a quality brand from one of inferior grade. All you need are a pocketknife and a sample piece of wire about 3 or 4 inches long.

Begin by cutting through the coating, entirely around the wire, about an inch from one end, as shown in Figure 11-1. Now try to pull that section away, much as if you were stripping insulation away from an electric wire. If it works, the coating is not fused to the metal as it should be. The only way you can remove the coating from a quality sample is to cut away a sliver at a time. Once you remove the sliver, see if the exposed part of the wire is galvanized. This is another indication of top-quality vinyl-clad fencing. If it is not galvanized, damaged places that appear on the installed fence will soon rust away.

BUILDING THE FENCE

11-2. The following steps show how this 78 x 120-foot fence, 10 feet high, was built around a single tennis court. The fenced area provides 21 feet of space beyond the base lines and 12 feet of space beyond the alley lines. The material ran slightly more than $2,000.

Note: The same construction steps apply equally to chain-link fences made of aluminum, aluminum-covered steel, and vinyl-clad steel.

11-2

Tools

Tools listed here are necessary for making proper installation, and you can rent them from most tool rental agencies. Also, some mail-order houses will loan hand tools if you purchase the fence materials from them.

> Posthole digger—hand or power operated
> Small level
> Pipe cutter designed to cut steel pipe
> Two pairs of fence stretchers—these can be stretcher hoists or ratchet-action wire stretchers
> Fence pliers
> Nonstretch tape measure, 10 foot minimum length
> 100-foot steel tape measure
> Hammer
> Nylon cord slightly longer than perimeter of fence

11-3. Determining your particular list of materials requires two steps. First, complete the sketch in Figure 11-3. The diagram was not drawn to scale: x, terminal post; y, gate post; z, line post. Secondly, list the amount of fabric and accessories required, referring to the following materials list. A fence 78 x 120 feet is recommended as these are the dimensions required by most professional tennis players. However, some recreational tennis players want a fence of slightly smaller dimensions. Therefore, actual measurements are left blank so you can indicate your own requirements.

Space line posts a maximum of 10 feet apart, closer if heavy close-knit wind curtains are to be used.

Two gates are recommended, as shown on the sketch. One gate should be a minimum of 12 inches wider than the width of the largest maintenance machine to be used on the court.

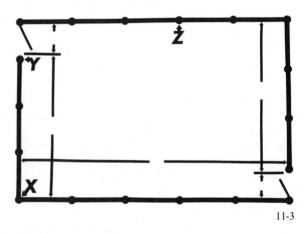

11-3

11-4. Begin building the fence by laying out the dimensions around your court(s) according to

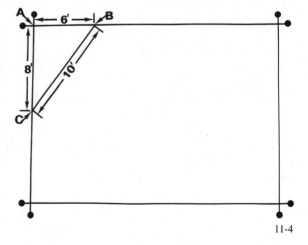

11-4

Chain-Link Fence Material

Parts and Specifications	Quantity
Fence fabric, #11 gauge and 1¾-inch mesh*	Perimeter of fence, minus width of gates
Terminal and gate posts, minimum outside diameter of 3 inches and minimum weight of 5.79 pounds per linear foot; or roll-formed sections 3½ x 3½ inches and minimum weight of 5.14 pounds per linear foot; or 2⅛-inch-square tubing and minimum weight of 5.79 pounds per linear foot	One for each terminal and gate post
Line posts welded and seamless steel pipe and weighing 3.65 pounds per linear foot; or H-column posts measuring 2 x 2¼ inches and weighing 4.1 pounds per linear foot	Minimum of one for each 10 feet of fence set between terminal and gate posts
Top and intermediate rails, outside diameter of 1⅝ inches and weight of 2.27 pounds per linear foot	Two for each 20 feet of fence
Top rail sleeves, minimum length of 7 inches	One for each interval of 20 feet or thereabouts
Line post caps, malleable casting	One for each line post
Intermediate rail connectors, #11 gauge, cold-rolled carbon steel	One for each line post
Terminal and gate post/rail connectors, #11 gauge, cold-rolled carbon steel	Four for each terminal post; two for each gate post†
Flat tension bars, #11 gauge, cold-rolled carbon steel	Two for each terminal post; one for each gate post†
Tension bar bands, #11 gauge, cold-rolled carbon steel	Fourteen for each terminal post and seven for each gate post†
Fabric tie wires, #9 gauge, soft annealed galvanized steel or aluminum wire (for all tying operations except tying fabric to tension wire)	Two pieces for each 2 feet of fence
Terminal and gate post caps, malleable casting extending at least 2 inches below top of post	One for each post
Tension wire, #7 gauge	Same length as fabric plus enough to make ties at terminal and gate posts
Tension wire fasteners, #11 gauge, galvanized steel hog rings	One for each 2 feet of fabric
Gate, welded and seamless steel pipe with an outside diameter of 1⁹/₁₀ inches or 2 inches square and weighing 2.72 pounds per linear foot. Fabric installed in frame with tension bars and hook bolts	One, more optional
Female gate hinge	Two for each gate
Male gate hinge	Two for each gate
Drop fork gate latch	One for each gate, fitted for accepting padlock

*Fasten pieces of chain-link fence fabric together by following steps in Figure 11-23 in reverse, with this exception: Before stringing the fabric wire down through the ends of both pieces, be sure diamonds are properly aligned so as to form a continuous pattern.

†Gate hinges substitute for terminal post fittings on one side of post.

plan. Then locate eight corner stakes as shown in Figure 11-4. Locate each pair of stakes about 2 feet apart and 12 inches above grade. Then stretch the nylon cord from stake to stake as shown. You can use a transit to get corners square, or you can use the 6–8–10 method, as shown. Measure 6 feet in one direction along the proposed line from corner *A* to point *B* and 8 feet from the same corner to point *C*, which is at a right angle to the first line. If the lines are square, *CB* equals 10 feet. Check all four corners for squareness. Also, if the four corners are square, diagonal measurements between opposite corner stakes are equal. (If edges of your surface material extend to the fence lines and it has square corners, skip this step.)

11-6

Dig the terminal postholes first. Then dig the line and gate postholes. Be sure holes are dug to a minimum depth of 3 feet and are 10 inches in diameter.

11-5

11-5. Starting at a terminal post location, use a nonstretch tape measure and a helper as you mark terminal, line, and gate post locations directly under the nylon cord. A spray can of light-colored paint speeds up the job. Where a gate is involved, divide the remaining distance equally along that side of the fence. For instance, suppose a 4-foot gate is planned for a 60-foot line. In this case, post measurements would be a minimum of 9 feet, 4 inches, apart, with the gate post marking 4 feet from the corner post location.

11-6. Even if you use a power-driven posthole digger, which can be rented from a tool rental agency, a hand-operated posthole digger is recommended for starting the holes exactly centered over each marking. Also, when hole is drilled, the use of a hand-operated posthole digger is an easy way to completely remove all loose dirt from the holes, which is essential for securing an A-1 job.

11-7

11-7. Next make a heavy pencil mark on each post 3 feet from the bottom. Now position each one in center of hole to within ⅛ inch of stretched cord. Pencil mark should be parallel to grade. Then use a level to line posts perpendicular or plumb. Terminal post height above top of fence is a personal matter. Some prefer them the same height as line posts. Others locate them 6 or 8 inches above the line posts.

11-8. Hold post in plumb position as helper fills hole almost to grade with six-bag mix concrete prepared by a ready-mix truck. If you want

11-8

to do your own mixing, *see* Appendix, Table I. Check posts for plumb position with level from time to time as hole is being filled with concrete.

11-9

11-9. When all posts are set, use a concrete sand mix (one part Portland cement to two parts sand, mixed with just enough water to make a puttylike consistency) to bring the concrete in the holes slightly above grade, with a convex top surface as shown in Figure 11-9. This procedure assures a perfect drain where the steel posts join the concrete, for it is at this point that post deterioration begins if shallow water holes are allowed to stand. Now remove the nylon cord and stakes. Allow the concrete to set a minimum of 72 hours before proceeding.

11-10

11-10. Next level tops of posts if needed. Stretch a nylon cord from tops of two terminal posts. The line serves to check posts for top alignment. Use a pipe cutter for lowering "high posts." If some posts are, say, a quarter of an inch to one inch short, cut a piece of like pipe to proper length to serve as a shim when the posts are capped.

Now using a wrench to tighten bolt nut, install terminal post rail end cup fitting to proper height. Then check remaining posts for proper height and attach two top rail end cup fittings to each terminal and gate post.

11-11

11-11. Run top rail through two line post cup fittings. Then slide end of rail into terminal post rail end cup fitting. Next position line post cups over line posts.

11-12. Use an outside friction-type sleeve coupling to connect top rails at intervals of 20

11-12

feet, or shorter distances if required. Then complete top rail installations.

11-13. Use intermediate rails for either 10 or 12-foot fences, installed midway between grade and top rails. Essentially, intermediate rails are installed in the same manner as top rails with one exception. Obviously, since intermediate rails must be cut to fit between posts, sleeve fittings cannot be used as connectors. Instead, use prepared split connectors (shown by arrow), fastened to line posts.

11-14

11-14. Terminal and gate post caps serve as decorative pieces as well as devices for keeping rain water and snow from getting inside the posts. You can slip the caps over the posts now or do it as the final installation operation.

11-13

Begin by cutting intermediate rail so it fits between posts. Then slide end of it into previously fastened terminal post end cup fitting. Next position opposite end of rail into split connector as you position the two pieces around line post. Now tighten connector bolts on each side of post. Repeat the operations until all intermediate rails are installed.

11-15

11-15. Wrap one end of the steel coil tension wire three times around corner post, 8 inches above grade, twisting tight with pliers. Then unroll wire just beyond opposite terminal post. Next connect fence stretcher cables to post and to tension wire. (Figure 11-15 shows a cable jack in use instead of a fence stretcher.) Tighten tension wire until it is taut, but don't overtighten. Using wire cutters or pliers, cut tension wire, leaving enough to wrap three times around post. Then twist end of wire tight with pliers. Next let out fence stretcher. Tension wire should still remain taut. If there is sag, restretch. Repeat operations on remaining sides of court.

gate post, as the case may be, with one clamp each positioned just above grade and slightly below top rail. Tighten clamp bolts, which hold tension bar and edge of fabric in vertical position as shown.

11-16

11-16. Beginning at a terminal post, unroll chain-link fabric slightly beyond opposite terminal, or gate post if one is involved. Be sure fabric is rolled on inside of posts and positioned so when installed barbs will be next to the ground.

11-17. With helpers raising fabric temporarily in place, weave tension bar in and out of diamonds at beginning of fabric. Now place tension bar inside tension bar clamps, which you position around post, being sure that seven clamps (10-foot fence) are evenly spaced on terminal or

11-18

11-18. Next bring fabric to vertical position to opposite terminal post, stretching hand tight. If fabric extends farther than one foot beyond post, cut as described in step 22.

11-19. Using piece of #9-gauge soft annealed galvanized steel or aluminum wire, wrap and twist a short piece through top diamond of fabric and top rail about midway between each line post, twisting with pliers only tight enough to keep fabric from falling. The trick here is to have

11-17

11-19

11-20

tie wire slack enough so that it easily slides along top rail during fence-stretching operation explained in the following step.

11-20. Now make ready for fence-stretching operations. First, with a helper, weave two 4-foot tension bars, one above the other, through the diamonds from top to bottom of fabric about 8 feet from terminal post.

11-21. Next fasten cables of two fence stretchers to terminal post and the 4-foot tension bars as shown. With a man working each stretcher, tighten fence evenly and taut, about 2,000 pounds pressure. Fence is tight enough when you can hand pull it only ¾ inch away from a line post. In approximately two weeks, fabric will lose some of its tension. Be sure fabric diamonds are stretched evenly from bottom to top.

Note: Position fabric approximately ¾ inch above grade. However, during the stretching process, bottom barbs and tension bars have a way of digging into the surface, causing top of fence to stretch ahead of bottom unless corrections are made.

11-22. With wire stretchers in place, cut fabric two diamonds away from terminal post when pliers are used to hand stretch fabric between stretchers and post.

Here is an easy way to cut the fabric. Trace same vertical strand of wire from top to bottom of fabric. Using wire cutters or heavy-duty pliers, cut wire at top and bottom. Then twist loose wire from fabric diamonds to leave a neat edge.

11-21

11-22

11-23

11-24

11-25

11-23. With the aid of helpers, weave tension bar through end diamonds of fabric, as shown.

11-24. Now place tension bar inside seven tension bar clamps, evenly spaced around post as described in step 17. Tighten bolts.

11-25. Next release tension on fence stretchers. Then remove them. Now remove the two 4-foot tension bars used to fasten one end of the fence stretcher cables. Finish stretching remainder of fence in the same way.

11-26

11-26. Tie fabric to top rails and intermediate rails at intervals of 2 feet with #9-gauge soft annealed galvanized steel or aluminum wire. Also, use five ties to fasten fabric to line posts, starting about 6 inches above grade and finishing about 12 inches from top rail. Space intermediate ties approximately 2 feet apart.

Be sure to leave ends of ties facing outside so a tennis ball with not be damaged if it comes in contact with them.

Complete fabric installation by fastening it every 2 feet to bottom tension wire with #11-gauge galvanized steel hog rings.

11-27. Now fasten the fabric, called a transom, over gates from terminal post to gate post, using tension bars and clamps as previously described for fastening fence fabric in place. Generally, hand stretching with the use of pliers and a helper provides satisfactory stretch. Complete transom installation by tying fabric to top and intermediate rails as previously described. No tension wire is required in this step.

11-27

11-28. Complete the fencing job by installing the gates.

Although a gate 5 feet high is used here, with nothing between it and the transom of fencing over it, I recommend using a gate 7 feet high, completing the opening with a transom of fencing extending the full height of the fence.

Bolt two female hinges *A* and *D* to post, then

11-28

bolt male hinge *B* to bottom of gate frame with pintle pointed down. Position gate with male hinge pintle fitting inside female hinge. Next position male hinge *C* around gate frame with pintle pointing up. Then slide the male pintle up into female hinge *D*. Tighten male hinge bolt *C* securely. Bottom of gate should be in line with bottom of fence and gate should open and close freely.

Complete gate installation by bolting two-way gate closer latch *E*, at a convenient height, to gate frame opposite hinges. Be sure closer latch is designed to accept padlock.

WINDSCREENS

Is it a *windscreen*, is it a *backdrop*, or is it *curtaining*? The way these terms are sometimes used synonymously, some players might think they refer to one and the same thing. But they don't, really. Recently, I heard a tennis court equipment manufacturer explain it this way. "Backdrops represent indoor courts, while windscreens represent outdoor courts. Curtaining is an all-inclusive term used to represent any material, such as canvas or synthetics, used as a windscreen or backdrop, or as between-court separators."

Perhaps these are not iron-clad definitions, but they serve as good conversation pieces to the following material on windscreens, backdrops, and curtains.

Advantages

Although windscreens are designed to be as unobtrusive as possible, they are almost as important to tennis players as the court itself, for they serve six important functions.

1. They dress up the court, much like a feather dresses up a hat.

2. Their dark color provides a pleasing background for the players.

3. Their existence prevents the ball from blending into nearby surroundings, such as light-colored objects or vehicles, making the game difficult to play.

4. They provide a certain amount of privacy and tranquility by blocking out spectators and other distractions.

11-29a

11-29b

5. They slow the wind speed so the game can be played under more favorable conditions.

6. They do much to deflect the sun's rays from the surface.

Making a Selection

Many windscreens are made of a vinyl material called polypropylene. This is a lightweight material that cleans easily, is resistant to the ultraviolet rays of the sun, and does not fade or dry out. For these reasons it has wide use for outdoor courts.

There are fiberglass windscreens, such as the ones manufactured by J. P. Stevens and Company. They are easy on the eyes, will not dent, shrink, stretch, burn, or disintegrate, and are resistant to salt air, sunlight, and industrial fumes.

11-29. Like so many other windscreens on the market, these fiberglass ones are procurable in either open pattern (*a*) or solid pattern (*b*).

Although a solid pattern offers more privacy, open patterns are recommended, and are becoming more and more popular, for areas known for their high winds.

Some owners of courts in extremely windy areas cut wind resistance by actually cutting windholes in open pattern windscreens. Other owners do not cut a complete hole. Rather, only the bottom and both sides of a given area are cut, leaving the top edge to serve as a hinge. This provides a series of flaps which are better than "open windows" because they maintain most of their protection from light and at the same time lose little of their privacy. When the wind blows, the openings serve to relieve wind buildup behind the windscreens. Of course there are some directed streams of air pouring through the holes, but these create only minor problems compared to damaged windscreens and possible fence damage during heavy blows.

Your personal tastes have priority when it comes right down to the bottom line in making a selection. How much area do you want to cover? For example, if yours is a fence 10 feet high, you might want a 6-foot curtain with 2 feet of fence exposure top and bottom. On the other hand, if more protection is in order, a 9-foot curtain centered would allow only 6 inches of exposure, top and bottom.

If you plan to handle the installation and removal of wind curtains by yourself, 60-foot lengths are about the maximum for easy handling. There's little point in trying to maneuver longer pieces, since joining them is a simple matter once they are installed.

Backdrops for indoor courts are simpler to select because wind, unwanted spectators, sunlight, etc., are not problems. Therefore, it is more or less a personal matter whether you select backdrops of canvas, fiberglass, or polypropylene, so long as the color is dark green, which is easy on the eyes.

Here's a claim worthy of consideration, made by a good many tennis players: "Sidekick" is a problem with a vinyl backdrop caused by a sheen on the material. This, they claim, causes the balls to spin off when they hit it. Also, they claim the film puts a glare across the backdrop. Of course, these criticisms are not true of canvas or fiberglass, both of which absorb light rays.

Conditions in your area should determine method of windscreen installation. If the area is constantly struck with gusty winds, shop around until you find a windscreen with a breakaway system of installation. Otherwise, there is always the possibility of wind creating a billowing effect, which could damage the windscreen or even bring down sections of the fence.

As you examine some of the common zinc-plated S hooks used for fastening windscreens, notice that some manufacturers "close" the ends of the hooks that are fastened through the grommets of the material, while the ends fastened to the fence remain open. When a high wind descends upon the court, the curtain will attempt to billow, causing the S hooks to straighten out. This automatically releases the curtain, saving both damage to it and the fence. New S hooks are dirt cheap if you compare their cost against possible curtain and/or fence damage. And the best part of it is they can be purchased locally from your hardware store.

Since wind is not a problem with indoor courts, any method of installation that meets your fancy is quite satisfactory for fastening backdrops in place.

12

Indoor Court Structures

If you're planning an indoor tennis facility, spend considerable time and effort in selecting the site, choosing a type of building to best serve your needs and pocketbook, and obtaining quality construction. If you're thinking about putting up an air-supported structure or a permanent building, spend several hours learning all you can about the ins and outs of different type structures and what they have to offer. It's a better investment than any gilt-edged security you can purchase. Becoming knowledgeable will enable you to enjoy the income from your securities and at the same time be reasonably sure of not having a "white elephant" cover your court.

Clear the site, excavate and fill, and install a drainage system, if required, prior to constructing a permanent building. Complete the court, including the surface, prior to erecting an air-supported structure.

Theoretically, all court surfaces designed for outdoor use can be installed indoors. From a practical point of view, however, most porous surfaces require moisture on a daily basis. Watering increases humidity, and, most likely, this is what you don't need. It may create condensation problems as well as complicate heating and air-conditioning systems. For obvious reasons, a grass court is much too difficult to maintain indoors.

SITE SELECTION

Select a site that is reasonably level. Otherwise, expensive excavation and filling could eat deeply into your budget. The site should be large enough to house the court structure, as well as to provide for expansion if you have reason to add additional courts later. Also, zoning generally requires a setback of a specified distance between a building and adjacent lots or streets.

If you are purchasing land for the court, check other zoning or deed restrictions for security against decline in desirability due to encroachment of inharmonious land uses, resulting in objectionable smoke, odor, noise, or unsightly buildings. Site location should not be endangered by flood water, conflagrations, erosion, or subsidence which might damage or even destroy your court and building.

Before signing on the dotted line, have a soil test made, or you can do it yourself with a posthole digger. Look for "filled" land, soil drainage, suitability of growing plants and trees if your plans call for this kind of landscaping. If filled land hasn't been compacted properly, or if a former junkyard was simply covered over with dirt, part or all of your court could become a poor excuse for a swimming pool.

Here are some additional points to consider when purchasing land:

Is the asking price complete, or are there assessment or other fees outstanding?

Is the title to the site free and clear? Check with your attorney to be sure.

Are taxes paid up to date on the site?

Have your attorney check title for any easements which give special privileges to individuals or companies. For instance, you couldn't afford to erect a building only to discover later that part of your building would be involved with telephone or electrical lines crossing your site. The playing surface wouldn't be improved if someday, just after an interesting match, you found out that a sewer or water line was scheduled to be laid right under your net.

Are the boundaries of the site correct as represented? A qualified land surveyor can tell you in a matter of minutes, and his fee will only be a drop in the bucket compared to your investment.

STRUCTURAL SOUNDNESS

"No worry for me about whether the structure is sound or not," recently remarked a neophyte tennis player. "I'm letting a contract for the complete structure. Let the contractor do the worrying," he boasted. How wrong he was. The contractor built the building, but it was substandard. He didn't worry, but the neophyte did enough worrying for both of them when his building literally fell apart at the seams. In the meantime the contractor dissolved his corporation, so there was no one to sue for damages and misrepresentation of facts.

Any structure you put up should be 120 feet in the clear to accommodate the length of the court in addition to the space behind the lines. The eaves should be between 16 and 20 feet above the court surface, and the center of the building should have a minimum height of 35 feet. Structural members projecting into the playing area, such as pillars or beams, should be well padded with shock-absorbent material, such as foam rubber, beginning at 12 inches and extending to 6 feet above the playing surface.

Here are some structural defects that you can expect from any type of poorly constructed tennis court buildings: damage by heavy winds; lack of proper stress and strain precautions during construction, causing the building to collapse under heavy snow or ice; the breaking and crumbling of concrete and masonry work. Water leaks of all kinds are a hazard of improperly constructed buildings, along with poorly fitted trim around doors and other parts of the building, doors that stick or don't operate properly, and peeled or blistered paint because of an inferior product and/or improper preparation of the surface.

Other major pitfalls are mechanical equipment, such as heating, air conditioning, plumbing, that is in constant need of repair or fails to provide proper service; electrical wiring or prewired equipment insufficient for usage and presenting an everpresent fire hazard.

What are all the causes? Generally, you can sum them up in six little words: *poor materials*, *poor workmanship*, and/or *poor design*. Carefully look through your building contract for flaws in construction specifications that could result in the three "poors." Have it evaluated by a disinterested contractor if necessary.

PNEUMATIC AIR-SUPPORTED STRUCTURES

If you have looked into the possibility of putting your court under cover and were stunned by the skyrocketing costs of constructing a conventional building, there's another way to go. It's the pneumatic air-supported structure, sometimes referred to as a "bubble building."

Bubbles are relatively new. During the early 1950s a need for low-cost buildings was recognized by a number of architects, engineers, and manufacturers. One such early pioneer was architect Frank Lloyd Wright, who demonstrated a full-sized dwelling that could be deflated and hauled away in a station wagon.

Air-supported structures are made of a thin skinlike material somewhat like balloons held up by air pressure; they are manufactured to shapes to meet almost every kind of housing requirement. Most coverings are made of vinyl-coated nylon or dacron.

The structures are kept inflated, ventilated, and heated by low-pressure air, supplied by a mechanical blower system. Most of the air is recirculated. In case of a power failure, a backup emergency generator automatically kicks in to furnish the power.

The first question most commonly asked is, "If I'm playing tennis and the building for some reason collapses, will I get hurt?" If the blower system should fail, the structure deflates very slowly, providing ample time to exit.

The second question is, "How safe are they?" The question could be answered with another question. How safe is any building, including your home, in a tornado? A far better answer is provided by the Canvas Products Association International, St. Paul, Minnesota, in their "Minimum Performance Standard For Single-Wall Air-Supported Structures," a twelve-page document originally issued in 1961 and approved by Air Structures Division in March of 1971. In part, it explains that with any new product, the design criteria and manufacturing methods are not uniform throughout the industry, resulting in some products offered to the public that are deficient in both design and performance. To remedy these conditions, major manufacturers policed their own industry. They recognized a need for proper controls to protect the public interest and safety and to provide recommendations for towns and cities to incorporate into their existing building codes. Therefore, a standards committee was organized, with seven companies represented, to standardize building and installation procedures.

One of the standards requires an air-supported structure to withstand winds up to 75 miles per hour. Some manufacturers say they can provide even more stable structures where greater wind velocities are experienced. To be on the safe side, be sure the structure you purchase was built by a member company of the Air Structure Association and will be installed according to their specifications. Then to be doubly safe, do as many other owners of air-supported structures are doing: Install a windometer nearby, and when the wind speed reaches 50 miles or whatever you judge unsafe, stop play immediately and evacuate the building. Edmund Scientific Company, Barrington, New Jersey carries several different styles of anemometers (measuring wind velocity), ranging in price from $2.50 to $47.

You may wonder what effect the jump in energy costs has on an air-supported structure. On an older one, the "bite" can be quite severe, because the thin-skinned bubble was not intended to serve as an insulant. Not so today. You can purchase a skin with an inner thermal and acoustical liner permanently fabricated into the membrane. As a result the trapped air insulation can cut heating and air-conditioning costs as much as 50 percent compared with older designs. Since a structure can be taken down and put up and inflated in a relatively short time, many owners store theirs during the summer months, cutting air-conditioning costs to zero.

In general terms, air structures cost in the range of 30 percent that of permanent structures. Like any permanent building, total costs depend upon what amenities you would want included. For example, Air-Tech Industries markets an

air-inflated structure large enough to house one tennis court for $35,775. This includes a 1,000,000 BTU heater. It does not include installation, a harness system, an anchor test kit, or a lighting system, which sell for an additional $5000.

There's also a bright side to the financial picture. You can start with just the basic structure and blower system. Then add other amenities and luxuries in the future. Cost pains can be further eased by seeking a company which has a lease plan in its offerings.

In summary, if you are looking for a way to play tennis in comfort the year round, rain or shine, but are prudent and ecology minded, investigate air-supported structures. After all, there are more than 1500 of them in use around the country, housing everything from college classrooms to tennis courts. Here's how an Air-Tech Industries air-inflated structure designed for a tennis court progresses from delivery to the site of completion.

Courtesy of Air-Tech Industries, Inc.   12-1

12-1. It used to be that buildings on the site went with the house, like the kitchen sink. When you sell your home, your tennis court building made of either vinyl-coated nylon fabric or vinyl-coated polyester fabric can be rolled up just as it is when delivered, and put into the moving van with the rest of the furniture.

12-2. The site requires no additional preparation, other than what is required for building the court. Here air structure and inflation equipment are placed on concrete pad. Inflation equipment is hooked up to fuel and electricity.

12-3. Workman uses 85-pound jack hammer to drive Air-Tech's Spearhead Anchor System

Courtesy of Air-Tech Industries, Inc.   12-2

Courtesy of Air-Tech Industries, Inc.   12-5

assembly (including steel cable) to a depth of 6 feet. Then with use of a jack or other lifting device and a scale, a pull is made until anchor holds and a reading is taken to be sure the assembly will do the job for which it is intended.

12-4.   First, the air structure is rolled out on the ground for joining at site and anchored.

12-5.   Next, the air structure is inflated with air, fed in at low pressure of .036 pounds per square inch (which also supplies ventilation) from blowers outside the structure. No other form of support is needed. Inflation takes only 15 minutes.

12-6.   The revolving door is designed for use as an entrance for high or continuous traffic ap-

Courtesy of Air-Tech Industries, Inc.   12-3

Courtesy of Air-Tech Industries, Inc.   12-4

Courtesy of Air-Tech Industries, Inc.   12-6

plications. It is bolted to a concrete pad poured adjacent to the structure ground line through the bolt-down tabs. Figure 12-6 shows fabric boot attachment sewn to the fabric envelope of the structure, and being attached to the door with fabric clamping strips provided. Available, too, are air locks and equipment doors in a wide range of sizes and designs to accommodate the passage of large equipment.

Courtesy of Air-Tech Industries, Inc. 12-8

given to the pole design so that when a structure is removed, the light poles and all connections are also removed, leaving no hazardous obstruction on the site.

12-8. Air-Tech has engineered a unique heating-inflation system combined in a single unit for maximum efficiency. Temperature in the Sportstructure can be thermostatically controlled, to maintain as high a temperature as 80°F. The heater-inflation system supplies all the air necessary to inflate and shape the air structure. During the heating season, the unit will automatically provide freshly heated temperature controlled air. Summer operation provides outside air for inflation only. Figure 12-8 shows caloric inflation ducts attached to inflation heater exhaust.

12-9. Here's the way completed air-

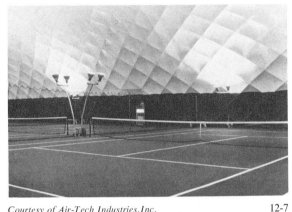

Courtesy of Air-Tech Industries,Inc. 12-7

12-7. The Sportstructure is translucent. During the day—although you don't see through it—it is as bright as daylight inside. Lighting for night use is easy because the structure is white and dome shaped. It has a highly reflective internal surface which, when lit indirectly, produces bright overall indirect illumination which is even and shadow free. Special consideration has been

Courtesy of Air-Tech Industries, Inc. 12-9

12-10

supported structure looks from the outside with the cable harness system installed. This is a network of plastic-coated cables that are interlocked and encapsulated over the entire fabric envelope in two directions.

Six or seven years is a conservative estimate of Sportstructure life expectancy without the cable harness system. After that it can be restored to "mint condition" for less than half of the original cost. However, the cable harness system significantly reduces tension on the fabric envelope. By reducing the tension and loadings imposed on the fabric (stress relief), the life and structural integrity of the fabric is increased by as much as 25 percent.

12-10. Stepping inside, there's nothing more to do. You just pick up a racket and play tennis anytime you want, year round. There's no cleaner sport anywhere.

STEEL FRAME/FABRIC MEMBRANE STRUCTURES

12-11. Portomod is a packaged clear span structure featuring an exceptionally high-strength tensioned fabric membrane cover supported by contoured arches of rigid steel. It is not an air-supported structure and is available on a lease contract basis for a minimum of 3 to 5 years

with options of renewal or outright purchase from the Seaman Building Systems (which also manufactures air-supported structures). At this writing, the lease costs approximately .08¢ per square foot per month, while the purchase price is listed at $32,959 for a structure covering one court.

The structure can be erected on a simple foundation on any level hard surface, earth, asphaltic concrete, or concrete. Authorized Portomod contractors are equipped to prepare your site and erect the structure in just a few days.

12-11

The structural frame utilizes heliarc welded steel trusses with light green zinc chromate.

Large volume, gravity ventilators with dampers are located at the vertex of each of the trusses.

The standard covering is a vinyl-coated fabric, woven from polyester yarns. It is weatherproof, fire-retardant, has exceptionally long life, and is maintenance free. This fabric, which is used as a roofing, is designed to support 30 pounds per square foot live loads and 100 miles per hour wind loads.

Portomod entries are steel framed and may be purchased with either manual or electrically operated overhead doors for vehicular traffic and similar framing for standard personnel entries.

Courtesy of Dome East Corp.   12-13

GEODESIC ALUMINUM FRAME/FABRIC MEMBRANE STRUCTURES

12-13. Tennisdome is a structure making use of the geodesic concept and is now available from Dome East Corporation at low cost and provides troublefree, clear span enclosures.

The fabrication of all components are ready for fast field erection, using a wide variety of materials in various colors, including metals, plastics, or wood.

This structure can be erected on any hard surface: earth, asphalt, concrete, even rooftops. It is lightweight, less than one pound per square foot.

The dome's continuous membrane is made of reinforced vinyl materials capable of withstanding hurricane force winds and heavy snow loads.

The membrane material is self-extinguishing and meets requirements of many tests such as ASTM D568, NFPA 701-1966, the California Fire Marshal test, and others.

If you like, a double membrane liner can be suspended to reduce the U factor from 1.2 to 0.6. A foam insulation liner can be added to further reduce the U factor to 0.15. Air can be circulated between the two membranes for cooling.

There are a minimum of two automatically controlled exhaust fans and intake louvers included per court. The sides of the membrane—bottom 12 feet—are removed or rolled up for summer playing and replaced with open mesh to restrain balls. Air conditioning is not necessary.

Tennisdomes are portable. At any time, the membrane can be taken down, the frame disassembled, and the entire structure easily moved or enlarged.

Courtesy of Seaman Building Systems   12-12

12-12. Tennis players at the Jackson Hole, Wyoming, Racquet Club play in perfect comfort, oblivious of the weather outside. Neither is lighting a problem, for the light interior acts as a reflector and provides a highly efficient lighting system when combined with artificial lighting.

Applications of the Portomod in varying climatic conditions are constantly proving the structure to be highly efficient in energy conservation. The opaque white-coated polyester fabric, comprised of white outside and white inside surface coatings, with a black layer sandwiched in between, provides an efficient barrier for reflecting cold and heat and preventing the "greenhouse effect" as well. Engineering evaluation has indicated the U factor in the vicinity of .53—better than 4 inches of brick masonry construction.

12-14

12-14. The picture shows the erection of Tennisdome's framework/membrane liner enclosure system that is designed for the single or multi- tennis court. Also, Tennisdome is a unique enclosure system whose sides are removable for rain and sun-sheltered summer use.

PERMANENT METAL BUILDINGS

12-15. The picture shows an American Buildings Company metal building housing the Boar's Head Tennis Club, Charlottesville, Virginia. Many shapes and designs are possible, so the owner can be as creative as he likes, ending up with a structure that is unlike any other in the country.

Metal buildings have wide clear-spans for maximum floor space usage. They are made of energy-saving wall and roof construction for lower utility costs. Generally, building occupancy is 60 to 90 days sooner than with standard construction, with original cost savings up to 30 per cent. Another important factor is that maintenance costs are minimal for years to come.

12-16

12-16. A crane makes erecting the structure a breeze, certainly not a job for the do-it-yourselfer. Note the block construction, which is being used as an add-on to this building. This is done quite often for shower and locker room facilities and sometimes used around the main building itself as a fire wall.

12-17. The framing shows the inherent advantages of clear span buildings for tennis, which can span up to 120 feet with 20-foot eaves and a 4-on-12 roof slope (which means it goes up 4

12-15

Courtesy of American Buildings Co. 12-17

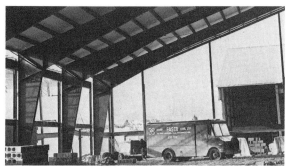

Courtesy of American Buildings Co. 12-18

inches for every 12 inches it runs horizontally up to one-half the width of the end of building). The structure gives the ideal clearance recommended by Lawn and Tennis Association for clearance under the net.

12-18. This picture gives one an overall view of sturdy construction as the building goes up.

12-19. Plenty of room here. The picture shows people playing on a five-court facility, following completion of the building.

Courtesy of American Buildings Co. 12-19

13

Maintenance

Almost everyone has done maintenance jobs of one kind or another—lawnmower, automobile, home, and yard, to mention a few. But did you ever stop to figure out how much time is wasted hunting up tools, putting them in working order, buying or chasing down materials for the job at hand? Any way you look at it, maintenance requires a certain amount of human energy. One tennis court owner put it simply, "It takes the sap out of me." Start by saving as much "sap" as possible. The old saw, every tool in place and a place for every tool, is improved upon when every tool is in proper working order, ready to use at all times.

Nothing is made to last forever and tennis courts are no exception. This is not to imply that your tennis court is headed for destruction within the foreseeable future. Just the contrary, for you can expect a lifetime of service from any type of well-constructed court, providing you give it TLC (tender loving care) and faithfully make minor repairs periodically.

COMMON PROBLEMS AND SOLUTIONS

Obviously, the majority of indoor courts fare much better than those outdoors for two very good reasons: They are protected from nature's harmful elements and people's carelessness and vandalism; because of the large investment, owners are prone to provide closer supervision.

On the other hand, outdoor courts are subjected to unwanted dirt, pebbles, grit, sand, leaves, twigs, and whatever else is usually brought in by the winds. As if this were not bad enough, people—sometimes thoughtlessly and sometimes purposely—play tennis in street shoes or sharp-edged basketball shoes, throw rocks or other debris on the court, break pop or beer bottles, and sometimes cut their initials or other grafitti on cushioned or other nonporous courts.

Of all the maintenance questions tennis court owners face, there are six problems that seem to be the most common. (Building trade solutions are found elsewhere in this book.)

1. I want to do the maintenance work myself, but where do I get the necessary equipment? See the section on maintenance equipment later in this chapter. It's necessary to purchase some of the equipment, but other pieces can be made by any do-it-yourselfer.

2. Watering the surface with a garden hose is one maintenance chore I am neglecting more and more. Isn't there some easier way to do the job? There most certainly is: *see* Chapter 9 for how to install an automatic sprinkling system to take the drudgery out of watering. There's even an inexpensive meter to install so you won't worry about spreading the correct number of gallons of water per hour as you sit in the shade and, perhaps, wonder if there really are 33,000,000 people in this country playing tennis—as recently reported by the editor of a leading tennis magazine.

3. How can I prevent leaves and twigs from getting onto the court? Trim back overhanging limbs. Sometimes, it's necessary to keep limbs properly trimmed from trees several feet from

the court proper. This includes dead limbs in close proximity to the playing area. At other times, the whole tree must come down. Trees are precious, but in some cases you'll have to decide which is worth the most—an open space free of blowing twigs and leaves, or a beautiful shade tree adding to your maintenance problems. Closely related to leaves and twigs are dirt and rocky areas that somehow have a way of cluttering the court. Planting grass or sodding the dirt area is easy to do, while the removal of rocks can be almost anyone's chore to keep pebbles from cropping up at the most inopportune time.

4. I don't want to hurt their feelings, but how can I prevent some of my best friends from playing tennis in street shoes? True, it is their feelings you stand a chance of hurting, but it is your pocketbook that is getting the beating. Sometimes it doesn't work, but diplomacy goes a long way most of the time in keeping friendships and at the same time extending surface life. Here's a starter: Have some signs painted stating "Tennis Shoes Only." Black letters on a yellow background can't be overlooked by the most color-blind players if you place the signs conspicuously, on each gate about head high. If the players are really good friends or even respectable patrons, they will usually abide by your wishes out of good sense. If a few still refuse to take the hint, meet them with a head-on confrontation that either they play in tennis shoes only or they don't play. So a few never come back, and you are money ahead. One tennis court club owner of my acquaintance solves the problem by carrying an assortment of tennis shoes in different sizes. These he rents for a not-too-modest fee, which has developed into an excellent motivating device for players to purchase their own shoes.

5. How can I extend the life of the surface and at the same time get the most use of the court? Good drainage is perhaps overlooked more than any other single factor. Good drainage is somewhat like having a baseball umpire call "four balls." Both keep the player in the game. Good drainage provides longer trouble-free surface life following showers; prevents delay or cancellation of games immediately after a heavy rain; prevents costly and unnecessary repair work by having flood water bubble up through the surface; prevents deluges from gradually undercutting edges of court, which may otherwise result in time-consuming repairs, often including re-

building the base as well as the surface. Usually, such erosion is caused by sudden falloff in the ground adjoining the court. Sometimes cures are effected by building a concrete trough to carry the water to a lower level. For a radical dropoff, the construction of one or more retaining walls—as described in Chapter 4—is the best solution.

6. I'm beset by vandalism. How can I eliminate it? Knowing that it is a menace to every kind of construction and that the national repair bill because of vandalism runs into millions of dollars each year is little comfort to the court owner facing a resurfacing job because a party or parties unknown made several passes over the court with a tractor fitted with lug wheels.

Closely related to vandalism is theft. For example, some nets are stolen for no other purpose than to discard them in the nearest garbage pail. Vandals and thieves, especially the amateurs, do not like to work their trade any harder than necessary. Therefore, make access as difficult as you know how. One of the best deterents is a regulation chain-link fence with locked gates completely surrounding the court. Although your fence dealer may tell you it is proper to position the barbed edge next to the ground, don't do it. Position the smooth edge next to the ground with the barbed edge just above the top rail, as recommended for the installation of industrial property fencing. If your fence has smooth edges on both top and bottom, string a strand of four-point barbed wire lightly above fence top. You may damage a few balls by so doing, but what's the cost of a few balls compared to the possibility of hundreds of dollars in damages due to vandalism? Most vandals and thieves think twice about possible body contact with the barbs as they contemplate vaulting over the fence.

Enclosing the court inside a steel building is another deterent. Knowing that such a building can be broken into if the vandals are determined, some owners further complicate unwanted visitations by encircling the building with a 6-foot chain-link fence, barbs up, with locked gates.

Supervision is another unwelcome sight to both vandals and thieves. Since it is virtually impossible for a family to provide personal supervision around the clock, some court owners, especially in suburban areas, pitch in with other property owners to hire a patrol person designated as an arresting officer by one of the local law-enforcement agencies. This can become quite costly, however. Personally, I've found the local police to be very responsive. Whenever a citizen with a valuable investment requests help beyond the call of duty, they provide patrols on an erratic schedule to make it as inconvenient as possible for shady characters to know exactly when they're around. Perhaps your police department will provide similar supervision.

Last but not least is lighting. Since thieves and vandals prefer working in the dark, don't cooperate with them. Keep the court lighted at night.

PERMANENT FIXTURES

The first order of maintenance business is to check out and correct any faulty permanent fixture that is unsatisfactory. If permanent fixtures check out to your satisfaction or have been corrected, your next step, applying the new surface, will assure you of a court as good as new. (Installation of permanent fixtures is described in Chapter 6.)

If the net-tightening mechanisms on the net posts are worn beyond repair, it's a simple matter to slip them out of their sleeves for replacement. Sometimes, however, it is not an easy matter to correct faulty net post foundations. Freezing and thawing, substandard concrete mixture, and substandard size are some of the causative factors that require corrections of net post foundations. If the net post foundation is not cracked and meets the specifications indicated in Chapter 6, but is out of plumb, remove just enough surface, base, and dirt materials so it can be restored to a plumb position when the net post is inserted inside the sleeve. If the net post foundation has deteriorated or shows signs of substandard construction, it's best to remove and replace it.

COURT MAINTENANCE AND RESURFACING

How much of a problem can a tennis court have before it is beyond the skill of a do-it-yourselfer? This is to say, at what point on a specific surface is the average tennis court owner well advised to turn the job over to a contractor? Sometimes, though, professional estimates can run into hundreds of dollars, so it is imperative to know two things: Recognize conditions or clues

that point to the need for cleaning, repairing, or resurfacing; and evaluate your own ability to perform necessary repairs and determine what jobs you should turn over to the pros.

Begin by taking a pencil to the basic checklist which follows. Once you have completed it, decide how many of the jobs you can do yourself. You may be able to effect a complete cure without costly professional help. This is especially true if you have built the court in the first place or have inherited one that can be repaired by an average do-it-yourselfer.

CHECKLIST

____Poor drainage adjacent to the court.

____Birdbaths in evidence when court is wet.

____Fast-dry court beginning to resemble a gravel pit.

____Surface in need of patching.

____Wear at base line great enough to cause trouble.

____Darkening or mottling of color on hard courts.

____Signs of shiny spots developing on hard surfaces.

____Playing lines fading or disappearing.

____Large structural cracks in surface extending through base below.

____Uneven settlement of court.

____Hairline surface cracks on hard courts, including concrete courts.

____Stains, especially on synthetic courts.

____Tears or cuts on synthetic courts.

____Worn spots on synthetic courts.

____Broken areas extending above or below grade on concrete courts.

____Signs of surface paint peeling on concrete courts.

____No specific fertilizing schedule for grass courts.

____Humpy, uneven grass court surface.

____Growth of algae in birdbaths on grass courts.

____Sporadic watering program for porous courts, including grass.

____Signs of weeds, such as broadleaf, crowding out the grass surface.

____Insects, such as cutworms, grubs, beetles, ants, etc., becoming troublesome on grass courts.

____Worn surface, including soil exposure, where players' shoes come in contact most often with the grass surface.

____Others.

POROUS TENNIS COURTS

Some owners of porous tennis courts are beating the high cost of maintenance by converting them into nonporous courts. On the other hand, many do-it-yourself owners have nothing but praise for their porous surfaces and for two good reasons: They provide luxurious underfoot comfort; maintenance costs are relatively inexpensive because, other than a few inexpensive materials, they can do it for nothing and get in some exercise at the same time.

For sake of improvement, however, there's always the possibility of converting clay and grit courts into fast-dry courts.

Courtesy of Robert Lee Co.   13-1

Fast-Dry Maintenance Schedule

The fast-dry court is gaining in popularity over other porous (soft) courts mainly because it allows play much sooner after rain. It has a low initial cost, medium ball bounce, and ease under foot, making it exceptionally popular with players of all ages.

Fast-dry courts require different maintenance operations at different times of the playing season to keep them in tip-top shape. The following schedule is designed to clarify the operations by bringing them out in the open, thereby making them self-evident.

Daily

Following play for the day:

13-1. Using a wide drag broom, before watering, hand drag it across the court. The picture illustrates use of an aluminum 7-foot Pro Drag Brush. It is wide enough to groom the whole court in nine sweeps, yet so lightweight a large child can handle it. It's also reversible, with straightedge top that doubles as a leveling scraper. Each day alternate direction of dragging operation. This violates the traditional principle of normal dragging and rolling following watering or a heavy rain, but by doing it you will have a velvety smooth surface. Here's why. During the course of play the surface is constantly developing hundreds of baby birdbaths due to players' shoes stopping, sliding, and digging on turns and stops. This leaves tiny bumps and lumps all over the court. Watering at this point would cause them to soak up some of the moisture, which would further cause them to "set up," thereby allowing the bumps and lumps to remain intact for the next day's players to contend with. But this one five-minute operation of dragging before watering breaks the lumps and bumps into minute particles, making a big improvement in the smoothness of the surface.

Water the surface until puddles form, as they will dry overnight. The idea here is to supply enough water to keep the fast-dry material "packed," thereby allowing for thorough penetration of moisture, including the top surface so it will hold enough moisture for the following day. This prevents the surface from becoming dusty and breaking up in small particles.

How much water will do the job is governed by two factors: the amount of rainfall, and the nature of the soil underneath the court. If there is an underlying dense or claylike formation, most of the water will remain within the court proper. On the other hand, if the underlying formation is sandy or consists of some other porous material, much of the water will filter down through it.

13-2. Sweep excess particles from the surface, including the lines. Figure 13-2 shows how the Pro line sweeper works. Clean tapes either before or after watering.

13-3. Using a 500 or 600-pound roller, roll the court when it is *moist* only. (A one-section water-filled roller should only be used in a straight forward-and-backward pattern, like a streetcar.)

If you want to speed up operations and still do a highly professional job, follow the practice of the lady in Figure 13-3. She is operating a Pro roller. This roller is designed to ready a battery of four courts in 20 minutes, with built-in brushes grooming the surface in the same operation.

Courtesy of Robert Lee Co.   13-2

How often to roll is a matter of individual choice. Some owners provide daily rolling. Some provide daily rolling on new courts for three or four weeks following dragging and watering. Others roll the court every other day. *Always* roll after a heavy rain. Then do it less frequently, something like three times a week.

Excessive rolling reduces drainage. If this is noticed, roll less frequently. Remove loose material from under the lines prior to rolling. Then the roller will keep them flat. Followup with nailing

Courtesy of Robert Lee Co.   13-3

loose lines as required. However, new synthetic tapes will lay flat anyway.

Weekly

Since running is heaviest in the baseline area, use a shovel to scatter (broadcast) a small amount of green granule material (usually about a half bag for the job) over the worn places. Then level with a 10-foot 2 x 4 or 7-foot drag brush scraper. To secure best bond between the surface and the new material, always do this job prior to a rain or watering. Sometimes this operation i's not required for several weeks. (Greenrock fast-dry material can be purchased from tennis court material suppliers, such as the Robert Lee Company.)

Periodically

Having one of the best fast-dry courts in the neighborhood calls for constant vigilance by the owner. Patching the surface and removing excess material are two of the most important maintenance operations in keeping the surface in A-1 condition. Categorically speaking, patching is either minor or major in nature.

Consider footprints or other small indentations, causing the surface to lose its smoothness, as indicators for making minor repairs. Spread some new green granule material in the depressions when the surface is dry. Then level and water the spots. Follow up by watering and rolling the entire court.

Sometimes major patching is necessary. For example, when the rock base and surface break up so that both materials are mixed together, to at least some degree, remove them. Then fill the hole with new green material, allowing it to extend level and about a quarter of an inch above the surface. Next water the patch. Then use a tamper to make it flush with the surface. If a number of holes are repaired, the use of a roller to level the repaired zones flush with the surface speeds up the operation.

Occasionally, a superfluous amount of "dead" green material builds up on the surface, bringing about bad ball bounce. Since the material has lost its binder contact, no amount of watering and rolling will compact it. It's easily recognizable by its "loose" look, along with an appearance of loosely scattered sand. Use a soft brush to gather it up for discarding.

Always keep the playing lines in good condition. For installing new lines, see Chapter 6.

Semiseasonal

To better keep the fast-dry court in a semidamp condition, evenly spread about 250 pounds of calcium chloride (secured from suppliers of fast-dry materials) over the court twice each playing season. With some courts three applications per season are necessary to do the job.

Annually

Each spring remove all loose material. Next true the surface by filling worn spots and indentations as described above. Then top-dress with from one to two tons of green fast-dry material; amount depends upon condition of the old surface. You can "broadcast" the material as explained above or you can use a mechanical fertilizer spreader either hand operated or attached to a riding lawn mower or a small tractor.

If you reside in a cold climate, you may want to protect the surface during the winter. Perhaps you have read or heard about using polyethylene and ordinary hay placed on top to a thickness of 8 or 10 inches. This may sound like a satisfactory procedure but it isn't. Robert Lee, President of Greenrock Fast-Dry Tennis Court Surfacing, has this to say about surface protection during cold weather: "Polyethylene is so slick it's almost impossible to keep the hay from ending up in one corner. One successful way is to use polyethylene, 8 inches of salt hay, then cover with chicken wire. This is an expensive procedure. Remember, if any heavy objects are placed on the court surface to keep the hay stationary, these will leave imprints in the court during periods of thawing. A practical, economical way to protect the court during the winter is to apply the salt hay directly to the court surface minus the polyethylene and heavy objects." If you decide to use polyethylene, use black since white is affected by the sun's ultraviolet rays and soon deteriorates.

Caution: When using power rollers, keep the speed to around 6 miles per hour. Make wide U turns to prevent damage to the lines and to prevent the wheels from "digging" into the surface.

Clay Courts

If the clay surface is worn, due to erosion or just ordinary wear, additional surface dressing is required. When the surface is brought to a satisfactory condition, a daily maintenance schedule of brushing, sprinkling, rolling, and cleaning the lines is necessary to maintain its marvelous playability.

As an owner of a clay court, you have a couple of options at your disposal: Set up a renovating program each spring and then maintain it during the playing season; changing the clay surface to fast-dry, maintaining it in accordance with the improvements made.

Renovating Program

1. If the surface isn't moist from a recent rain, thoroughly sprinkle the surface.
2. Using a 4-foot roller or one 36 inches in width filled with water, roll and cross the surface when the clay is still moist. Do not roll if puddles form on the surface. A roller attached to a large riding lawn mower or a small tractor makes rolling a breeze.
3. Spike the rolled surface with a spiking device, fitted with iron rakes, to a depth of ¾ inch.
4. Next use a bamboo rake to rake the loose clay, removing any small stones which may have worked to the surface.
5. Spread enough fresh-screened clay over the surface to replace any lost by wear or erosion. It's possible for the surface to be "dead" after several years of play, caused by too much sand in the clay. This is especially true if new clay has not been recently added. If this is your case, spread on additional clay to a depth of approximately ½ inch. Then spike the surface to a depth of 2 inches to bring clay to the surface. See Chapter 5 for properly preparing the clay.
6. Drag a grading device or a mat over the screened clay to restore a smooth surface.
7. Roll and cross roll with a lighter roller, weighing approximately 300 pounds. Here the advantage of owning a water-ballast roller filled or partially filled with water, as weight changes are required, is self-evident.
8. Now sprinkle a thin layer of screened clay over the rolled surface.
9. Drag and cross drag a light grading device over the surface to fill in small depressions such as birdbaths.

10. Again roll and cross roll, using a heavy roller of around 400-pound capacity.

11. Again sprinkle the rolled surface. When the live water in the surface has drained or evaporated, but is still moist, roll and cross roll.

12. Finalize the spring renovating program by spreading a thin covering of screened sand. Then level by dragging and cross dragging, followed by rolling and cross rolling. Put down the playing lines as described in Chapter 6.

Improving Clay Courts

I find many owners of clay courts improving them in one of two ways: upgrading the court, and converting existing courts to fast-dry.

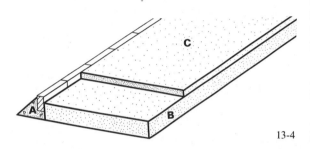

13-4

13-4.   The sectional view shows how to upgrade a clay court. Begin by installing a brick curb or wood header *A* as explained in Chapter 4. Allow the curbing to extend ½ inch above clay surface. Next begin the first operation by using a spiking device to loosen clay surface *B* approximately ½ inch deep. Then drag and cross the surface to powder and level the clay. Next spread a ton of fast-dry material *C* evenly on the surface. Then using rakes or a spiking device thoroughly mix fast-dry material with the clay. (It is best to spread the fast-dry material in four or five applications.)

The second operation calls for spreading evenly another ton of fast-dry material over the surface. Then roll and cross roll with a roller weighing approximately 400 pounds. Next spread evenly over the court 500 pounds of flake calcium chloride, purchased from fast-dry distributors, such as Robert Lee Company. When it has soaked in, roll and cross roll, completing up-grading of the court.

Each spring hereafter apply and roll an additional half ton of flaked calcium chloride to the court. Since fast-dry material protects clay, the

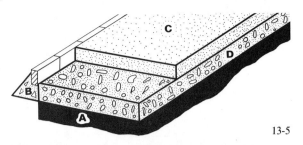

13-5

up-graded court is much easier to put in condition each spring, and the cost is small for the benefits gained.

13-5.   This sectional view shows two methods of converting existing clay or asphalt courts to fast-dry: The first thing to do is to evaluate clay or asphalt sub-base *A*.

If it is in good condition, build curb *B* so 1¼ inches extend above it. Then apply 1¼ inches of fast-dry material *C* directly on sub-base *A*. Make the application the same way as described for building a fast-dry court in Chapter 5.

Note: When clay or asphalt surface *A* is in good condition, stone screening base *D* is not required.

If the court is old and clay or asphalt *A* is in poor condition, build curb *B* 2¾ inches above it. Then construct stone screening base *D* 1½ inches thick directly over old surface *A* as indicated in the picture. Next apply 1½ inches fast-dry material *C* over sub-base *D*.

Note: Construct curb *B*, screening base *D* as described in Chapter 4. Make application of fast-dry material *C* as described in Chapter 5 for building a new fast-dry tennis court.

Grit Courts

Because cost, rather than playing characteristics, was foremost when building tennis courts twenty or more years ago, many of the installations have been allowed to deteriorate to the point where they are unacceptable to the demands of today's tennis players. Older grit courts serve as good examples. Perhaps, because they were built during the days of the great depression of the 1930s or shortly thereafter, they were built by the hundreds because both the original cost and the maintenance cost were cheap.

Once the grit court is evaluated (*see* Checklist), the owner has one of three options open to him: (1) Tear it out and start over by building a more modern court, such as a nonporous noncushioned or cushioned type as described in Chapter 5; (2) Improve or renovate it as described above for improving or renovating clay courts; or (3) make repairs to put it into good playing condition, which follows.

Do a repair job each spring. Playing and erosion has a way of wearing some areas of the surface more than others. If your grit court has numerous eroded and worn areas, use a straight edge about 10 feet long, such as a 2 x 4, to check the surface for levelness.

Use equal parts of good quality clay, which crumbles or powders, and sharp sand thoroughly mixed together to fill the worn areas and to give a new ½-inch topping to the surface. Drag and cross drag, checking with the straight edge to determine uneven areas. Next sprinkle. When the free water has evaporated or filtered into the surface, roll and cross roll with a heavy roller.

Once the surface is in good playing condition, maintain daily by sprinkling, rolling, and sweeping sand, including any on the playing lines, off the court.

To conserve water as well as to keep the court in semi-damp condition, apply approximately 400 pounds of flake calcium chloride to the surface two or three times during the playing season. Sprinkle and, after the water has had a chance to soak into the surface, roll and cross roll.

Grass

Grass courts are considered one of the most luxurious of all surfaces only if they are kept in good condition. This means a schedule of almost daily care during the playing season and a program of intermittent care during the winter season in cold climates. Ideally, of course, grass courts should be rested by alternating play between two courts. This is out of the question in most cases. Even so, a sound maintenance program is a must.

Most likely, the items you noted on the checklist can be corrected without too much difficulty. On the other hand, if the surface has been totally neglected it needs complete renovation. To keep the surface continually in good condition, let's concentrate on two main areas; namely, *renovating a grass surface and keeping a grass surface in good condition.*

Sometimes maintenance operations require the same techniques required to build a new court. Therefore, how-to-do-it techniques not described here can be found in the section on building grass tennis courts in Chapter 5.

Renovating a Grass Court

To cultivate a perfect grass surface, the soil is the most important consideration. So check by removing an 8-inch plug of it. If it is thick, black and crumbly, your court is in perfect shape to support deep roots, the secret of supporting a good stand of grass.

If the topsoil is thinner than 4 inches, you're in for an endless battle if you try to keep the grass alive. On the other hand, the right kind of topsoil will provide a better grass surface with much less work. Here's what to do. Before reseeding, spread a 2-inch-thick top dressing of sedge humus, leaf mold or compost and roto-till it into the soil. An alternative is to roto-till a 4-inch layer of good topsoil into the court. If in doubt about the topsoil quality have it checked (*see* Chapter 5 for methods of testing). You can rent a roto-tiller from a local tool rental agency. If compost is used, be sure all weeds and their seeds are completely rotted. Otherwise, you'll do a perfect job of reseeding the surface with weeds of one kind or another.

Courtesy of Montgomery Ward and Co. 13-6

13-6. Assuming your topsoil is now in good condition, level and without birdbaths, here are the steps necessary for renovating the court. Since seed sprout fastest in cool weather and grass grows faster, renovate the court during the autumn season if possible.

1. Set the lawn mower to its closest setting. Then mow the old stand of grass, being sure to remove the clippings. The purpose here is to destroy all unwanted growth.

2. Apply weed-killing chemicals that do not poison the soil.

3. Cultivate with a spiker or an aerator as shown in Figure 13-6.

4. Apply fertilizer and lime in amounts indicated by your soil tests.

5. Seed.

6. Roll.

7. Water.

8. Mow as soon as grass reaches height to cut, recommended by the seed manufacturer.

Conditioning a Grass Surface

Now that your grass court is ready to use, here are ten steps necessary for keeping it in tiptop shape:

1. Fertilize in the proper season, generally when the grass is thin or unthrifty. General practice calls for 20 pounds per 1000 square feet or about 50 pounds for each tennis court. Use commercial fertilizer of 5–10–5 or one close to this ratio. The numbers refer to percentages; i.e., 5 percent nitrogen, 10 percent phosphoric acid, and 5 percent potash. Since we are talking about averages for the country as a whole, it's best to check with local authorities as cited in Chapter 5. Apply the fertilizer in spring and early summer in warm humid regions and in early fall and early spring in cool humid regions.

2. Make annual soil tests. If the addition of lime is required, the best time for making application is late fall or early spring.

3. Mow frequently with a sharp, properly adjusted mower. Mowing does more than just cut the grass. It promotes tilling and causes the spreading of grass plants, making for a better surface on which to play.

4. Grass requires an inch of water once a week during a single watering. When the rains do not equal this amount, supplement with water from a hose or a watering system. It takes 2000 gallons of water distributed over the court to equal a one-inch rainfall. By all means, do not substitute a little sprinkling each day, since this forces the grass roots to turn upward for the water, thereby doing more harm than good. Also, constant sprinkling makes for excellent crabgrass growth.

5. When the ground is moist in the spring, give the surface a good rolling. This helps to firm the soil that has been loosened during the winter. This is particularly true in cold regions where the soil has been heaved by heavy frosts. If the ground "puddles," it's too wet to roll. Also, use a light roller or you stand a chance of compacting the soil too tightly.

6. A good crop of grass also acts as a weed preventive. However, to grow a weed-free surface, you should also apply artificial weed-control measures intelligently. Herbicides, crabgrass killers and the like all have their place in a weed-control program, but they must be used with care. Since conditions vary from region to region, find out what kinds of weed killers are best suited for your problem from your county agent or other professionals, mentioned in Chapter 5.

7. Closely related to a weed-control program is an insect and underground animal control program. Insects most troublesome in tennis court grass are mole crickets, chinch bugs, sod webworms, ants, army worms, cutworms, grubs, beetles, ticks, and chiggers. Ticks and chiggers won't harm the grass, but they'll make most tennis players take to the high country about as fast as anything. Again it makes sense to check with your county agent or other professionals on the best preventive measures for your particular problems.

Earthworms, any one of numerous annelid worms, are not insects, and they do serve a useful purpose by keeping the topsoil aerated, but if they become numerous enough to make the grass unsightly with their casts, the use of lead arsenate at the rate of 20 pounds per 1000 square feet, almost 60 pounds for one tennis court, is effective against them and grubs. There are other, newer insecticides your county agent most likely will recommend.

Caution: Lead arsenate, as well as many other insecticides, are poisonous to humans and animals. Keep them under lock and key when not in use, particularly if young children are around.

Moles, any of various small insectivorous mammals, are both good and bad, depending upon how one reacts to their work. They are good in that they keep the soil loose and rid the turf of many insects; they are bad in that their presence continually raises the topsoil due to their runs. Not only is ball bounce affected by them, but players continually run the risk of spraining an ankle everytime they step in a run. How to get rid of them? Some people trap them with mole traps. This, of course, is most inhumane. Others kill them with poisoned bait, which is no more humane than trapping them. Still others, like myself, dig them out of the ground alive and unhurt.

Here's the way to do a good turn for ecology and rid your court of moles at the same time. All you need is an empty gallon bucket and a garden spade. Moles have rather regular working hours, particularly during the morning. As they work, you can see the ground heaving upward. With spade and bucket in hand, tiptoe softly to about 3 feet in back of the new end of the run being made. As quick as lightning, ram your heel tightly into the run, blocking off the mole's retreat. Then start digging carefully forward. You should uncover the mole somewhere between your heel imprint and the spot where he was seen working. Using the shovel, gently place him inside the bucket. Because of the smooth sides, escape is impossible. What to do with him? Here's what I do. I have an arrangement with a farmer whereby I transport the animal to his large acreage, where I release it. Before pushing your heel into the run, be sure there is no intersecting run between you and the mole. If there is, he will use it as an escape route.

8. Grass surfaces are sometimes subject to disease. For example, bent grass is susceptible to attacks of dollarspot and brownpatch. Cadmium or mercury products are used to control dollarspot, while Tersan works well to check brownpatch. Use these materials only as directed by the manufacturer.

Since diseases attacking turf grasses are difficult to control, it's wise to secure professional help from your county agent or other specialists as indicated in Chapter 5.

9. Growths, such as algae, sometimes are mistaken for harmful diseases. Algae is caused by water standing in birdbaths. Filling the birdbaths with topsoil followed by reseeding or sodding again provides an environment suitable for healthy turf. Of course, correcting overall drainage is necessary if it is poor (*see* Ch. 5 for details).

Organisms called *slime molds* cause gray, unsightly patches in grass surfaces during wet weather. Actually, these are primitive fungi and are not harmful to the grass. When the surface is dry, brush them off the grass blades. You can

recognize the fruiting bodies of the fungi because they emit a "dust" or "smoke" when disturbed.

Grass roots must have air for the grass to survive. There's a procedure called spiking, guaranteeing air reaching the roots if you do it every autumn just prior to fertilizing the court. To do the job both quickly and effectively calls for two operations: Rid the surface of thatch, a tough fibrous mat of old grass clippings, leaves, etc. that has gradually built up under the blades and is smothering the grass, even acting as a device to carry water away instead of allowing it to percolate down to the root system. Do not use a garden rake to clean out the thatch as it will rip out the grass roots as well. By renting a power rake from a tool rental agency, you can loosen the thatch without harming the root system. This is a one-time operation if, in the future, you equip your lawnmower with a clipping catcher. To be on the safe side, every spring use a bamboo rake to go over the surface. This rids it of winterkilled grass. Use a power-operated spiker or a spiked roller. Both are rentable at tool rental agencies. If you own a power lawnmower, you can use an aerator attachment to it as shown in Figure 13-6.

NONPOROUS, NONCUSHIONED COURTS

Asphalt Types

No tennis court is absolutely immune from maintenance, and nonporous noncushioned courts are no exception. However, there is a difference in requirements from surface to surface and from court to court. Each one requires some form of a maintenance program that eventually leads to a point of resurfacing.

Having a no-maintenance tennis court is wishful thinking. After all, players grind sand, grit, and dirt into the surface as they play the game. If you have not experienced air pollution, small rocks, pins, nails, tree sap, leaves, and other foreign matter having a way of getting on the surface, you are one of the lucky few. For instance, if your outdoor court is several years old, it is bound to show signs of wear if for no other reason than from nature's elements, as ice and snow in the north and blazing sun in the south are doing their best to deteriorate the surface.

Systematically cleaning, repairing, and periodically resurfacing a hard court plays an important role in having at one's disposal a lifetime tennis court as relatively free of problems as is humanly possible.

Cleaning the Surface

The prerequisite to putting into effect a cleaning schedule is the keeping of an "eagle eye" open for minor damages as they occur, then repairing them to save expensive major repairs later. Frequently the "eagle eye" pays dividends in preventing damage from happening in the first place. For example, it is common practice in the north for some owners to flood their courts in the winter for ice skating. It is a simple way to make the playing area multipurpose, but it may result in surface damage if the ice isn't thick enough or skaters are permitted to enjoy themselves as the ice is melting. Another common example is damage caused by lack of supervision where players wearing improper shoes get onto the court.

By now, your checklist probably indicates a number of reasons to clean the court. Let's think about a regular cleaning schedule which should drastically reduce emergency cleaning in the future, and you'll have a better playing surface for it.

First, using a stiff-bristled brush, give the court a good scrubbing every other week. Check with the manufacturer for cleaning instructions recommended for your type of court. However, a mild detergent and water can be used for general cleaning as well as for removing ordinary run-of-the-mill stains and normal contamination. Follow up with a thorough rinsing of clean water. It is imperative that you flush *all* detergents or other cleaning agents off the surface. Otherwise, you run the risk of residue creating a dangerous, slippery surface.

It's considered good practice to remove stains immediately. Unless your cleaning instructions state otherwise, use 2 ounces of tri-sodium to a gallon of clean water to remove the stains. Then follow up by rinsing the area with clean water.

Second, avoid the grindstone effect between shoes and surface, creating an abrasive effect. Although rains usually do a good job of surface washing, they can also leave a residue of mineral content brought on the court from surrounding areas. Air-borne dirt is another problem to consider. So how often to hose off the court? Some authorities say every other week; others, every week. Actually, you'll have to set up a rinsing schedule to suit existing surface conditions.

You can drag out a couple hundred feet of garden hose every time you clean the court if you like doing things the hard way. On the other hand, you can do it the easy way by installing enough hose bibbs so a 50-foot hose is long enough to do the job. Still, if you want to cut the use of human energy to almost zero, you can install a sprinkler system. Then all you do is to open a valve to start the court rinsing job, sit in the shade until it is finished, then close the valve (*see* Ch. 9 for installing a sprinkler system).

Resurfacing

If your checklist indicates a need for court repairs or a complete resurfacing job, here are some suggestions to consider in making the restoration almost as good as new.

First, let's consider resurfacing the court, the most expensive of the renovating jobs. If the surface is beyond the point where an addition of a color coat will not do the job and the basic structure, including drainage, is in good condition, resurfacing is in order. For information on resurfacing, see Chapter 5. Follow the resurfacing with repainted playing lines (explained in Ch. 6); this should provide a satisfactory tennis court for at least another five or six years.

As when building a new asphaltic nonporous surface, this is a job for the pros. Before resurfacing, however, check with the manufacturer about definite requirements so the new surface will give satisfactory service. I've found most manufacturers willing to cooperate by furnishing complete specifications which their crews or local tennis court contractors should follow when resurfacing.

Second, let's consider repairing the court surface. If it is badly worn, only a resurfacing job can restore it to its proper playing condition. Fortunately, however, sometimes the surface isn't as badly worn as it first appears. If the damage is slight, a light application of acrylic coating can give the appearance of a resurfaced court.

How long has it been since a sealer was applied to the surface? As most tennis court contractors will attest, the asphalt is oxidized by the rays of the sun. Occasionally, a sealer applied to the surface protects the asphalt, thereby keeping it in top condition.

Making surface repairs have at least two pleasantries. They are reasonably inexpensive and you stand a good chance of doing some, if not all, of them yourself.

Like any other highly specialized field, the pros differ on making spot repairs. They can be done claim some, but they are quick to point out that repairing cracks or birdbaths always leaves noticeable spots on the court because fresh color cannot be matched exactly with older colors due to fading caused by rays of the sun. Such an argument leaves a question with the owner. Is it better to place a greater value on aesthetics than on making minor repairs with off-color spots showing up here and there? Most court owners couldn't care less about having a few spots slightly off-color, so they make minor repairs when needed if for no other reason than to save costly, larger repairs and premature resurfacing later. Because of this feeling, some manufacturers offer their customers repair kits including filler materials and an assortment of colors to select from. Perhaps the manufacturer of your court surface has such a kit for sale.

Hairline Cracks

Recently, I heard a reliable tennis court contractor say, "A properly constructed surface will not have hairline surface cracks." Comforting words, indeed, but unfortunately they do occur. If you're one of the unfortunate ones and want to make repairs, the best time to do it is in late fall or early winter. During cold weather the cracks are larger due to surface contraction, making it easier to get repair material down inside them.

Structural Cracks

Having structural cracks in the court is somewhat like having ghosts in the closet. For when either break out of hiding, you're in for real trouble. To find out whether or not cracks are structural, cut the bottom end of a wire clothes hanger near one end. Then poke it lightly into the cracks at several points to find out if you have only wide surface cracks or structural cracks.

Here's the way to bridge structural cracks so as to stop progression. Begin by using the manu-facturer's recommended crack filler, following instructions to the letter. Some companies advise repairing structural cracks when it is raining or just before a rain and the temperature is at least 50°F. Other companies recommend doing the job when the temperature is over 55° F.

Miscellaneous Cracks

There are any number of reasons, in addition to the ones given in this chapter, why tennis court surfaces crack. The important point is to try to determine the cause of cracking. Then take proper steps to correct the cause.

If you reside in a cold climate and the drainage around the court area is poor, surface cracks could be caused by the base or portions of it heaving upward and downward due to freezing and thawing of the soil and/or base. Signs to look for are net posts off the perpendicular and a slight up and down hill cracked surface, checked by using a straight 2 x 4 about 10 feet long and a carpenter's level.

If the cracks are by the hundreds and form patterns resembling jigsaw patterns, most likely the surface was not properly applied. Here it is best to obtain a surface manufacturer's recommendations on proper steps to take. Otherwise, you may end up with a large expenditure of time and money and still have an unsatisfactory surface.

If the surface was put down over a cracked base or over a concrete base with joints other than one at the net line, the problem usually shows up as cracks resembling the surface characteristics of the base. So if the cracks resemble joints, large blocks, or irregular patterns, there is a likely chance the problem lies in the base or in the soil underneath, especially if you live in a cold climate. However, if the surface is one of the asphalt types, the problem could be one of change in volume in the surface itself. If the surface is solid, you can lick the problem once and for all by installing a module surface, such as the Mateflex surface described in Chapter 5.

Patching Birdbaths and Voids

If your checklist indicates a number of birdbaths, it's better and probably cheaper in the long run to resurface the whole court rather than to spend an endless number of hours making repairs. Fortunately, if only a few birdbaths exist, you can repair them yourself.

The following steps show how to build up depressed surface areas, commonly called birdbaths, to keep water from standing in puddles, thereby speeding drying following a surface rinsing or following rains.

There are several good products on the market used for patching tennis courts. The product described and illustrated here is called Acrylic Plexibinder, manufactured by the California Products Corporation, which is an associate member of the U.S. Tennis Court and Track Builders Association.

Courtesy of California Products Corp.   13-8

Courtesy of California Products Corp.   13-7

a helper for this operation, one person at each end of 2 x 4.

13-11. Using a cement finisher's trowel, smooth the patch, being sure to feather edges so

13-7. Flood the court with water. As the court dries, birdbaths and worn areas are evidenced by standing water. Using a piece of chalk, outline each depression where depth of water is more than 1/16-inch deep.

13-8. For large jobs, pour factory mixed binder in a mechanical mixer. For small jobs, pour estimated amount from a 5-gallon pail into a clean wheelbarrow. Using a clean shovel, mix with enough water to bring the binder to a smooth-flowing consistency.

13-9. Now spread binder inside chalk line surrounding void.

13-10. Next, using a 2 x 4 (minimum length about a foot longer than void is wide), level the binder by slowly moving 2 x 4 to and fro, from one side to the other, as it is moved forward. Use

Courtesy of California Products Corp.   13-9

13-10

they blend into adjoining surface without leaving ridges or high places. No roller is required.

One final word. Whether your court requires repairs, recoloring, resurfacing, or just repainting of the playing lines, the best in materials and labor is none too good. Therefore be sure to select only a reliable tennis court contractor to do the jobs you do not do yourself.

13-11

Concrete Courts

If your checklist indicates a need for repair, there are three things that could have put it out of commission: it cracked, it settled irregularly, or it scaled or pitted.

Cracks

Are there cracks in the surface? If so, with a little time and a small amount of inexpensive materials, you can do the repairs as good as anyone.

13-12. First, chisel or saw out the uneven cracks to form a slight inverted V-shaped indentation as shown in Figure 13-12. The inverted V serves three functions: (1) Soiled concrete will not bond to newly mixed concrete, so forming the inverted V provides a clean surface suited for bonding; (2) it makes it easier to insert patching material deeper into the cracks; and (3) it prevents the cured patches from later working out of the cracks.

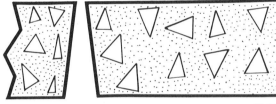

13-12

You can use a cold chisel and a hammer to form the inverted Vs if you have only a few small cracks to repair. If the number is large or even small in number but long in size, use a portable power saw fitted with a masonry blade. Set the angle of the blade at approximately 15°. As you saw down one side of a crack, one side of the inverted V is formed; returning along the crack forms the opposite side.

Caution: Wear safety glasses while using either the cold chisel and hammer or the portable power saw.

Preparing the mortar comes next. Using a wheelbarrow or small mixing box, mix two parts Portland cement to one part sand with just enough clean water to make a pliable working material similar in consistency to pancake batter. (*Always* mix the dry ingredients first; then mix with water to suit.) You can substitute a prepackaged sand mix, carried by most lumberyards. Some court repairmen object to using prepackaged mixes because they come only in 25, 45, and 90-pound bags, making them expensive products for small jobs.

Lightly rinse the inverted V cracks with clean water. Then using a pointed trowel (a large putty knife makes a good substitute) force mortar into moistened cracks, leveling off tops flush with tennis court surface. Do not have water standing in the cracks as you apply the mortar. Otherwise, the sand and cement will separate.

Before the mortar sets, clean excess on surfaces adjoining cracks with a moist rag. Here again, excess water has a way of getting into the repaired cracks where it separates the sand from the cement, making the patch useless. Let the court stand idle for 48 hours before playing on it.

Irregular Settlement

Does your court have an irregular surface because it was built with several section joints? If so, don't let anyone tell you "this is the way they were built in the old days." Unfortunately, some courts are built this way today. I personally know of a concrete tennis court that was built two years ago where an uninformed contractor constructed each half court with five section joints. As any expert would predict, each section acted independently of the others as they raised during freezes and settled during thaws, resulting in a most irregular surface.

Of course, there are other causes of concrete surface irregularities, to name a few: (1) Failing to properly compact either or both the aggregate base or the subsoil underneath it during original construction; (2) building the aggregate base over matter subject to decay, such as tree stumps, old land fills, etc; (3) land sinks caused by cave-ins of rooms and entries in abandoned mines of one kind or another; (4) originally constructing the court without the use of reinforcement rods or reinforcement wire, or during construction permit reinforcement materials to lie directly on top of the aggregate base rather than positioning them approximately 2 inches above it during the concrete-pouring operation.

If each half of the playing area is satisfactory with the exception of having different elevation, chances are the builder failed to install a concrete beam under the joint at net location (*see* Ch. 5 for beam construction details).

Older courts with irregular surfaces and many section joints may continue to cause problems after making repairs. If the surface of your court is relatively level and the irregularities seem to have stabilized, it has possibilities of being restored to good playing condition.

There are two methods of resurfacing an irregular concrete tennis court with new concrete: *thin bonded resurfacing* and *unbonded resurfacing*.

The *thin bonded* method is recommended if the court appears solid and there are only slight surface irregularities.

Begin by repairing the cracks as described in this chapter.

Next prepare surface for bonding to the resurfacing concrete. Mix one part muriatic acid (supplied by most hardware stores, some paint stores, and some ready-mix concrete companies) to five parts water. Mix well in a plastic container, since the acid will react with a galvanized container, leaving it in a blackened condition. Apply mixture freely to concrete surface with a cotton mop or a mop made of discarded rags securely fastened to a handle. The idea here is for the diluted muriatic acid to react with the surface, thereby giving "teeth" for bonding to the resurfacing concrete. When the court has been covered, begin rinsing with a hose at the starting point on the court. Be sure to rinse court until entirely free of acid.

Caution: Since muriatic acid reacts with human tissue, an ounce of precaution is worth a pound of cure. Work slowly and carefully. Wear rubber gloves, protective eyeglasses, and old shoes or rubber boots. If by chance the acid comes in contact with your skin, immediately drench affected area freely with clean water. *See* Chapter 5 for steps used in pouring concrete.

Form edges on outside of court with 2-inch lumber wide enough to extend ¾ inch above old surface. Hold form in place with 2-inch stakes spaced about 3 feet apart. Set up screeds. Then pour concrete topping and finish as described in Chapter 5 for building concrete courts.

Since the old surface presents a problem, screeds here are 1- x 2-inch (actually ¾ x 1½-inch) lumber. Hold them in place, flat side down, by first applying construction adhesive, then press the 1 x 2s in place. Use just enough adhesive so the screeds can be moved and reused down the court as you pour succeeding bays of topping until each half of the court is resurfaced.

Prepare topping by mixing one part Portland cement to 2½ parts sand with clean water in a mixing box to a consistency of pancake batter.

You can substitute a prepackaged topping mix in 90-pound bags secured from a lumberyard. Also, you can have a ready-mix company deliver topping mix to the site.

To further increase the bond between the old surface and the new topping, use a stiff scrubbing brush with an attached handle to scrub a slurry of Portland cement and water mixed to a consistency of house paint on the old surface. Here success lies in keeping the slurry of cement just ahead of the topping as it is being poured in place. You can't pour topping too soon, but if the slurry of cement turns white, it's drying and you are applying it much too far ahead of the topping application. Complete the operation as described in Chapter 5 for finishing a newly poured concrete tennis court, e.g., striking off, edging, finishing, and curing.

The 4-inch (actually 3½ inch) *unbonded resurfacing* method can be used if the thin-bodied method described above is impractical for your court, but yet is solid enough to act as a suitable base for resurfacing.

An unbonded resurfacing job boils down to using the old slab as a base onto which the new slab is built. Begin by covering the old court surface with 2-mil polyethylene. This serves as a bond breaker preventing control joints or other separations in the base slab from "telegraphing" up, thereby cracking the new slab. Next position 2-inch-thick form lumber on outside of court and 3½ inches above it. Hold in place with 2-inch stakes approximately 3 feet apart driven into the ground. Use 2 x 4s for screeds placed on top of old surface. Then proceed to pour and finish the resurfacing job exactly in the same way as when building a new concrete court (Ch. 5).

Scaling or Pitting

Does your surface show signs of scales or pitted places? Too much troweling in certain areas of the surface during construction can cause sand to work to the surface. In a short time the grains of sand work loose, leaving rough or pitted

places on the surface. Air bubbles not troweled out of the surface during construction leave large pit holes. De-icing chemicals containing ammonium sulfate and ammonium nitrate set up a chemical reaction with the concrete, causing the surface to disintegrate. For this reason they should never be used for melting ice on any concrete surface.

Use a cold chisel and wire brush to loosen partially fastened concrete chips from the surface. Next flush it thoroughly with water until all traces of loose concrete are gone. Then apply a bonded surface to the court as described previously in this chapter and in Chapter 5.

NONPOROUS, CUSHIONED COURTS

If you must maintain a synthetic court, the first thing to do is to recognize it as one of three types: (1) The newest type is manufactured in pieces and is installed somewhat like a patchwork quilt over a well-prepared base. In fact, some are so new that their manufacturers, without hesitation, brand them as experimental; (2) the asphalt-bound type consists of a cushioned surface installed over a concrete or asphalt base; and (3) the rubberized surface is squeegeed onto an existing base, then rolled smooth.

Maintenance is reduced to a bare minimum on all cushioned courts. Nevertheless, for the first month, good practice calls for cleaning them three or four times a week. After that a weekly cleaning is all the maintenance required.

How long before they require resurfacing? Because they are new on the market, many manufacturers like to say, "varies from court to court." However, they are quick to admit their products have not been on the courts long enough to give an accurate prediction of life expectancy. Nevertheless, from all indications they have a relatively long life, and maintenance is just about as close to zero as one can get with a tennis court. However, there does come a time when resurfacing is in order. When that time comes around, you may be in for a surprise, because manufacturers of synthetic courts have certain policies regarding who does the work. So check with the manufacturer to find out exactly how you can get the job done satisfactorily. Some sell their surfaces directly to court owners and recommend contractors. Others sell only to approved contractors who are authorized to install their product. There are others who have their own crews and will permit no one else to make installations even if they must travel halfway across the country to do it.

At first glance such stringent requirements may seem a bit severe. However, the reputation of any manufacturer is built upon how well his surface wears and how players enjoy playing on it. So at second glance, tight controls by manufacturers often are understood. After all, it's your interest and investment they are thinking about.

Synthetic Carpetlike Materials

Sheet plastics, small plastic squares, grasslike surfaces, and carpet materials come under the synthetic carpetlike materials. Instead of resurfacing with a traditional surface material, some owners are now having carpetlike materials installed right over their old surface. Ease of replacement and making repairs are the reasons cited for so doing. Actually, the surface never dies, since worn parts of the modular design are quickly removed and new modules installed, making the court like new again.

Carpet surfaces, too, aren't difficult to keep in tiptop shape. First, a good scrubbing does wonders for many of the courts where at first owners are positive they need complete resurfacing jobs. If your court has not had periodic cleanings, try a thorough scrubbing. You may be surprised at the results. Tears, cuts, unremovable stains, and worn spots present no major problem. Simply cut out the damaged areas and sew in new pieces of the same carpetlike material. If the base is sound, you may want to install a surface like Mateflex on top of it, as described in Chapter 5.

Asphalt Bound

If a regular surface cleaning schedule is followed, either a full acrylic or an asphalt emulsion and acrylic surface may last as long as six years before requiring a new top dressing. Otherwise, three or four years may be all you can expect before it's time for a new one.

There comes a time when all courts require resurfacing, and an asphalt-bound type is no exception. Also, like other courts, methods of re-

surfacing are different, depending upon a particular court's requirements. For example, a worn acrylic surface may require two or more coats to renovate it. Sometimes, though, releveling of the court is required. In such a case it may take several applications of asphalt emulsion applied and rolled prior to applying a new color surface.

For additional information, see sections on cleaning the surface and resurfacing asphalt-type courts, earlier in this chapter.

Synthetic Poured

After several years of play, one thing to watch for is the wearing off of the glass beads in the surface, caused by the ball hitting certain areas much more than others. If this is your problem, simply clean the affected areas. Then respray them with material recommended by the manufacturer.

If you discover the surface losing traction, this could be caused by worn spots produced by continuous play. Correction calls for resurfacing followed by applying a new color.

Before trying to repair or resurface urethane or other synthetics, contact the surface manufacturer for his recommendations before actual work is begun. These kinds of courts require different techniques, each one suited to a particular surface.

PLATFORM TENNIS COURTS

Set up a periodic inspection for examining the whole structure for loose or warped flooring boards, loose bolts, decayed lumber, scaled and worn paint, and termite invasion. The time between inspection periods varies from area to area, so you will have to decide when it's best to inspect.

Renail loose flooring boards, replace warped lumber, and replace decayed lumber; tighten loose bolts, use a steel brush to remove scaled paint, then paint as suggested in Chapter 7.

Although termite treatment is suggested in Chapter 7, never take it for granted that termites will never invade your platform tennis court.

13-13. Don't worry if you see termites swarming on the structure. Just know it's time for an inspection. Actually, termites cannot sur-

13-13

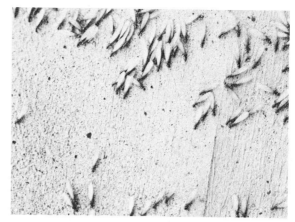

13-14

vive unless they are able to travel from the wood to the ground where they partake in large amounts of water, necessary for digestion.

Figure 13-13 shows what is left of floor joists in a house where termites were allowed to live without interference. The same kind of damage can happen to wood platform tennis courts.

Termites are somewhat like human thieves in at least one respect. Both like to work under cover of darkness. Therefore, remove any skirting material you may have between edge of floor and ground, allowing as much light as possible to penetrate underneath the floor.

Long before serious damage is done to the wood, however, telltale signs of small tunnels (about ¼ inch OD) are found from the infested wood along the piers to the ground through which the termites travel in perfect darkness. Start termite elimination by raking away these tunnels. Then treat for termite infestation as described in Chapter 7.

13-14. Don't let anyone tell you, "A few termites can't do much damage." They just don't come that way. Figure 13-14 is an example of only part of a termite colony on the move after man tore out just one infected wood timber.

Appendix

TABLE I.   Concrete Mixes and Functions

Proportions of materials*		Type of mixture	Where used
From ready-mix†	Use when mixing concrete your-self‡		
6-bag	1–2½–3½	High stress	Tennis court sur-faces, retaining walls, piers, roads, columns
5-bag	1–3–4	Standard	Sidewalks, arches, roofs, beams, gutters, footing pads, foundations, footings, filler for posts

*The first figure stands for cement, the second sand, and the third refers to the number of parts of stone or gravel. Do not use stone larger than 1½ inches for driveways and roads, ¾ inch for all other mixes. A bag of cement contains one cubic foot. Thoroughly mix the dry ingredients. Then mix again, using enough clean water, free of alkali, acids, or other foreign matter, to form a completely plastic and workable concrete. To add more water than needed weakens the concrete.

†Specify either 5 to 6-bag mix. The company takes care of properly mixing the correct amounts of sand and rock.

‡These proportions make approximately 4¾ cubic feet of concrete, depending upon grading of aggre-gate and amount of water added. Here's the way to figure number of cubic yards of concrete required: length x height x width. First convert inches to feet or fractions thereof. Then divide number of cubic feet by 27 (27 cubic feet in one cubic yard) to give amount of concrete required in cubic yards. For example, 18 piers 4 feet high x 12 inches square = 18 x 4 x 1 foot = 72 cubic feet or 2⅔ cubic yards.

TABLE II.   Mortar Mixes

Proportions of materials*	Where used
Packaged mortar mix†	Laying bricks, concrete blocks, etc.
1 part masonry cement‡ to 3 parts clean, fine sand	

*Be sure dry ingredients are thoroughly mixed. Then mix again, using enough clean water, free of alkali, acids, or other foreign matter, to form a completely plastic workable mortar. Do not skimp on water, it is essential to a good bond. One check for a good mortar is that it does not slop off the trowel when picked up. Clinging to the faces of masonry units even when they are inverted is a second check. Mixing additional water with stiffened mortar to keep it workable is acceptable for up to two hours, less time on extremely hot days. Discard mortar that begins to set.

†Purchase from lumberyards. Mortar mix is not to be confused with gravel-mix or sand-mix concrete.

‡Purchase from lumberyards. Masonry or plastic cement is not to be confused with Portland cement.

TABLE III.   Lumber Sizes

Specification sizes	Actual dimensions
1 x 2	¾ x 1½
1 x 3	¾ x 2½
1 x 4	¾ x 3½
1 x 6	¾ x 5½
1 x 8	¾ x 7¼
1 x 10	¾ x 9¼
1 x 12	¾ x 11¼
2 x 2	1½ x 1½
2 x 3	1½ x 2½
2 x 4	1½ x 3½
2 x 6	1½ x 5½
2 x 8	1½ x 7¼
2 x 10	1½ x 9¼
2 x 12	1½ x 11¼

Note: Where ⁵/₄ material is specified, its actual thickness is the same as specification size: 1⅛″ or 5 quarters. The actual dimensions of finished lumber is less than specification size because of drying and planing. When placing orders, list the specification sizes and not the actual dimensions.

Glossary

Aerator An apparatus used on soil so air can reach the roots of the plants.

Algae Simple green plants known by the scientific name of *pleurococcus* or *protococcus*.

Alternating current Back-and-forth movements of electrons through a conductor, such as an electric wire.

Ampere A unit used for measuring the rate of flow of electricity.

Apron Area adjoining a tennis court, usually 3 to 5 feet in width.

Band The strip of canvas fastened to the top of the net.

Birdbaths Small depressions in which water settles on a nonporous court surface following a rain or melting snow.

Bucksaw A frame consisting of two uprights or a curved pipe, to which a blade is fastened for cutting limbs and small tree trunks.

Building code A list of building trade rules and regulations designed for a specific community.

Building permit A document issued by a municipal government granting permission to build a certain type structure within certain boundaries of a particular zone.

Center mark The mark dividing the base line, defining one of the limits of the service position.

Center service line The line separating the right and left service courts by dividing the service court into halves.

Circuit Two or more wires through which electricity flows away from a source of supply to one or more pieces of equipment, such as a light, service outlet, motor, etc., and then returns.

Circuit breaker A safety device which automatically breaks the flow of electricity whenever a circuit becomes overloaded.

Conductor An electrical term used for denoting materials able to carry electricity.

Conduit A special galvanized pipe through which electric wires are run.

Coupling A plumbing fitting used to join two pipes.

Cross bridging Transverse rows of diagonal boards or struts positioned at right angles to the joists and fitted snugly between them.

Crosscut timber saw Usually two handles with an attached blade, for cutting trees and sawing limbs.

Crown Upper edge of a board having the form of a crown or convex surface due to warping.

Deed covenant A series of building and construction regulations written into property deeds intended to perpetuate the wishes and desires of the original owner.

Direct current Continuous movements of electrons in one direction through a conductor, such as an electric wire.

Edging tool A small rectangular steel blade curved at a right angle on one side and fastened to a wood handle, used to give a professional look to edges of freshly poured concrete walks or driveways.

Fabric Fence material.

Fast court A smooth surface court, such as wood or concrete.

Fence stretcher A device consisting of a block and tackle or ratchet-action mechanism, used to stretch fence material.

Fish tape A tape fastened to a reel, used to fish electric wires through conduit and walls.

Foot-candle Illumination produced on an object at a distance of one foot from a standard candle.

Footing A base on which a foundation rests.

Footing pad Small, level concrete slab onto which piers are poured or concrete blocks laid.

Framing square A steel square with the widest part 24 inches long, called the body, and the narrowest part 16 inches long, called the blade, each divided into fractions of inches.

Fuse Device that protects a circuit from overheating

147

by melting when an over-supply of electricity flows through the circuit, thereby preventing the flow of electricity to continue through the conduit.

Grade   Ground level on a building site.

Grommets   Eyelets of metal or other material used along the edges of windscreens, backdrops, and curtaining through which S hooks are inserted to hold the materials in place.

Grounding   A means of connecting the electric system to the earth.

Grubbing hoe   A handle with an attached hoelike blade, for digging up stumps and small trees by their roots.

Horsepower   One horsepower equals 746 watts.

Hot wire   The electric wire carrying electricity, usually black or red.

Insulation   A protective covering placed over wires to prevent escape of electricity.

Kerf   A shallow cut made by a saw in a piece of wood.

Kilowatt   One thousand watts.

Knockout   A round plate partially fastened to a metal electric box, such as a switch box, outlet box, or service panel cabinet, for easy removal to allow passing of wires into box.

Light meter   Device containing a photoelectric cell, used for measuring illumination.

Meter box   Box housing the electric meter.

Mortise   A slot made into a piece of wood to receive something, such as a slot made into a door frame to accept a hinge leaf.

Multipurpose court   Used here to denote surfaces, adaptable for playing games other than tennis.

Multipurpose tool   An electrical tool used to cut and strip wire, attach terminals, etc.

Nail set   A tool used by woodworkers for driving heads of brads, casing nails, or finishing nails below the wood surface.

Neutral wire   The electric wire purposely grounded.

Nipple   A plumbing term referring to a short piece of pipe, usually between 2 and 8 inches long.

Nonmetallic cable   Nonmetal material used for covering electric wires.

Nonporous court   Any court not permitting water to penetrate through its surface, but constructed so that water runs off.

Ohm   Unit for measuring electric resistance.

Outlet   An electric device designed for tapping off electricity at specific locations for appliances and lights.

Philips screwdriver   A hand tool designed for turning a screw manufactured with a double kerf cut into its head.

Pintle   A bolt or pin on which something turns, such as the attachment on a female hinge turning on the attached pin of male hinge.

Pipe bender   A metal tool used for bending pipe and conduit to some preconceived shape.

Pipe cap   A plumbing fitting used at the end of a water supply pipe to terminate water flow.

Plumb bob   Consists of a metal weight with a point at one end and a hole for attaching a cord at the other end, used for establishing one point vertical with another point.

Porous court   Any court permitting water to filter through its surface.

Ready-mix concrete   Special trucks mixing Portland cement, sand, rock, and water enroute between source of supply and job site.

Receptacle   A type of outlet used for plugging in electric cords to a circuit.

Reducer bushing   A plumbing fitting designed to receive a pipe of one diameter at one end and to receive a pipe of another diameter at the opposite end.

Rod   A light pole marked with gradations, held upright by a helper while a surveyor reads through a transit in leveling or stadia surveying.

Screed   A guide of wood or one made by supporting an iron pipe on top of wood stakes driven into the ground to a designated elevation, used in smoothing a freshly poured concrete surface.

Sedge   Any rushlike or grasslike cyperaceous plant of the genus *carex* with sawlike edges growing in a wet environment.

Service line   The line 21 feet from the net, bounding the back of the service courts.

Service panel   The main panel through which electricity is brought from the power lines and then distributed to the various branch circuits in the electrical system.

Shoe   Acts as a plate to hold studs at equal spacing and as a straightedge to the frame.

Shutoff valve   A metal valve installed in a water supply line for the purpose of cutting off supply when repairs are required.

Sideline   The line at either side of the court, marking the outside edge of the playing surface.

Side service line   The service courts boundary line at the right and left sides. In singles, the side service lines are also part of the sidelines.

Single-phase   An electric device, such as an electric motor, that is energized by a single electronic force with one phase or with phases differing by 180°.

Single-purpose court   Used here to denote surface especially designed for playing tennis only.

Slow court   A rough surface court, such as clay and fast dry.

Solderless connectors   Devices used for connecting electric wires together by mechanical means, rather than with solder.

Solid bridging   Single boards or blocks set at right angles to the joists and fitted snugly between them.

Stolons   Prostrate stems below or just below the surface of ground level that produce new plants from buds at their nodes or tips.

Stringers The supporting members of steps or stairs, sometimes called *carriages, horses,* and *strings.*

Studs Upright frame members, such as 2 x 4s, used in outside walls and partitions as part of the building frame. Also used in framing retaining walls.

Temperature relief valve A metal safety valve installed in top of hot-water heater to automatically relieve the pressure if overheating occurs.

Terminal post The post located at the end of a piece of fence in a continuous line, such as at a corner or opposite a gate post.

Three-phase An electric device, such as an electric motor, that is energized by three electronic forces differing in phase by one third of a cycle or 120°.

Tillering Putting out new shoots from the roots or bottom of the stalk.

Transit An instrument used by surveyors to establish grade lines and establish various angles used in the building trades.

Transom The fence area above a gate.

Trap A plumbing fitting designed in the form of an S to allow waste fluids to pass into drain line and at the same time retain enough fluid to block sewer gas from entering the building.

Trowel A concrete finisher's trowel consists of a rectangular steel blade fastened to a wood handle, used to produce a slick finish on freshly poured concrete. A bricklayer's trowel has a triangular steel blade fastened to a wood handle, used to handle mortar during masonry work.

Voltage drop An electrical term used to indicate the voltage loss which occurs when wires in a circuit are overloaded.

Watt Unit of electric power, equal to the power produced by one ampere in a one-volt circuit.

Wedge A piece of hard material, such as wood, plastic, or metal, with two principal faces meeting in an acute angle, the narrow end of which is used by woodsmen to drive into a saw kerf to prevent pinching of saw.

Zoning regulations Special restrictions as to the type of buildings that may be constructed in each of several areas of districts making up a town or city.

Sources of Supply

The following list of manufacturers and companies selling supplies is not intended to be complete. It was compiled from a random sampling of hundreds of reputable companies.

Add-In
9200 Cody
Overland Park, KS 66215
Accessories, rackets, apparel

Advance Machine Co.
PO Box 275
Spring Park, MN 55384
Ball-throwing machines

Air-Tech Industries
9 Brighton Road
Clifton, NJ 07102
Air-supported structures

Allen A. Co.
803 N. Downing St.
Piqua, OH 45356
Apparel, socks

Allied Chemical Corp.
PO Box 787
Cheshire, CT 06410
Surfaces

American Buildings Co.
Eufaula, AL 36027
Metal buildings

A.M.F. Head Ski
4801 North 63rd St.
Boulder, CO 80301
Rackets

Anchor Fence
6500 Eastern Ave.
Baltimore, MD 21224
Fence materials

Ashaway Mfg. Co.
Ashaway, RI 02804
Racket string

Automatic Tennis, Inc.
2296 Meyers
Escondido, CA 92025
Automatic practice alley units

Apple Manufacturing
1307 Roosevelt Ave.
Havertown, PA 19083
Luggage

Bancroft Sporting Goods Co.
Bancroft Court
Woonsocket, RI 02895
Accessories, rackets, apparel, shoes, balls

Beconta Inc.
50 Executive Blvd.
Elmsford, NY 10523
Shoes, socks, visors, grips, T-shirts, headbands, apparel

Book Brothers, Inc.
PO Box 145, Forest Park Station
Springfield, MA 01108
Sports books and prints

B.S.T. Sports
1210 Park Newport
Suite 402
Newport Beach, CA 92660
Apparel, accessories, bags

California Products Corp.
169 Waverly St.
Cambridge, MA 02139
Surfaces, court equipment

Carron Net Co.
1623-17th St.
Two Rivers, WI 54241
Court equipment, accessories

C-E Elsco Lighting Products
633 San Juan Ave.
Stockton, CA 95208
Lighting systems

Century Sports, Inc.
400 Park Ave., P.O. Box 47
Plainfield, NJ 07061
*Everything needed for tennis, platform tennis, and
    squash*

Champion Glove Mfg. Co.
2200 E. Ovid
Des Moines, IA 50313
Gloves, accessories, racquet ball equipment

Chevron Asphalt Co.
PO Box 7643
San Francisco, CA 94120
Court surfaces and equipment practice alley

Children's Wear Corp. of America
2641 N.W. 5th Ave.
Miami, FL 33125
Children's tennis wear

Chris-Cross Courtwear
19643 Castellana Plaza
Yorba Linda, CA 92686
Accessories

Cidair Structures Co.
143 West 154th St.
South Holland, IL 60473
Air-supported structures

Clossco, Inc.
PO Box 299
Santa Clara, CA 95050
Shoes, apparel, bags, rackets

Converse Rubber Co.
55 Fordham Road
Wilmington, MA 01887
Shoes, apparel

Court and Slope
1224 Remington Road
Schaumburg, IL 60172
Electro-matic racket stringer

Creative Awards by Lane
32 W. Randolph
Chicago, IL 60601
Gift items, jewelry, trophies

Curley-Bates Co.
860 Stanton Road
Burlingame, CA 94010
Rackets, string, apparel

Dally Tally
Overlook Park
Montclair, NJ 07042
Score cards

Devoe Tennis Systems
800 Eastern Ave.
Carlstadt, NJ 07072
Lighting systems, platform tennis courts

Dome East Corp.
325 Duffy Ave.
Hicksville, NY 11801
Tennis dome buildings

Dunlop Sports Co.
PO Box 1109
Buffalo, NY 14240
Rackets, apparel, shoes, balls, accessories

Dura-Fiber, Inc.
2300 Arrowhead Drive
Carson City, NV 89701
Rackets

Dynaturf Co.
1770 Joyce Ave.
Columbus, OH 43216
Synthetic court surfaces

Edgeroy Co.
Box 494
Ridgefield, NJ 07657
*Accessories, gift items, tennis ball life-maintaining
    equipment*

Edwards Sports
1311 Rue Ampere
PO Box 220
Boucherville, Quebec J4B 5J6
Nets, accessories, court equipment

Ektelon
7079 Mission Gorge Road
San Diego, CA 92120
Stringing machine, rackets

Elanne Products, Inc.
209 West Chestnut
Marianna, AR 72360
Women's apparel, children's apparel, hats

Fashion T—Racquet Squad
1350 Broadway
New York, NY 10018
Women's apparel

Flintkote Co.
5500 South Alameda St.
Los Angeles, CA 90058
Surfaces

Fox Tool and Die Co.
3420 Oakdale Rd.
Modesto, CA 95355
Ball-throwing machine

Fun Fads of Palm Springs
210 San Rafael Drive
Palm Springs, CA 92262
Apparel

Futabaya Racket Mfg. Co., Ltd.
9250 Wilshire Blvd.
Beverly Hills, CA 90212
Rackets

Garcia Corp.
329 Alfred Ave.
Teaneck, NJ 07666
*Rackets, strings, stringing machine, surfaces and
    accessories*

Gardco Manufacturing, Inc.
2661 Alvarado Street
San Leandro, CA 94577
Court equipment, lighting systems

Gold Crest, Ltd.
12307 Ventura Blvd.
Studio City, CA 91604
Gift items, jewelry, trophies, apparel

Goshen Mfg. Co.
612 East Reynolds St.
Goshen, IN 46526
Benches

G. R. McKinley and Associates
222 So. Bemiston
St. Louis, MO 63105
Apparel

Hang Ten
1010 Sycamore Ave.
So. Pasadena, CA 91030
Apparel

Head Ski, A.M.F.
4801 North 63rd St.
Boulder, CO 80301
Rackets

Hoag-Co.
1062 North Vinedo Ave.
Pasadena, CA 91107
Ball pickup equipment

Holophane
Greenwood Plaza
Denver, CO 80217
Lighting systems

House of Haist
1540 N.W. 65th Ave.
Plantation, FL 33313
Apparel, ball pickup equipment

Ideal Steel
9735 West River Road
Gansevoort, NY 12831
Steel lockers

Jacobs Corp.
5735 Arapahoe Ave.
Boulder, CO 80303
Children's and teens' apparel, rackets

Jay Display Fixture Corp.
1045 Tenth Ave.
San Diego, CA 92101
Display fixtures

Jayfro Corp.
Box 400
Waterford, CT 06385
Court equipment

Jez of California
105 W. Union St.
Pasadena, CA 91101
Apparel

J. H. Spaulding
3731 Dirr St.
Cincinnati, OH 45223
Outdoor lighting systems

Jockey International, Inc.
2300 60th St.
Kenosha, WI 53140
Men's apparel, socks

Johns-Manville Sales Corp.
PO Box 5108
Denver, CO 80217
Lighting, puncture-resistant insulation

Johnson & Johnson Athletic Division
501 George St.
New Brunswick, NJ 08903
First-aid products, thirst quencher

Juneman Sports Co.
210 Los Molinos
Suite D
San Clemente, CA 92672
Strings, grips, racket stringing machines, rackets

Kimberton Co.
Phoenixville, PA 19460
Apparel, custom embroidery

Kim Morgen
1407 Broadway
14th Floor
New York, NY 10018
Apparel

K-Lin Specialties, Inc.
812 Fifth St.
Manhattan Beach, CA 90266
Ball-throwing machines

K-Swiss
14641 Arminta St.
Van Nuys, CA 91402
Shoes

Lily's Boutique of Beverly Hills
8512 Whitworth Drive
Los Angeles, CA 90035
Accessories, bags, hats, women's apparel

Linder-Euro-Imports, Inc.
5837 West Adams Blvd.
Culver City, CA 90230
Rackets

Little Miss Tennis
PO Box 17442
Memphis, TN 38117
Children's apparel, accessories

Mac Levy Products Corp.
92–21 Corona Ave.
Elmhurst, NY 11373
Sauna rooms, whirlpool baths, steam baths, health, exercise, fitness, and rehabilitation equipment

Manufacturers Specialty Co., Inc.
2501 South Jefferson Ave.
St. Louis, MO 63104
Accessories

Matchmate
8643 Darby Ave,
Northridge, CA 91324
Ball-throwing machine

Mateflex by Mele
1712 Erie St.
Utica, NY 13503
Polyethylene interlocking-module court surface

Miracle Recreation Equipment Co.
PO Box 275
Grinnell, IA 50112
Bleachers, seating

Model Display & Fixture Co., Inc.
1405 East McDowell Road
Phoenix, AZ 85010
Display fixtures

Modern Sports, Inc.
1347 West Trenton Ave.
PO Box 5148
Orange, CA 92667
Apparel, children's apparel

M. Putterman Co.
2888 S. Archer Ave.
Chicago, IL 60608
Backdrops

NJP Sports, Inc.
PO Box 1469
Glendale, CA 91209
Court equipment

Omnitec Products Corp.
8505 Tanglewood Square
Chagrin Falls, OH 44022
Home ball-throwing machine

Pacifico Co.
1630 Cotner Ave.
Los Angeles, CA 90025
Apparel, rackets, strings, stringing machines, accessories

Paramount Construction, Inc.
9250 Wilshire Blvd.
Beverly Hills, CA 90212
Surfaces

Pegasus Luggage, Inc.
7575 N.W. 82nd St.
Miami, FL 33166
Bags, covers

Precision Tennis Systems, Inc.
21 West 86th St.
New York, NY 10024
Air-supported structures

Prince Manufacturing, Inc.
PO Box 2031
Princeton, NJ 08540
Ball-throwing machines

Pro Groups, Inc.
1809 National
Anaheim, CA 92801
Rackets, shoes

Prolite
9005 Southern Blvd.
West Palm Beach, FL 33411
Lighting systems

Rawlings Sporting Goods Co.
2300 Delmar Blvd.
St. Louis, MO 63166
Sporting goods

Robert Lee Co., Inc.
999 Grove St.
Charlottesville, VA 22903
Fast-dry materials and maintenance equipment

Rol-Dri, Inc.
7331 Long Point Road
Suite 4
Houston, TX 77055
Court equipment

Royal Athletic Surfacing Co. Inc.
120 Hopper St.
Westbury, NY 11590
Synthetic court surface

Russell Corp.
1114 Avenue of the Americas
New York, NY 10036
Fabrics

Scarborough Group
1345 Avenue of the Americas
New York, NY 10019
Gift items, accessories, jewelry, bags

Seaman Buildings Systems
2028 E. Whitfield Ave.
Sarasota, FL 33580
Portomod buildings

Seamco Sporting Goods
253 Hallock Ave.
New Haven, CT 06503
Sports equipment, including platform tennis

Sewing Factory, Inc.
13311 Beach Ave.
Venice, CA 90291
Racket covers, bags, accessories, contract sewing

Spalding
Meadow St.
Chicopee, MA 01014
Rackets, balls, apparel

Sonoco Products
Hartsville, SC 29550
Sonovoid fiber tubes and other building products

Sports Pal Co., Inc.
10440 German Blvd.
St. Louis, MO 63131
Gut, nylon string, grips, nets, court line tape and equipment, tennis machines, ball pickups, windscreens, backdrop curtains, apparel

Supreme Court Products Co.
PO Box 1385
Monterey, CA 93940
Court equipment, ball pickup equipment

Tail, Inc.
2630 N.W. 5th Ave.
Miami, FL 33127
Women's apparel

Tennis Ball Saver
1459 Thousand Oaks Blvd.
Thousand Oaks, CA 91360
Accessories, gift items

Tennisman Sportswear
30 W. 26th St.
New York, NY 10010
Men's apparel

Tennis Masters
PO Box D
San Rafael, CA 94903
Jewelry

The Field Co.
360 S. Los Angeles St.
Los Angeles, CA 90013
Sports and casual headwear

The J. E. Francis Co.
3040 State Street
PO Box 30303
Santa Barbara, CA 93105
Court equipment

Threads & Things
1663 Mission St.
San Francisco, CA 94103
Apparel, jewelry, fiber manufacturer

Tony Trabert Division
Pro Group, Inc.
99 Tremont St.
Chattanooga, TN 37405
Rackets, shoes

Tropitone Furniture Co., Inc.
17101 Armstrong
Irvine, CA 92705
Furniture

Tru-Flex Recreational Coatings
1760 Revere Beach Parkway
Everett, MA 02149
Acrylic court surfaces

Uniroyal, Inc.
1230 Avenue of the Americas
New York, NY 10020
Accessories, shoes, bags, apparel, socks

Uni-Spray
31225 Kenall
Fraser, MI 48026
Watering systems

Universal Athletic Sales
1328 N. Sierra Vista Ave.
Fresno, CA 93703
Physical conditioning equipment

Viking Sauna Co.
909 Park Avenue
PO Box 6298
San Jose, CA 95150
Saunas

Viking Whirl-Spa, Inc.
1014 NE 42rd St.
Fort Lauderdale, FL 33334
Whirlpool units

Whimsicals
1411 Broadway
New York, NY 10018
Women's apparel

Wilkinson Enterprises
2434 N. State Road 39
La Porte, IN 46350
Tennis trainer Perma-Partner

Wilshire Book Co.
12015 Sherman Road
North Hollywood, CA 91605
Books

Wind & Shade Screens, Inc.
706 Kellog Ave.
Glendale, CA 91202
Windscreens, net posts, nets, center straps

Win Mark, Inc.
(The Winners Mark)
10 Corbin Drive
Darien, CT 06820
Testing and motivation systems

Yamaha International Corp.
6600 Orangethorpe Ave.
Buena Park, CA 90620
Rackets

Yonex, Inc.
521 Superior Ave.
Newport Beach, CA 92660
Rackets, accessories

Index

Page numbers in **bold** indicate information in illustrations;
page numbers followed by t indicate information found in tables.